Sid Caesar and
Your Show of Shows

Sid Caesar and *Your Show of Shows*
The Birth of the Television Sketch Comedy Series

KAREN J. HARVEY

McFarland & Company, Inc., Publishers
Jefferson, North Carolina

LIBRARY OF CONGRESS CATALOGUING-IN-PUBLICATION DATA

Names: Harvey, Karen J., 1947– author.
Title: Sid Caesar and Your show of shows : the birth of the television sketch comedy series / Karen J. Harvey.
Description: Jefferson, North Carolina : McFarland & Company, Inc., Publishers, 2021 | Includes bibliographical references and index.
Identifiers: LCCN 2020049158 | ISBN 9781476671499 (paperback : acid free paper) ∞
ISBN 9781476641836 (ebook)
Subjects: LCSH: Your show of shows (Television program) | Caesar, Sid, 1922–2014.
Classification: LCC PN1992.77.Y65 H37 2021 | DDC 791.45/72—dc23
LC record available at https://lccn.loc.gov/2020049158

BRITISH LIBRARY CATALOGUING DATA ARE AVAILABLE

ISBN (print) 978-1-4766-7149-9
ISBN (ebook) 978-1-4766-4183-6

© 2021 Karen J. Harvey. All rights reserved

No part of this book may be reproduced or transmitted in any form or by any means, electronic or mechanical, including photocopying or recording, or by any information storage and retrieval system, without permission in writing from the publisher.

Front cover image: shown from left: Sid Caesar, Imogene Coca, Carl Reiner in *Your Show of Shows* (NBC/Photofest)

Printed in the United States of America

*McFarland & Company, Inc., Publishers
Box 611, Jefferson, North Carolina 28640
www.mcfarlandpub.com*

For my mother, who was as big a Sid Caesar fan as I am—genetics, obviously.

And for Gary, who introduced me to the comedy of Sid and *Your Show of Shows*— for that and so much more, my thanks.

Table of Contents

Preface	1
Introduction	3
Part I—"Ladies and Gentlemen, the star of The Admiral Broadway Revue, Sid Caesar"	9
1. Origins	11
2. *The Admiral Broadway Revue*: Broadway Right into Your Home	28
Part II—"Ladies and Gentlemen, the star of *Your Show of Shows*, Sid Caesar"	37
3. Brought to You in Living Black and White: Television in the '50s	39
4. The Writers' Room: Comedy in a Pressure Cooker	51
5. Scripts Versus Performance: Whose Line Is It Anyway?	60
6. The Sketches: "Show Me the Brilliance"	67
7. Jewishness and *Your Show of Shows*: White Bread or Rye?	108
Part III—Rendering Unto Caesar	113
8. Caesar as Physical Comedian	115
9. Caesar as Comic Actor	132
Part IV—The End of *Your Show of Shows*	151
10. "Well, this was it"	153

Afterword	167
Appendix: Comedy Sketch Guide	171
Notes	227
Bibliography	237
Index	239

Preface

This is where a writer usually tells you something about the book. However, let me start with a few words about what this book is *not*. It's not a biography of Sid Caesar, although I explore much of his early life to explain why and how he became a comedian and ultimately the star of *Your Show of Shows*. It's also not a treatment of every part of the program, the singing and dancing and big production numbers for example. I'm concerned primarily with its comedy, how it was written and how it was performed.

So, what *is* it about? Think of it as a kind of dual biography of a performer and a show: the story of how a brilliant comic actor and a superb cast, writing staff and director combined, in the earliest days of television, to produce a ground-breaking program that would influence all successful TV comedy after it.

Central to my research has been watching all of the *Your Show of Shows* episodes, some 142 of them, that are viewable at the Paley Center for Media in New York, but are otherwise, for a variety of reasons, relatively inaccessible to the public. The experience was not only enjoyable—how often do you laugh while doing research?—but vital in answering two important questions: Does the program deserve its reputation? Are there sketches that are very difficult to see that are just as good as those that *can* be seen?

The answer to both is, happily, yes. It's the reason I wrote the book and, in it, provide descriptions of those frequently brilliant "forgotten" ones. Besides that vital visual source, I consulted the Sid Caesar Papers and those of Max Liebman, the producer/director of *Your Show of Shows*, both deposited in the Library of Congress; and additional Liebman materials and the papers of Lucille Kallen, the only female writer on the show, held in the New York Public Library for the Performing Arts. The Library of Congress also has microfilmed copies of the NBC Master Books that recorded everything broadcast on a particular day, specifically those of WNBC in New York from 1950 to 1954. All of these collections contain original scripts for the show's episodes and provide valuable insights into the difference between what was scripted and what aired live on Saturday nights. I have also made extensive use of articles and interviews from newspapers and magazines of the period along with, of course, later interviews with the principals of the show both in print and on video.

The result, ideally at least, is a book that will be of interest to two kinds of readers. For those familiar with *Your Show of Shows* or Caesar only by their reputations, it's an introduction to a classic of early television; for those who are already knowledgeable, it will, I hope, provide new material about and insights into both show and star.

This is also where a writer gets the chance to acknowledge those people and institutions whose help has been instrumental in writing the book. In terms of research, the following are owed thanks: the staffs of the Library of Congress (especially Loretta Deaver of the Manuscripts Division, who tracked down an important sketch script for me and Rosemary Hanes, Reference Librarian in the Moving Image Section, who brought to my attention two episodes that have recently been digitized that I would otherwise not have seen); the New York Public Library for the Performing Arts; and Mark Quigley of the Archive Research & Study Center of the UCLA Film and Television Archive, for information about the kinescopes Caesar deposited there. And special thanks to the librarians of the Paley Center for Media in New York, which holds *Your Show of Shows* episodes in both digitized form and on tape. Patricia Lunde and Todd Kmetz were unfailingly helpful and patient in retrieving "just one more tape" and very tolerant of my chortling while seated in front of a computer screen in the back of the library.

In terms of putting the book together, thanks to: my editor at McFarland, Dylan Lightfoot, who was not only very helpful but exhibited patience, worthy of several saints, in seeing this through to completion; Barry Jacobsen, Max Liebman's last assistant, whose generosity in sharing his materials and reminiscences about Max, has been both incredible and greatly appreciated; Richard Camhi, who indefatigably proofed the chapters and provided valuable feedback; and Candace Kent, who assisted with the task any author dreads—indexing.

And in a special category, thanks to Gary Westin, who was a wonderful combination of sounding board for ideas and enthusiastic booster for the project. Above all, it was he who introduced me, through his YouTube channel, to the comedy of Sid and *Your Show of Shows* and, after much enjoyable discussion of both, asked the obvious question, "Why don't you write a book?" So, here it is.

Last, but certainly not least, my gratitude to my family and friends who heard all too much about this book as it was being written, but nonetheless still listened to—and tolerated—me.

Introduction

Black and white images on a TV screen: A tall man in white tie and tails and a diminutive woman in evening dress, miming percussionists in a symphony orchestra playing the 1812 Overture. All starts calmly enough as they test and tune their instruments. Then the man, carefully checking to make sure the conductor isn't watching, breaks into a decidedly non-classical riff on the drums—and musical mayhem begins. She ruins his dramatic preparation to hit a gong by striking her tiny triangle just as he's in his final wind-up; he hits her head as percussive punctuation in his tambourine solo. Bored with the long interval between their parts, the man suggests a game of rummy, interrupted repeatedly however by the need to solemnly stand every time a strain of the *Marseilles* is played. After almost missing their cue for the Overture's thunderous finale as they're arguing over the game, they finish in a frenzy of bell-ringing, kettledrum playing, cannon-firing, and for good and absurd measure, spraying machine-gun fire and flinging hand grenades. After one final grenade toss, they pin medals on each other, kiss on the cheek in grand French military style, and end by saluting the audience. Perfectly mimed, it's a marvelous sketch performed on January 17, 1953, by Sid Caesar and Imogene Coca on *Your Show of Shows*.

That, for decades, was my only memory of *Your Show of Shows* and even it has been magnified through the lens of recent viewing. Where or when I first saw the sketch, I don't know—only that it would not have been on live TV during the show's 1950–54 run. But I knew *of* Sid Caesar and *Your Show of Shows*—or thought that I did. Caesar was a typical '50s comedian, maybe like Milton Berle or Red Skelton, and the program was probably funny in its day. The sketch was, yes, but the show in its entirety? After all, its comedy was now over 60 years old. It was not until after Caesar's death in 2014 that, my interest piqued by the online tributes to him, I followed the video links provided in many of them and saw the relatively few sketches that had been digitized from the kinescopes that, thankfully, had preserved them. I soon discovered that my assumptions about both Caesar and the show were wrong.

Those six-decade-old sketches and routines not only hold up but are among the funniest television writers have ever produced. And what a group of writers. Mel Tolkin, Lucille Kallen, Mel Brooks, Danny and Neil Simon, Tony Webster, Joe Stein—all were on the staff recruited by Max Liebman, the show's producer/director, and by Caesar himself, who presided over the shark tank known as the Writers' Room. Putting together a live weekly show in 5 days for 33 to 39 weeks a year was, in retrospect, an insane undertaking, but as Brooks and Tolkin often remarked, they didn't know they couldn't do it.

Not only did they do it, in the process they created the Ur-television comedy, providing a template for all that followed. What kind of comedy did they produce? Parodies of Hollywood movies (*From Here to Eternity, Shane, A Streetcar Named Desire*) as well as foreign films, and other TV programs (most notably, a wicked skewering of *This Is Your Life*, generally regarded as the funniest sketch on *Your Show of Shows*). Domestic comedy in the form of the battling Hickenloopers, played by Caesar and Coca. Comedy song and dance numbers. The "Strangers" sketches, in which Sid and Imogene met and traded observations in fluent cliché. Silent film recreations. The Professor sketches, in which Caesar as a self-proclaimed expert in everything was interviewed by "your roving reporter" Carl Reiner on a variety of topics, ranging from self-defense to mountain-climbing. The humor ran the gamut from slapstick to the sophisticated to the surreal.

Of course, the writers were also producing material for the best troupe of comedy performers ever assembled on one show: Caesar, Coca, Carl Reiner, and Howard ("Howie") Morris. Coca, a dancer as well as a comedian, had a face almost as mobile, and eyes almost as expressive, as Caesar's. Hilarious as a vamp or as one of the slightly deranged women a bewildered Caesar would periodically encounter in a park or, more ominously, on the observation decks of tall buildings, she could hold her own in the sketches against her overpowering comedic partner. At 6'1", he loomed over her by almost a foot, but she could wield a dour look as a weapon that would have cut a lesser man down to size. Together, they would develop an intuitive, almost ESP-like, comedy relationship. Carl Reiner was television's best Second Banana (and also a member of the Writers' Room). He could do much more than just straight-man duty: he was a key actor in the sketches (more than able to keep up with Caesar in motor-mouth delivery of lines) and adept at physical comedy and impressions. Howie Morris was not only a fine sketch player, he also frequently supplied the broader comedy of the show. Not much taller than Coca, he was the perfect physical foil for Caesar, who could lift him over his head, toss him about, and commit other acts of comedic assault with ease.

However, the biggest revelation in watching those videos was Sid

Caesar himself. He was anything but a typical '50s comedian (and most definitely *not* like Berle or Skelton). Younger than most of the TV comics of the period—he was only 26 at the beginning of his television career—he did not have vaudeville or radio experience, nor did he do stand-up. Rather, he was a comic actor, coming from a theatrical revue background, and with limited, although highly successful, experience in that.

Yet he did just about everything. Carl Reiner would later call him the greatest single sketch comedian who ever worked in television. He was a skilled pantomimist, television's Chaplin. He was a riveting, as well as side-splitting, monologist. The monologues were a great showcase for his amazing comedic energy (check out the sketch *Five Dollar Date* on YouTube for an example; it's almost exhausting to *watch*) as well as his acting abilities. He could be manic, as the husband who suspects his wife is having an affair with his best friend, or introspective, as a man who is pondering a breakup with his girlfriend. Or play every role in a parody of a Western: from the hero, the hero's horse, the heroine, an entire wagon train, and the cigar-smoking villain, to attacking Indians and—why not?—their smoke signals, which somehow he managed to anthropomorphize. Oh yes, he could also be non-humans: a housefly or the family dog. He was a dialectician with an uncanny skill of mimicking the sounds of foreign languages without knowing any of them. He was a master of sound effects. In fact, he could be his own sound-track, from the commonplace—the now almost forgotten sound of a rotary telephone dial, liquid poured into a glass, nails hammered into a board—to the more esoteric and challenging—not just *a* horse but an entire herd, a slot machine, or a punching bag. He was also a professional musician, playing both swing and jazz on tenor saxophone and, occasionally, the clarinet. His musical background was not only a key component in the development of his incredible sense of timing, it also led to the creation of one of his funniest characters, the hip jazz musician who floats above interviews with a beatific—and very stoned—smile. The protean Caesar made every other TV comic look one-dimensional.

Was there anything he *couldn't* do? Rather sadly, be himself. It was the one role he had difficulty mastering and was least comfortable in. It's all too easy to attribute adult psychological issues to childhood trauma, but in Caesar's case, this is probably an accurate assessment. His childhood was not always a happy one. The youngest of Max and Ida Caesar's three sons, he was emotionally neglected by his Jewish immigrant parents and physically disciplined by his stern father in ways that tended to inflict, if not serious bodily injury, the maximum psychological damage. Not surprisingly, he grew up seeking attention and approval. Making people laugh, a talent he developed early, elicited both. As well, comedy allowed the almost painfully shy Caesar to assume outgoing characters that people liked. Of course, many actors and comedians, unhappy with themselves, are more comfortable assuming other identities. But, as in most things Caesarean, he tended to take it to the extreme; the contrast between stage personae and the real-life Caesar was almost jarring. He also, and again not surprisingly, grew up with suppressed rage and resentment, which could manifest itself in volcanic eruptions of anger, made more frightening by his immense physical strength. Not many comedians then or since could rip sinks from walls or doors from cabs. Or, for that matter, dangle one of his writers from an 18th-story hotel room window (Mel Brooks forgave him). Yet, that same barely suppressed anger would also make his comedy distinctive, in its intensity and the sometimes dark edge to his humor.

Richard Corliss, writing in *Time* shortly after Caesar's death, was indeed on to something when he described him as TV's first Method comedian. He inhabited his roles like no other comic of his era and conveyed his characters' emotions to a degree that, even in a comedic context, could be startlingly real. His "anger" could be positively unnerving. In the sketches, his intensity and immersion into a role draw your eye to him, even when he had no lines. And, in many of the monologues, when he has fully become his character, roaming or pacing the stage, with hair falling over his forehead and beads of sweat rolling down his face, the small screen seems almost unable to contain him.

This then was *Your Show of Shows*, a comedy three-ring circus with Caesar as slightly unbalanced ringmaster. Was all the comedy hilarious or was Caesar always top-notch? Of course not, given the demands of writing and performing material under such incredible time constraints. Some of the sketches could be repetitive, some fell flat, and some leave the distinct impression that the writers just couldn't figure out a way to *end* them. With weaker material, both Caesar and Coca tended to rely too heavily on facial expressions to sell it. The real marvel was not that it was all good, but that so *much* of it was.

But *Your Show of Shows* was not all comedy. To have filled 90 minutes of live TV weekly with nothing but, would have overtaxed the creative abilities of the writers not to mention the stamina of the performers, even that of Caesar, who had the constitution of an ox. There were songs and musical numbers by The Billy Williams Quartet, Bill Hayes, Judy Johnson, and Jack Russell (who also appeared frequently in the comedy sketches) among others; opera excerpts performed by Marguerite Piazza and Robert Merrill; and dances by The Hamilton Trio and Mata and Hari. Each program ended with a big production number with usually all of the singers and dancers and, frequently, Coca. (Both she and Caesar would occasionally team up for a brief comedy appearance in the finale as well.) All of this was Max Liebman's department and specialty. And production values were

Introduction 7

generally superb. *Your Show of Shows* simply *looked* better than most of the other programs on the air in the early '50s. Some of the non-comedy segments hold up well; others, not so much, unless you happen to be particularly fond of '50s dancing and song.

However, it's the comedy that people remember about the program, deservedly so, and it will be the focus here. Why a new treatment of it? First, because there have been surprisingly few full (or even medium) length ones. *Esquire* published a multi-page retrospective in 1972 (the popularity of which may have prompted Max Liebman to plan the theatrical release of *Ten from Your Show of Shows* a year later). Ted Sennett wrote *Your Show of Shows* in 1977 (rev. 2002). It's a valuable compendium of photos and script excerpts and is the best source for discussion of the non-comedy parts of the show, but on balance a rather uncritical assessment. Caesar, of course, devoted several chapters to it in his autobiography *Where Have I Been?* (1982, with Bill Davison), and discussed the show in a memoir about his life in comedy, *Caesar's Hours* (2003, with Eddy Friedfeld). I think there might be room for another book-length, more recent, treatment of the comedy of Caesar and the show.

There's a second reason. This book will be based on what of *Your Show of Shows* can still be seen widely—sketches on the Sid Caesar channel on YouTube and the various VHS tapes and CDs that are still available—and also on what, unhappily, is inaccessible except to a relatively small number of people, among which I count myself fortunate to be one. One of the enduring myths about *Your Show of Shows* is that most of the episodes have been lost. Not the case. Although most of the studio kinescopes were destroyed, Max Liebman and Sid Caesar had almost complete collections of their own. Today, the Paley Center for Media in New York and Los Angeles has over 140 episodes (not all complete), donated by Liebman's heir; a large number have thankfully been digitized, but some have not and can be seen only on tape. There are 121 kinescopes from the same source at the Library of Congress, which also has a collection of the syndicated *Best of Your Show of Shows* on tape, but individual sketches are not listed, nor are they complete episodes. Caesar donated his collection of 152 kinescopes to the UCLA Film and Television Archive; some programs are intact, others are only partial.

So the episodes are not really "lost," but might as well be unless you are in New York, Los Angeles, or Washington, D.C., and can get extended access to them—and in the case of the Library of Congress and UCLA, are willing to see them, with a few exceptions, only on kinescope. For that reason, the Paley Center's digitized collection is, simply, invaluable. There has been sporadic discussion of making some of the Paley collections available through internet access, but they have bogged down in issues of copyright and potential future release by owners or donors. However, no sketches from *Your Show of Shows* that were not included in previously issued collections have been released for profit for almost two decades. There might be profit in a fee for internet access in some form; none in essentially letting them sit there to be seen for free (with some restrictions), but only by a regrettably small group of people. If this book can begin a new discussion of these issues, for no other reason, it will have been well worth writing it. *Your Show of Shows* was genuinely *television* comedy at its earliest and best, and Caesar was the first genuine television comedian. Both the show and its monstrously talented star deserve to be seen more widely.

Part I
"Ladies and Gentlemen, the star of The Admiral Broadway Revue, Sid Caesar"

1

Origins

Comedians are people whose father never listened to them.
—Mel Tolkin[1]

Owners of television sets in 1949 who tuned in to the NBC or DuMont networks to watch the debut of *The Admiral Broadway Revue* could well have wondered who exactly this star was. Some of those watching in New York, where most TV households were, or in the audience at the International Theatre at Columbus Circle, where the *Revue* aired, might have seen him before in an act at the Copa or a stage show at the Roxy Theatre in Rockefeller Center. Or in a Broadway revue, *Make Mine Manhattan*. But that was a New York audience and a limited one at that. In comparison with other headliners and hosts on television at the time—Milton Berle, Arthur Godfrey, or even Ed Sullivan—Sid Caesar, at 26, was a relative unknown.

The Admiral Broadway Revue would make Caesar's TV career, even though the show ran for barely over 4 months, from January 28 to June 3. It was not only a hit; it would lead directly to *Your Show of Shows* and nationwide stardom. For someone whose comedic career up to 1945 had consisted of being a teenage *tummler* in the Catskills and a saxophone player and entertainer in a Coast Guard revue during World War II, it was a rapid rise to success—and one not especially predictable for a man who was, when you consider his shyness and emotional makeup, an unlikely comedian. A superlative comedian he would indeed become, but his psychological complexities would often make it difficult for him to handle that success. Caesar was hardly the first entertainer to exhibit neurotic tendencies or frequently dwell in emotional dark places, but, as he would excel in comedy, he would unfortunately excel in these areas as well.

Sid is often described as a "tortured genius." It's a shopworn trope: the creative artist tormented by inner demons, prone to emotional instability, substance abuse, and self-contempt. The description fits him almost uncomfortably well; however, the concept itself can lead to an overly facile linking of creativity and discontent, with the implication that the latter promotes the former. In Caesar's case, his inner demons—and he indeed had them—played a role in driving him to a remarkable comedic career; they also contributed to his addiction to alcohol and pills that would ultimately derail it.

Another problem with the "tortured genius" trope is its suggestion that life for the creative artist (and for the comedian; cf. the Sad Clown Syndrome) must be one of almost unremitting gloom and suffering. This was certainly not the case for Sid: he had a wife and children whom he loved, and he took a genuine joy in performing and the applause it brought. Yet, those who knew him spoke of an often troubled man, one who was delicately balanced and whose temperament was mercurial, at times volatile. He felt insecure, even at the height of his success; he didn't know where his talents had come from and feared losing them. Mel Brooks once commented that "Sid was never comfortable with life."[2] Nor was he comfortable with himself, often discontent and unhappy with who the real Sid Caesar was. In fact, he would come to believe that no one could possibly like him for himself. Neil Simon's *Laughter on the 23rd Floor* is a play based on his experiences as a writer on *Your Show of Shows*. In it, one of the denizens of the Writers' Room observes that the TV star "Max Prince," for whom they write and to whom they are devoted, has no enemies besides himself: "Nobody hates Max the way Max hates Max."[3]

Sid also contained enough contradictions for at least two people: appealingly shy and annoyingly imperious; given to morose and sullen moods, that would then be broken by infectious laughter; capable of great rage and great generosity; incredibly difficult and self-centered at times, yet immensely likeable. (Caesar came to fully acknowledge these very different sides of himself in the late 1970s. In the DIY talk therapy he devised to overcome his psychological issues and addictions, he called them "Sidney," the angry, wayward wild child, and "Sid," the calmer, rational adult. Getting them to communicate with each other—literally—brought a large measure of success. Afterward, Sid's son Richard, who had seen all too much of "Sidney" when he was growing up, said that it was like meeting an entirely different man.)[4]

These emotional complexities, contradictory behaviors, and dual—and dueling—personalities did not appear suddenly at age 22, when Caesar had his first major comedy success in the film *Tars and Spars* (filmed in 1945, its release was delayed until the following year). Occasionally, brief sketches of Sid's life make reference to a troubled childhood from which his demons and dark places originated, one in which he grew up often unhappy with and angry at the world—and himself. So it becomes both a legitimate and necessary question to at least attempt to address: what was his childhood like and how did a comedian with all that complex emotional baggage emerge from it?

1. Origins

Isaac Sidney Caesar was born on September 8, 1922, in Yonkers, a New York city that borders the Bronx. He was the youngest of the three sons of Max and Ida Caesar, both Jewish immigrants. Max came from what was, before World War I, Austrian Poland; Ida Rafael from Russia. At the time of Sid's birth, they ran a 24-hour diner, the St. Clair, and rented out the rooms above it, catering to the local factory workers.

A few comments about Caesar's given and family names, because there has been no little confusion and misinformation about them: First, it was common for Jewish immigrants to give their sons two distinct names—one for ritual occasions and a second secular "American" one, hence "Isaac Sidney." Most likely the last time Sid was called "Isaac" was at his bar mitzvah; he appears in the census records of 1930, when he was 8, as just Sidney Caesar and in records onward always as that. (Although "Isaac" was an almost prescient choice for his Jewish name; it means "laughter," or "to laugh" in Hebrew.) Second, the family name was originally Ziser and, contrary to cherished melting pot lore, would not have been changed by immigration officials, who simply recorded the names of immigrants from the manifests of the ships that brought them. As there were no New York laws at the time that prohibited voluntary name changes, someone in the Ziser family, after their arrival in 1881, simply changed the name to what people heard if it was pronounced correctly in German: "tsezer," thus Caesar.[5] In a period when many major Jewish comedians would adopt stage names less ethnic or more "mainstream" than their real ones, Sid would be among the relatively few who didn't; his performing name would be the one he was born with.

What was this future comedian's childhood like? Any attempt to answer the question, particularly some 80 years later, immediately runs into difficulties. The source materials are limited and often highly subjective, and the intervals between them huge: magazine articles and interviews from the 1950s and '60s; Caesar's autobiography from 1982; and a subsequent memoir from 2003. Moreover, in the latter, there is considerable softening and sanitizing of childhood experiences, particularly when they involved his father Max. Nonetheless, by examining not only what the sources say but what they imply, and looking for similar patterns in both, it may be possible to reconstruct a childhood from which those inner demons emerged.

There was a family version of that childhood and two from Caesar himself, at times so contradictory it's like *Rashomon* set in Yonkers. All the versions are at least in agreement that young Sid adored his Russian mother, whom he would come to resemble greatly in height and facial features, and that he respected and admired his hard-working father Max. In his reminiscences, he describes happy occasions of family dinners; accompanying his parents on shopping excursions to the Lower East Side where they would later go to a restaurant and perhaps a movie; and summer trips to visit Ida's mother and father in Asbury Park along the Jersey shore. His oldest brother Abe, in perhaps a bit of sibling rivalry of the "Mom always liked you best" variety, would tell a reporter doing a story on Caesar that Sid as a child was treated differently from the way he and his other brother Dave had been: Sid got material things and treats they had not. "Mamma would say, after all, he's the baby. Papa hit Dave and me when he got sore at us, but nobody ever hit Sid."[6] The reporter noted that when she mentioned Abe's comment to Caesar, he looked surprised. As well he might have. Because that was not the way Sid would recall it, remembering that "my father would hit me occasionally,"[7] and being on the receiving end of cuffs and wallops, usually when he did something that Max thought might reflect badly on his standing with the important members of the local synagogue. And the delivery of the discipline followed a predictable pattern: young Sid misbehaves, usually in a relatively minor way; Max poses a sarcastic question about whether he'd like to repeat said behavior; then, *Cuff*. It usually went something like: "You missed part of *shul* because you were watching an electronic baseball scoreboard and forgot what time it was? Would you like to go back to check the score?" *Smack*. Hardly Dr. Spock-approved child-rearing or discipline, but those were different times. On the whole, this can certainly be seen as a plausible version of a fairly normal upper working-class New York childhood of the period.

However, it doesn't quite account for a child who didn't talk until he was almost 4 and then, outside of his family, spoke only when he was spoken to. Or for one so painfully shy that at least one of his teachers thought he was stupid and a boarder thought him stuck-up because he wouldn't meet his eyes when he greeted him. Or for a young teenager whose temper was already so hair-trigger that his usual response to frustration was to slam his fist against a wall.

And there *was* another, not-so-happy version of that childhood. Caesar once said that he was called a "make-up" child, "meaning, I assume, that [my parents] were mad at each other for a long time, then made up, and I was the result."[8] Whether he was told this or just came to believe it, that he would even mention it in an account of his childhood says a great deal about his perception of his parents and his own place in the Caesar family. And there are enough details in his account and in what we know about that family to understand why he formed it. Ida was 14 years younger than Max, who was almost 50 at Sid's birth, and there are indications that the two didn't always get along. The intervals between which their children arrived—Abe was 16 years older than Sidney, Dave almost 11 years older—also suggest that Sid may have been not only a "make-up" child but one neither entirely anticipated nor planned for.[9] This circumstance of being the much youngest child in the family would have a major impact on Caesar's early life and could account, at least in part, for what was a complex and problematic relationship with his father.

To his credit, Caesar refused to blame all of his later adult problems on his parents, acknowledging they had difficulties of their own. Yet a comment he made in his autobiography that "I loved them very much and they loved *me* very much—but not very well,"[10] is significant. If there is one dominant motif that runs through every account he gave of his childhood, it is one of abandonment, both physical and emotional. The demands of running the diner meant that his parents and brothers spent most of their time there, and at a very early age, he came to regard it as the place that took away his family. His brother Dave could provide occasional baby-sitting, but his help was more often needed at the St. Clair. Until Sid could start school, he was simply left in the house alone—a lot.

Even this isolation might at times have been preferable to extended babysitting by his much-older brothers. Carl Reiner told a story he heard from them about Caesar's childhood and thought it was one of the reasons "he was who he was." His brothers used to give the very young Sid pennies, which was undoubtedly charming, until the day one of them decided it would be amusing to heat them on a stove before putting them into his hand. The appalling, but apparently desired, result was screams and tears. (You have to wonder why they thought it was a funny story to tell.) As Reiner put it, "When you're 3 years old and somebody does that to you? Who do you trust if you can't trust your own brothers?"[11]

Sid also started running away—a lot. His family seems to have regarded this as a source of amusing stories about his retrievals. Nowadays of course this would be interpreted as an obvious cry for attention, particularly from a pre-school-age child. It may also have been something else—a young boy's desire, unable to be articulated, to punish his parents. This was suggested by Caesar, whether he was conscious of it or not, in an interview in 1950 when he mentioned that he was indeed "always running away" as a child and mused that he was still running away as an adult: "Everybody has something driving them. You know, something happens in your life and you want to get even."[12]

When he grew old enough to help at the diner in his turn, bussing tables, even though his head barely reached them, brought two-fold satisfaction. He began to listen to, and imitate, the sounds of the different languages he heard spoken by the immigrant factory workers who ate there. It would not only be the beginning of a remarkable talent at mimicking languages, it brought approval and laughter from the workers. Perhaps more important: "I soon found out that my mimicry could get the attention of my mother and father and make them laugh, too."[13]

This need for approval and attention was rarely met by Max, however, although it's clear the young Caesar sought it from his father. Max was not only stern and sarcastic, he was also cold and emotionally distant. Another motif in Sid's autobiography is about his father, one of "he really loved me, he just couldn't show it," repeated often enough to suggest he was trying to convince himself of it. Unfortunately, some of the things Max did—or didn't do—only reinforced the young child's insecurity and feelings of abandonment.

In a magazine article from the 1950s, Caesar told a story about one of his parents' fights that ended, or at least entered a cooling-off period, with Ida leaving to visit friends in Asbury Park for a while. Because Max was "too busy to look after me," he put the 6-year-old Sid on a train, by himself, with a card around his neck labeled "Asbury Park," to join his mother. However, "my father had not bothered to call her," so as the young boy was travelling to New Jersey, his mother was on another train going back to Yonkers, and he arrived at the station with nobody there to pick him up. It could almost have come out of a scene in a novel by Dickens (who knew a thing or two about childhood feelings of helplessness and abandonment by adults). Fortunately, his mother's friends came to rescue him, and called his parents—who told them to keep him for a while. The adult Sid recalled: "If my mother and father had beaten me with baseball bats, they wouldn't have hurt me half as much."[14]

Max as disciplinarian also contributed to the young Sid's insecurity and disappointment at failing to please a father whose approval he wanted and needed. His pattern of dealing with a transgression—irritation, then sarcasm (difficult for a child to interpret), preceding a hit—as well as the things he punished the boy for (usually activities that made Sid happy), was a psychologically toxic combination. In Caesar's last memoir, there's a telling example, both in the situation itself and Sid's way of relating it. He loved going to the movies; when old enough to go by himself, he would spend many weekends going from one theater to another. On one occasion, when he was eight years old, Sid stayed from the beginning of the showings in the late morning, watching everything twice, until 6 that night. He described Max as being worried because he was late and relieved when he finally showed up at the diner. "He put his hand in his pocket as if he were going to give me money and said: 'Would you like to go back for the evening performance?'" And in 2003 Sid ends the anecdote, abruptly. The benign portrayal of Max is a bit suspicious, particularly in light of the sarcastic question he asks, usually part of his disciplinary pattern. And Caesar did provide an all too believable end to the story, but as part of an interview with a reporter from 1963: when Max took his hand out of his pocket, it was not to give him a coin to return to the movies, but to deliver a slap across his face hard enough to bounce young Sid off a wall. It's a story that makes you wince—and an incident Caesar never forgot. Moreover, the reporter suggested that there were other experiences like this one that the adult Sid told him about.[15]

Which version of his childhood is the more accurate? At this remove, it's impossible to tell. Did Sid dream up or exaggerate the darker one? It's highly doubtful. One story maybe, but not several (which he would repeat more than once), and he goes out of his way, in his later reminiscences, to tweak or even omit earlier ones that put Max in an unflattering light.[16] Maybe both are accurate: Happy times as well as lonely ones. A mother who indulged him even though she couldn't always be with him. A father frequently frustrated with a sensitive, dreamy youngest son he perhaps hadn't planned on and couldn't spare much time for, but whose future he was at least concerned about (he seemed relieved to hear from Sid that he was making $500 a week after filming *Tars and Spars*—"he didn't have to worry about me anymore").[17] It would be a suitably complex childhood for a complex man.

Seaman First Class Sidney Caesar in the Coast Guard revue *Tars and Spars* (ca. 1944).

Yet, in one of those dark interviews from the 1950s, Caesar would say candidly and almost matter-of-factly that as a child he never felt wanted. Certainly, all of that insecurity, need for attention and approval, and anger was evident at a very early age. Making people laugh, in his comedy career as an adult, could satisfy in part the need for attention and approval, but the anger and resentment at being denied it as a child would remain. It would be internalized as self-discontent and all too frequently externalized in his violent temper. You can't help but think the circumstances of his childhood not only led him, but drove him, to become a comedian. And created and fueled those inner demons noted by anyone who knew him well.

Given that need for attention and approval, it's somewhat surprising that Sid did not become a needy, "love me" type of comic. Instead, he sought admiration and respect for his professionalism and talents, a different verification and validation of who he was. Moreover, unlike the popular comedy identification of miserliness with Jack Benny, or mania with Jerry Lewis, or brashness with Milton Berle, he never developed a distinctive Sid Caesar comedic persona. Because with Caesar, the "actor" part of comic actor was just as important as the "comic." He was always someone else—Charlie Hickenlooper; the Professor; or in his monologues, Everyman with his everyday problems—and always more comfortable *being* someone else. You are always left with the feeling that he needed a character to get into—or hide behind.

To appreciate the differences between Caesar and his comic contemporaries, the analysis of David Marc is most helpful. Marc, a shrewd and perceptive analyst of early television, posited three general modes that a television personality develops: the representational, in which he assumes the role of a fictional character; the presentational, in which, as "himself," he addresses the audience, usually in an opening monologue; and the documentary, in which his "real life," i.e., his lifestyle, opinions, etc., becomes the topic of other media coverage and encourages television viewers to feel that, whether accurately or not, they really "know" him and often regard him with affection. Marc regards—and how could you possibly disagree?—Jackie Gleason as the embodiment of all three.[18] Other critics, following and expanding on Marc's "modal" analysis, see Jack Benny and, to some extent, Red Skelton, as exemplars of the presentational and documentary modes.[19] And where does Caesar fit in? Not in the presentational mode: on *Your Show of Shows*, after his introduction, he quickly presented the guest host and exited without any kind of opening monologue as himself. Nor in the documentary: he was certainly the subject of numerous magazine and newspaper articles in which you could learn about his background and his family life (or as much as he chose to reveal about either in the early to mid-'50s). In them, Sid comes across as personable and often appealing, but although he and Gleason shared superior skills in the representational mode, he was never going to be the larger-than-life Great One. The articles' usual focus was on his prodigious talents rather than his personality. Nor was he a constantly-appealing-for-audience-love Skelton. In neither case was that who he was, or who he could be. Caesar operated almost exclusively in the representational mode—not only was he most comfortable in it, as a skilled comic actor, it was what he did superbly.

However, there *were* times an audience saw the "real" Sid Caesar. For

1. Origins

example, in those frequently stiff, almost endearingly awkward introductions of the guest host at the beginning of *Your Show of Shows*, where his entire demeanor suggests he'd rather be having a root canal. All that was required of him was to say "Thank you, ladies and gentlemen, and welcome to *Your Show of Shows*. Our guest host for tonight is—" And then give a plug for whatever the host was currently doing. The writers would hold their collective breaths until he got through it (he would generally flub at least one intro out of every four or five) and could, with palpable relief, get off stage and into his character for the first sketch. Nanette Fabray once asked him why he continued to do the introductions when they obviously made him uncomfortable. His response was almost poignant: "That's the way I practice being me.... Sid Caesar is the hardest thing for me to do. I can be anything but it's very hard to be myself."[20] The audience could also see the real Caesar in his frequent nervousness in setting up a brief explanation for a monologue, often twisting his wedding band to occupy his hands. On one memorable occasion, this master of rapid-fire dialogue in sketches becomes almost tongue-tied when Melvyn Douglas introduces him to perform one. His response was an awkward "Thank you, Melvyn ... Uh...." Of course, this is the same man who once, rather remarkably, mangled his own name ("This is Cae—Si—Sid Caesar") when introducing himself.

They also saw the real Sid Caesar in his shy grin when audiences applauded a solo routine. And at the end of a show, still on a performance high, when he would occasionally joke with guest stars or clown around killing time when the program had run short. (Once by, rather charmingly, introducing everyone down to the "sound man" and then asking, "Did I forget anybody?") Above all, viewers could catch a glimpse of the real Caesar at the end-of-season shows in which he would become visibly emotional when addressing the audience at the curtain call. At the end of the last episode of *The Admiral Broadway Revue*, he looks like he's tearing up and has to bite his lip to keep control. In those moments, he could display a sensitivity and vulnerability that were not part of a character, but his own.

What then, were the circumstances that would launch a shy, troubled kid into an unlikely comedy career? The one thing Max Caesar did provide for his youngest son (besides fodder for future psychoanalytic sessions) was an ultimate ticket out of Yonkers and an entrée into performing. A boarder at the St. Clair left behind a saxophone. Max presented it to Sid, told him he was going to play it, and paid for music lessons. The 11-year-old took to the sax immediately and his role models became professional musicians. In a typically mordant example of his humor from the '50s, Caesar would comment, "I've often been glad that no one ever left a sawed-off shotgun."[21] Max might have come to wonder what he had wrought, however.

At a junior high school musical recital, Sid had a sax solo. When the spotlight was put on him, it was bright enough to make him shift his music stand slightly so that he could see the sheet music. The spot followed ... he shifted away ... the spot followed ... he shifted ... the spot followed relentlessly ... and he began to turn its pursuit and his evasion into a routine. The parents in attendance thought it was funny; it probably beat the tedium of watching kids other than yours play and was a bit of comedic aplomb you wouldn't expect from a young teen soloist. Max, observing the whole thing, was predictably furious—"They laughed at you!" Sid thought the laughter, the first he received from a genuine audience, was great.[22]

This earliest instance of Caesar's combining music and humor is a significant one. It's not at all difficult to imagine that had he not become a musician, he might never have become a comedian. It was one thing to make factory workers in your father's diner laugh by mimicking languages or trying to entertain your parents with imitating what you saw in the movies, another to turn a bent toward getting laughs (and a desire for approval) into a vocation. The saxophone would draw him into comedy with much larger audiences—in the Catskills and the Coast Guard—and put him on a career trajectory that would have been hardly predictable otherwise. Certainly, not by his mother or father. You get the distinct impression from Sid's autobiography (whether he intended to give it or not) that the Caesars never really knew what to *do* with their shy and offbeat youngest son.

Quiet and different he may have been, but Caesar had both ambition and plans; both precluded staying in Yonkers. At first, music predominated. Not only was he good at it, playing the sax seems to have drawn out to at least some degree someone who wasn't exactly the most outgoing of teenagers. (Any social unease was probably not helped by the fact that he was a good year younger than most of his classmates. Max had enrolled his shy son in school early, "just to get me out of the house," according to Sid. That resentful-sounding "just" coming from an interview some 30 years later is rather telling.[23]) He was in dance bands in both junior and senior high school and his bandmates are the only school friends he ever mentions. And he took music very seriously. He studied with a member of the NBC Symphony and audited classes in both saxophone and clarinet at Julliard. His dream was to play classical music and study in France with a renowned saxophonist; however, limited finances and, ultimately, World War II, put an end to it. Moreover, by 1935, in the depths of the Depression, the Caesar family's finances were at low ebb. Max lost the St. Clair and two successive diners went under as well. Much of the money Sid got from small engagements in Yonkers bars and restaurants (which, if he was lucky, was $5 a week) he "gave to the house."

When he graduated from Yonkers High School in 1939 at age 16, he moved to a boarding house in Manhattan; it meant one less mouth to feed

1. Origins

at home and, for him, the chance to join a musicians' union and get engagements that were not only more professionally satisfying but also more lucrative. His fellow musicians at the boarding house with whom he would jam (the landlady was both very tolerant and somewhat deaf) described him as serious and hard-working, and a musician talented enough that "Caesar never had to look for a job with a band—the jobs came looking for him."[24] At age 17, he landed a booking with the Shep Fields Orchestra, whose arrangements, fortuitously enough, featured reed instruments, particularly saxophones[25]; he would go on to play with the bands of Art Mooney, Charlie Spivak, and Claude Thornhill, all nationally-known in the Big Band Era.

However, Caesar had developed another interest and the sax would be an entry into it. Starting when he was 14, he had begun to spend summers playing in house bands in the Catskill Mountains resorts fondly known as the "Borscht Belt." They were particularly popular with Jews from the New York area, who in an age of overt anti–Semitism were often excluded from other resorts. So many major Jewish comedians got their start in the "Jewish Alps" providing entertainment for vacationers that a list of those who didn't would be shorter than one of those who did. Caesar would be among the latter. Observing the *tummlers* and comedians, he decided to offer his services, starting as a straight man for the resident comics. Very soon, he developed his own ideas about what was funny, which didn't include the old vaudeville routines and rapid-fire stand-up that was the usual comedy fare at the hotels and lodges. With the approval of Don Appel, the social director at Vacationland where Sid was playing in the house band, he began to work up routines based on the language mimicry he had been doing since childhood and added what would become a hallmark of his comedy: finding humor in real-life situations which he would then exaggerate for comic effect. By the time of his last Borscht Belt summers, he was playing at top-line resorts like Kutscher's Hotel not as a saxophonist who also did comedy, but a comedian who also played sax.[26]

Nor did military service in World War II interrupt the combination. Caesar had enlisted in the Coast Guard in early 1942 and got lucky in his deployment; he was assigned to the Brooklyn Barracks (for him, it was practically in his back yard), patrolling the piers and guarding their materiel. Although he and his base mates were grateful for the coastal assignment (as opposed to, say, convoy escort duty in the North Atlantic), it was not the most exciting. As Sid put it, "What are you going to do after you check out the pier, stand there and look at the stuff?"[27] The answer to boredom was obvious, at least to Caesar: with the approval of his commander, he formed a dance band and put on variety shows with Vernon Duke, the composer, also in his unit. One of them, *Six On, Twelve Off* (the schedule for patrols), became very popular and the show was put on at various bases in the Coast Guard and Navy districts. Sid played sax and clarinet, led the band, and was the chief comic in the sketches. The latter included the germ of what would become one of his best-known comedy routines, the airplane number, a parody of wartime aviation movies. In it, he spoofed the improbable heroics of a lone pilot taking on an entire Luftwaffe squadron, complete with sound effects and German doubletalk. (Sid would do the airplane number several times on *Your Show of Shows*. His performance of it was always funny, but the one of 3/1/1952 is perhaps the best.) When Duke, along with Howard Dietz the lyricist, began to develop *Tars and Spars*, the Coast Guard's answer to the Army's service show, he arranged for Caesar to be transferred to Palm Beach for rehearsals for the revue; he was to play sax and do some of his comedy routines.

It was during the development of *Tars and Spars* that Sid would meet the man who would become the mentor and supporter he had always sought, but never found, in his father Max. It would be another Max who, in a nice psychological touch, was old enough to be his father—Max Liebman. Their association would last until 1954 and it was one of mutual respect and admiration for each other's talents. And for Caesar, it was something more: Greg Garrison, one of *Your Show of Shows*' television directors, commented that "He truly loved Max—and he trusted him. He trusted him. Max was probably the only man that really could ever get into and communicate with Sid artistically."[28]

If Caesar could have chosen someone to be discovered by, he couldn't have done any better. Liebman was a well-known director and producer at Camp Tamiment in the Poconos where he had been social director since 1933. His organizational skills and eye for talent were already legendary in the resort area. At Tamiment Playhouse, he would mount weekly productions each summer that were comparable to New York shows; under his leadership, Tamiment would eventually be referred to as "Broadway in the Poconos."[29] His discoveries included Danny Kaye, Imogene Coca, Jules Munshin, and Betty Garrett. He would employ Lucille Kallen and Mel Tolkin as writers at the Playhouse, Jerome Robbins as a choreographer, and Sylvia Fine (future wife of Danny Kaye) and Jerry Bock as writers and composers. Taking a leave from Tamiment during the war, Liebman had been serving as a director and sketch writer for USO shows when he was approached by the Coast Guard to produce and direct *Tars and Spars*. Max had heard from Vernon Duke about Caesar's airplane number and, overhearing Sid joking around and doing improv with the other band members, approached him. In one of those almost-too-good-to-be-true discovery stories, Liebman actually told him the equivalent of "You're too good for this, kid." Recognizing Caesar's raw talent, Max began to work with him in

1. Origins 23

refining the airplane number into a 9-minute monologue, which became a feature of the revue as it toured the country. Although Quartermaster Second Class Marc Ballero, an impressionist, was supposed to be the main comic in the show, he was soon overshadowed by Seaman First Class Sidney Caesar. When *Tars and Spars* reached its terminus on the West Coast, Columbia, which held an option on it, decided to make a movie based on the revue. Sid was the only original cast member to appear in the film.

From 1945 on, he would be a full-time comedian, but he would never entirely give up the saxophone, the instrument that led him into that career. At least once, it would be used as a comic prop in a sketch: in the very funny *Your Show of Shows* parody "Young Man with a Lip" (9/15/1952), Caesar is a prize fighter who has given up the sax to box. Imogene Coca is his girlfriend Shirley who hauls it around with her and at every other moment, always the most inopportune, reminds him of the professional career he might have had. Nonetheless, it turns out to be his salvation. In a championship fight, during which he's being beaten to a pulp, he rallies to knock out his opponent—when he hears "Humoresque" (of all things) being played by Shirley on sax from ringside. However, using it solely as a prop to get laughs was rare (the writers probably couldn't resist the parallels). Far more frequent were the instances in which he played the saxophone seriously. Both Carl Reiner and Mel Brooks thought that Sid could have made a good living playing it if he had continued as a professional musician[30]; on the basis of what can be seen on video and tape, they were probably correct. Caesar and his sax would occasionally appear in brief numbers on *The Admiral Broadway Revue* and *Your Show of Shows* (where he also played the clarinet on one episode—he was good on that, too). On an episode of *Caesar's Hour* in 1954, he joined Benny Goodman's band in a rendition of the classic swing number "Sing, Sing, Sing." Although he hadn't played professionally for almost ten years at that point, he could still rip off an impressive sax solo. And on another episode, as Progress Hornsby the hip musician, he would also do a more than competent jazz improvisation.

Tars and Spars, sans sax,[31] would be Caesar's first major comedy success. Other than the use of his airplane number, the movie itself, which starred Alfred Drake and Janet Blair, had nothing in common with the revue it was based on except its title, and the reviews were mixed. However, they all mentioned Caesar, who played the best friend role. *Variety* declared, in its review of January 10, 1946, that the film "uncovers a comer in Sid Caesar." Bosley Crowther in the *New York Times* of February 25, summed it up well: "*Tars and Spars*, or boy meets girl in the same old way even in the Coast Guard, is mighty lucky that it has a fellow named Sid Caesar to break the monotony of juvenile romantic misunderstanding, listless songs, and commonplace dance routines." Although Crowther could have been a bit less scathing in his assessment of the full-scale dance routines, some of which weren't bad, he was certainly accurate in his assessment of Sid's performance. He provided what life there was in the picture. He had three showcase numbers, including the airplane movie parody and a crazed as well as physically impressive song and dance bit in a mess hall (and on top of its tables). Was he funny? Yes, although far more frenetic than he would be later in his career (he could still do frenetic when called for, but in only a year's time, would learn to dial it down for nightclub audiences and, eventually, a TV one). What is perhaps more impressive for a 22-year-old in his first film is his assurance on camera and his ability, even at that early stage of his career, to play it straight if called for and to genuinely listen to other actors. It was clear that he wasn't just going to be a comedian waiting for his next line, but someone who could become a legitimate comic actor.

After filming of *Tars and Spars* was completed, its director Alfred Green suggested Caesar try out for *The Al Jolson Story* at Columbia. The conversation apparently went something like this—Caesar (before screen test): "That's ridiculous. I can't play Jolson." Green (after screen test): "You're right."[32] The part would go to Larry Parks. It *might* have been an interesting casting choice. Sid seems to have been the only Jewish actor even vaguely considered to play someone who was also a Jew and whose religion is an integral part of the story. However, the role would have been totally wrong for him. Caesar lip-synching to Jolson's recordings? The mind boggles. Above all, there was the nature of the material, particularly Jolson's song standards: first, in their saccharine sentimentality (of a sort that Sid would later parody) and second, in the need for any actor to put on blackface to perform some of them. Parks was a great success in the role but watching him perform "Mammy" induces a cringe today. Even though he wanted a leading role very badly, Sid was perhaps fortunate in not getting this one.

While waiting for the release of *Tars and Spars*, delayed by an industry-wide film crew strike, Caesar did land a part in *The Guilt of Janet Ames*, which starred Rosalind Russell and Melvyn Douglas. In the post-war period, there was a good movie to be made about the trauma experienced by women whose husbands or lovers died in combat. This wasn't it. The film is a psychological/semi-Freudian/fantasy mishmosh about a war widow (Russell), bitter and resentful, who is trying to track down five men whose lives were saved by her husband at the cost of his own. A newspaperman (Douglas), who unbeknownst to her, is one of the five, uses a form of hypnotic suggestion to enable her to enter their lives, showing her that her husband's sacrifice was worth it. These mental excursions are presented in the form of dream sequences acted out on expressionistic sets. Sid is the last she "sees," a comedian—hardly a stretch—performing in a fantasy nightclub.

Caesar, hanging around the set during filming, was distinctly unimpressed with the plot, and decided, along with the writers for his sequence, Allen Roberts and Doris Fisher, to go for comedic broke. Playing a psychiatrist and his patient, his routine is a satire of "psychological" movies within a "psychological" movie (you'd think the director would've noticed). It's Sid at his most frenetic, at one point almost turning himself into the human equivalent of a Chuck Jones cartoon character, but he's also rather engaging in the few straight lines he has with Russell and Douglas at the end of his segment. As in *Tars and Spars*, he received favorable notices, even if critical reception of the film was lukewarm. *Variety* (3/5/47) thought that "Sid Caesar gets across with a bang," and noted that the monologue was a pretty good review of the picture in itself. The *New York Times* review (5/23/47), although critical of the film's script and story development, was positive about him: "Three of the lady's four dreams are unfortunately mundane affairs, but a lunatic note of comedy is attained when the elastic-faced Sid Caesar appears doing an energetic burlesque of psychiatrists and psychoanalysis. A very funny man, this Mr. Caesar."

However, this would mark the end of an early Hollywood career for Sid. He would not appear in a movie again until 1963 in *It's a Mad, Mad, Mad, Mad World*. (Although there were many discussions and tentative plans for pictures when he and Coca were on *Your Show of Shows*, none ever came to fruition, one reason, besides finding the right vehicle, being the difficulty in filming one in the brief summer hiatus of the program.) Despite appearing in two films in two years, with good reviews and featured billing in both, he was also, at least from his perspective, idle a lot.[33] Moreover, he didn't want to make a film career out of just performing routines or playing comedic sidekicks. Nonetheless, his success in *Tars and Spars* would bring about an opportunity to go back to New York. A booking agent for the Copacabana who liked his performance in the film offered him a two-week engagement. There were only two slight snags—Caesar had never done a nightclub act before and he didn't have material for one. He reached out to his wartime mentor Max Liebman, who not only helped him put together an act, but took him to the William Morris Agency to get further bookings in nightclubs and theaters, including the Roxy in Rockefeller Center. The *Variety* review of his opening at the Copa on January 1, 1947, was both positive and prescient: "Caesar has genuine comedic talents that depend on characterization rather than gags. It's the type of material that will probably distinguish him from other funnymen...."[34] Even though these early engagements were successful, he seems never to have been entirely comfortable in a club atmosphere. Once again, it would be Liebman who would be his mentor and guide.[35] Max would provide the opportunity for Sid to return to comic acting, first on the stage, a venue

Publicity shot for *Make Mine Manhattan* (1948). The "Noises in the Street" number, with Sid on garbage can lids. The Manhattan noisemakers, left to right: Joshua Shelley, Julie Oshins, Caesar, Max Showalter, Perry Bruskin.

with which he was already familiar (and comfortable with), and then in a brand-new setting which he would make his own—television.

In 1947 Max was sketch director for an upcoming revue, *Make Mine Manhattan*. It seems clear he was influential in persuading its producer Joe Hyman to sign Caesar, then playing the Roxy, for it. The revue was a success even in road try-outs; when it opened on Broadway in January of 1948, it was a hit, running for 429 performances, and Sid was the breakout star. He had three solos and appeared in over half the sketches. Reviews of his performance were all he could have hoped for in his Broadway debut: "An innate knack for character delineations," "shows off his virtuosity," "most original item in the program," "imaginative and clever."[36] And it also won him a Donaldson Award (think pre–Tony) for Best Male Debut in a Musical. Despite its success, *Make Mine Manhattan* was probably one of the best musical revues you never heard of. Unfortunately, there was no cast album and, as its title suggests, it was very New York-centric. Although many of the songs and sketches were about New York at any time in the 20th century, others were far less "timeless," including one about the opening of the United Nations, in which Sid played three different delegates.[37] After almost a year, Caesar had had enough, becoming bored doing the same numbers over and over. However, he left the show with not only more theater experience and a Donaldson but considerably more money (he had wangled a contract of $1500 a week plus 5 percent of the box office).

Meanwhile, Liebman had returned to Tamiment with big plans: putting together a package for television. As a popular medium, it was just beginning to come into its own, and he wanted to recreate Broadway revues and the shows he had been putting on in the Poconos for its growing audience. It would be something different for TV in the late '40s, a revue with a stock company to provide comedy, songs, and dance. It was also a conscious attempt to elevate the tone of what TV audiences saw; the dance would include both ballet and modern, and the song segments would feature operatic excerpts as well as popular music. Tamiment alumni would be prominent parts of it—dancers Mata and Hari, choreographer James Starbuck, and musical director Charles Sanford. Lucille Kallen and Mel Tolkin would provide the writing for comedy sketches. And Liebman already had his leads in mind: Caesar and Imogene Coca.

The concept attracted two potential backers: the Admiral Corporation, makers of radios and phonographs and a major manufacturer of television sets, and Sylvester "Pat" Weaver, an advertising executive with Young & Rubicam who had a client ready to invest in TV shows. (The CBS head of programming, probably to his everlasting regret, wasn't interested.)[38] Liebman successfully sealed a deal for sponsorship with Admiral. Meanwhile, Weaver had just become the chief of programming at NBC; like Max, he saw potential in TV as a cultural as well as entertainment medium and arranged for the network to carry the new hour-long show. (So too would DuMont, a fledgling TV network founded in 1946.) Throughout negotiations, Liebman insisted on top billing for Caesar. Sid had started a comedy career in a Coast Guard revue in 1944; by 1949, he had been in films, performed in nightclubs and on Broadway, and made two television appearances on *Texaco Star Theatre*, doing the airplane number and a bit from *Make Mine Manhattan*. Now he would be the star of a TV show. Caesar had chosen a career in comedy to satisfy a deep-seated desire for attention and approval; now he was about to receive it on a scale he probably couldn't have imagined—and it would be the infant medium of television that would give it to him.

2

The Admiral Broadway Revue: Broadway Right into Your Home

The Admiral Broadway Revue would be *Your Show of Shows* in embryo. Max Liebman was the *Revue*'s producer and director, Caesar was the headliner, and Imogene Coca was a featured performer. Howie Morris was a member of the cast, appearing in comedy sketches as well as song and dance numbers. Mel Tolkin and Lucille Kallen were on the writing staff; Mel Brooks, although neither on salary nor credited, supplied material for Caesar. The program featured parodies of operas and Hollywood film genres (although none of specific films, a hallmark of *Your Show of Shows*). The Professor first made his appearance in a regular roving-reporter bit, "Nonentities in the News." Caesar did a weekly monologue and Coca did solo dances and musical parodies. A good half of the show was devoted to variety acts that included singers, comics, even a trained seal that shook "hands" with Caesar at the end of one episode (you can imagine Sid storing that in his memory bank for a later pantomime on *Your Show of Shows* where he was a frustrated performing seal and Imogene his demanding trainer). There were regular featured dancers—Marge and Gower Champion, as well as Mata and Hari. Each episode ended with a big production number, followed (if time permitted) by a curtain call of the stars. Anyone who has seen an entire episode of both the *Revue* and *Your Show of Shows* will immediately recognize the similarities in both personnel and format.

However, in other respects, *The Admiral Broadway Revue* was definitely the beta version. As the chorus in naval costumes (just in case you forgot who the sponsor was) sang at the beginning of each show, "We try to bring Broadway right into your home." The program was basically a televised theatrical revue, as Liebman had intended, and much more rigid in that format than its successor, which was more of a comedy-variety show, would be. The TV audience saw almost exactly what someone with a good seat in the theater would see, with only a few exceptions—there were close-ups of Caesar during his monologues, which were effective, and of the dancers in production numbers, which were less so (critics complained they cut off the visual flow of the dances). Jack Gould, TV critic of the *New York Times*, while finding the show promising, accurately observed that a filmed presentation of a stage show resulted in the actors playing to the studio audience and not to the cameras; there was a need for the intimate approach that a genuine television show could provide.[39] *Your Show of Shows* would eventually have far more sophisticated camerawork and technique and its cast, especially Caesar, learned very quickly how close-ups could enhance sketch comedy for a home viewing audience rather than just one in a theater. There was one more major difference between the *Revue* and its successor. The announcer promised a "happy blend of music, song, and comedy," but the emphasis on comedy, at least the sketch variety, was far less than it would be in *Your Show of Shows*. Above all, there was also no fixed comedy ensemble. In the 17 episodes of the *Revue* that can be seen today, Caesar, Morris, and Coca are never all together in a sketch.

In fact, Coca's role in the *Revue* was initially very different from the one she would assume on *Your Show of Shows*. Fourteen years older than Caesar, she had vastly more theatrical and revue/cabaret experience, including working with Max Liebman in a 1939 Broadway musical, *The Straw Hat Revue*, which was based on a summer production at Tamiment. After beginning her career as a dancer, she developed a specialization in musical comedy—parodies of ballet and opera, a striptease done under a huge overcoat (which is as funny as it sounds)—rather than sketch comedy. The sponsor was initially reluctant about using her, preferring a name player, so Mary McCarty, a Broadway actress with Hollywood experience, was given billing over Coca; it was McCarty who was supposed to be the principal female comedian. In the early episodes, the writers were not even doing material specifically for Imogene; she relied on numbers she had done in earlier revues.

Moreover, there was no real Second Banana to Caesar. If you're expecting to see Carl Reiner in the sketches, you won't—he was not a member of the cast. The closest the *Revue* came to a straight man was journeyman actor Tom Avera. He was fine as a singer and dancer; less so in the sketches, where his characterizations tended to be of the one-note, overwrought twit variety. Nonetheless, he would follow Caesar and Coca onto *Your Show of Shows* for the earliest episodes before being replaced by Reiner. Max Liebman had noticed his talent when he was brought in as a play doctor for a short-run Broadway comedy in which Carl appeared. Avera had been satisfactory, Reiner would be superb. (One of the few things Avera and Reiner had in common was that they were both taller than Sid. Liebman had a theory, based on who-knows-what, that the Second Banana should be taller than the principal comic. As this particular principal comic was over six feet tall, it presented an obstacle in auditioning for actors otherwise qualified but height-challenged. You have to thank the comedic gods that Carl was at least 6'2".)

Howie Morris, who would become an invaluable Third Banana on *Your Show of Shows*, didn't even appear in the *Revue* in its earliest episodes. He came on board for a distinctly Caesar-related reason. As Morris told it, he heard that Max Liebman was looking for someone Sid Caesar could lift by the lapels. When he showed up at Liebman's office, Max introduced him to Mel Tolkin and Lucille Kallen and "this hulk standing in the corner." The hulk lifted him up and said, "I want him."[40] Caesar got him. On the March 4 episode, Morris appears in a sketch about a mobster—Sid naturally—who seeks psychiatric help because he's beginning to feel sorry for the rivals he has to bump off. (Yes, exactly 50 years before *Analyze This*.) As an associate who angers Caesar, Howie finds himself lifted off the floor by, of course, his lapels. From that point forward, even though he wouldn't receive billing until almost the end of the *Revue*, Morris would appear in sketches and song and dance numbers.

Perhaps the most striking difference between the *Revue* and *Your Show of Shows* was in its comedy. The *Revue* would have witty numbers satirizing modern art, opera, and psychiatry. The closing one on the first episode was a clever parody of an opera. Performed in English for "mass appeal," it was entitled "No, No, Rigoletto." It threw in every expected opera motif—a bit of *The Valkyries, Carmen*, and the *Barber of Seville*—as well as the unexpected—a Can-Can and, for good measure, a Western saloon song. Caesar as the villain provided *recitativo*, breaking into full song for "It's a Good Day"—to commit foul deeds. It's a witty and funny pastiche and one remarkably sophisticated for television in 1949, particularly in comparison to, say, the usual fare on Milton Berle's *Texaco Star Theatre*. However, anyone expecting *Your Show of Shows*' sustained quality of sketch comedy will be disappointed. The sketches tend to be broader and funny only in spots, somewhat surprisingly, as Tolkin and Kallen would be the major contributors in the writing for *Your Show of Shows*. Certainly, there were exceptions: there's a good one about Radio City Music Hall ushers preparing for a premiere as if for a military operation. Caesar is the chief usher in an elaborate braided uniform who wields a pointer to a huge map of the theater to assign the ushers to their various posts: "We may lose the mezzanine but we shall hold the orchestra pit." Meanwhile, "I myself will take my commandos into the ladies' lounge and wipe out all resistance." To calm a nervous rookie, he performs a rapid-fire and very funny history of the movies in under two minutes. It culminates in what he describes as the apex of film-making, which he identifies by emitting an unexpected (and unenhanced) Tarzan yell. Another, as part of a Hollywood-themed episode, is about actors on a movie set with a director (Morris) who insists on repeating one scene: Caesar is a rich playboy who attempts to seduce the girlfriend of one of his employees and gets slapped by him. Over and over ... and over, thanks to the director's insistence on getting it right. It's worth watching even to a tiresome ending to appreciate Sid's facial expressions and physical comedy as he reels in increasingly dramatic fashion from each successive wallop. It also includes his first extensive manhandling of Howie when the director yells "Take it from the slap" just once too often. But overall, the humor in the sketches frequently comes as much from Caesar's talents as it does from the writing—he could simply elevate weaker material.

And those with Caesar and Coca? Apart from occasional appearances as part of a comedic ensemble, some of which involved no interaction between them at all, they worked together exclusively on only five sketches during the *Revue*'s 4-month run. And these are among the broader, less funny ones. They almost act past each other and more to the audience at times, particularly on Coca's part. After all, they had never worked together before. Nor did they apparently know each other all that well in the beginning of the *Revue* (at the curtain call of an episode in February, Sid introduces Imogene as "Miss Imogene Coco"). In any event, there simply was no immediate or dramatic comedic connection. In only two bits before the next-to-last episode of the show are there glimmerings of what the two together might be capable of, and neither was a comedy sketch in which they spoke. Rather they were opportunities for the dancer and the musician to move together and in them you *can* see the beginnings of an extraordinary working relationship. The first was a sketch in which Tom Avera is seated at a typewriter pounding out a play, "Breakfast," about a young married couple, Caesar and Coca, who are seated at a table. As he reads out loud what he's typing, they mouth his dialogue and follow his directions. When he changes his mind repeatedly, speeds things up and slows them down, or comes to a dead halt to think, they follow perfectly, including some impressive stop-action sequences (try freezing for ten seconds sometime as you're bent over, or as you're about to drink a cup of coffee). The second is a brief comedy segment at the end of a Latin dance production number. Sid and Imogene perform, with appropriate passion (and some very funny anguished expressions), a series of dramatic tango-like moves—so dramatic they keep missing each other. He finally halts her circling around him by sticking a huge palm in front of her face to gently push her back to the routine. It would be the first example of the kind of comedy dance sequences they would later perform together on *Your Show of Shows*.

Max Liebman, with his usual unerring eye for comedic pairings and possibilities, apparently noticed something in these bits too, because he was responsible for bringing about their first genuine pantomime together. As

Coca recalled, she asked Liebman to do a sketch called "Better Go Now" that she had done in a revue, expecting that her husband Robert Burton would be used as her partner. Instead, Max said, "Good idea. Do it with Sid." Not having seen very much of Caesar's solo routines, she replied, "but we'll have to teach him pantomime." Obviously, they didn't. "Sid came in and looked at me peculiarly [it was her material, after all], and I looked at him and I said 'this is a pantomime I did.' I told him the story. I said, 'These people are going to see a movie. It's about the cliché things that people do.' He did it as if he had done it all his life."[41]

"Better Go Now" was indeed a breakthrough. It was the first indication of the ability they would develop to communicate with each other on an almost uncanny, ESP-like, comedic level. The scene in a movie theater is entirely in pantomime and their synchronization of movement and expression is almost perfect. It begins with their attempts to cope with particularly inedible pieces of candy, actually engaging in mirror image chewing. Their reactions to various parts of the movie—a funny sequence, a sad sequence (with Sid looking around furtively to see if anyone notices he is crying), an exciting sequence, and finally a steamy sequence—are impressively identical. Both of them are surprised, then wide-eyed, at the love scene. You can see the wheels turning in Sid's head as he figures out how to take advantage of it. Using the time-honored stratagem of yawning and stretching to put his arm around Imogene, his checking out of the corner of his eye to gauge his success and Coca's "oh, no he *isn't*" facial expression when she realizes what he's doing are classic. There's a bit of subtle cuing (that they would never need again), but for a first pantomime together, it's an amazing performance. And everyone realized it. As Imogene would later say, "From then on Sid and I worked together."

If it took until the next-to-last episode of the *Revue* for Caesar and Coca to forge a pairing made in comedy heaven, Sid showed comic brilliance in solo routines immediately. His monologues are just as energetic and intense as they would be on *Your Show of Shows* and you can see more of them from the *Revue* on video today. On the earliest episodes, he reprised the airplane number from *Tars and Spars* (in a slightly different version—Caesar never repeated a sketch in exactly the same way) as well as the Penny Gum Machine routine and "Five-Dollar Date," both of which he had done in *Make Mine Manhattan*. Both are classics and make abundantly clear why he won the Donaldson Award.

In the first, he is an incredibly perky and polite, incredibly honest gum machine in the West 57th Street subway station—"Juicy Fruit, Ma'am? Surely." When he runs out of gum and is force-fed a penny, despite his attempts to refuse it, an angry customer shakes and hits him. Realizing honesty doesn't pay, the polite machine turns cynical and sarcastic—"Hey, you over there? You want gum?" When none comes out, he snarks, "No gum? Sue me!" After the vending owners discover a surfeit of money in his innards—"Hey, this kid's got talent!"—he's made into a Downtown quarter slot-machine luring suckers into depositing their quarters without paying off. He ultimately comes to a bad end, destroyed in a police raid. Throughout, Caesar's comic acting ability is on full display—not only does he make the penny gum machine appealing and its transmogrification into the crooked slot machine funny, you feel sorry for the inanimate object's tragic demise. And the only prop he uses for both is himself—his arms as a lever and delivery slot for the gum machine, his eyes blinking to mime the spinning of the reels of the slot machine and making ticking sounds as they slow. (The only "real" prop he would ever use in one of his solo routines was a straight-backed chair to suggest a bed or, well, a chair.)

"Five-Dollar Date" is about a guy with his girl on a date in 1939, then on the same date in 1949. In 1939, prices are low, cab drivers accommodating, restaurateurs polite and effusive, a movie usher pleads for business ("Free turkeys, free cheese. Buy your tickets, please!"), and he goes home with change from his five-dollar bill. Ten years later, prices have skyrocketed, cab drivers are surly ("Wherever you're going, I'm not going there"), there are no seats in the restaurants, and the usher is interested only in herding patrons into block-long lines. In 6 minutes, Caesar plays the man, his date, three cabbies, French and Italian restaurant owners, and the movie usher—twice. And most of it is done in rhyme. The first version of the date is fast, the second approaches Mach 1. Sid's machine-gun delivery is incredible (yet coherent) and his comedic energy is staggering—it's hard to believe that the *Make Mine Manhattan* version was actually longer.

Of the monologues he would first perform on *The Admiral Broadway Revue*, few are weak, all are funny, and some are brilliant, a series of comedic *tours de force*. In them, the writers, not always up to the *Your Show of Shows* par for sketches, click perfectly with Caesar solo. And all of Sid's considerable comedy skills are used in them—acting, mime, sound-effects, and language mimicry (French, Russian, Italian, and in one brief bit where he is an auctioneer in a slave market, no known language, but it sounds convincingly Arabic). Not to mention sheer out-of-my-way energy: a jive version of *Cyrano de Bergerac* is five non-stop minutes of patter singing, fighting a duel, and miming playing a bass and drums and supplying the sound effects. Somehow, he finds sufficient breath to finish with a saxophone solo—and belt out an end to the song.

When you consider that the monologues were written and memorized weekly, their variety as well as the skill with which they were performed is all the more impressive. "A Man Getting Up in the Morning" has some of Sid's most skillful miming: testing the water in the shower, painstakingly adjusting it until it's just so, stepping in—and getting scalded. Or, as he's dressing, going through the world's most complicated tying of a necktie. In "Technicolor Western" aka "California or Else," he is not just 2 or 3 but at least 16 characters, including a horse. "Zero Hour," a play about World War I, is performed first in a stiff upper-lip English version (a wounded Tommy shakes off aid: "No. No water, Gunga Din.") and then in an extremely impassioned French one in which he employs doubletalk in one of the faux languages he did best.

Both Caesar's and his writers' love of movies resulted in two of the funniest monologues of the *Revue*. The first is "The Schmo," a parody of boxing movies with a hefty dollop of *Body and Soul*, as well as every other fight film you can think of. Every cliché of the genre is fondly ticked off. Caesar is a poor and, as the title suggests, none too bright kid who wants to be somebody. After decking a bully in a pool hall, he's approached by a boxing manager who asks him if he's ever considered becoming a fighter. His response: "What? And get my brains knocked out? I'm gonna be a chemistry teacher." Instead, he does indeed become a boxer and a successful one, but then a gangster who won a controlling interest in him in a pinochle game tells him to take a dive in the title fight for $60,000. Sid decides to return to the old neighborhood to talk to his aged mother and tell her how well he's doing: "I'm gonna take ya outta this damp, dark, dirty dump. I'm gonna take ya someplace where there's light, fresh air, and sunshine—I'll move ya across the street." On his way to the fight, he's surrounded by neighborhood kids who have bet their entire savings of 19 cents on him. After a brief, very brief, wrestle with his conscience ("they bet their last 19 cents on me and I'm gonna throw the fight for a measly 60 thousand?—Ah, I'll give 'em their 19 cents back"), he takes the dive. With one knee on the canvas waiting for the ten-count, it suddenly occurs to him that he can make more money if he wins the fight and he gets up to knock out his opponent and become the new champ—happier if not necessarily any brighter.

The second is a semi-parody of a film noir, from opening credits to the end. Besides being gut-bustingly funny, it's a stunning display of Caesarean sound-effects. Sid usually used them in monologues; this one featured them. The melodramatic plot: A man gets up in the morning and goes to work to find a letter from his lover Mary demanding he divorce his wife. He panics and calls her to suggest a picnic at "our favorite spot, down by the cliff." After telling her "Just remember I love you," he pushes her off. Discovering to his horror that he's being followed by a man who has seen him do it, he flees to a carnival to lose him amid the attractions, but he's cornered. Then he wakes up. It was only a dream. Reunited with Mary (appearing from who-knows-where), he kisses her and tells her he's always loved her. The End. Sid performs the whole thing first with dialogue and action, then again with music and sound-effects. The first version is funny, thanks to his facial expressions and body language in reaction to every plot twist, and he has to interrupt audience applause to continue. The second is hilarious, starting with the over-the-top music he supplies for the credits and at every melodramatic moment. His sound effects? Among others, bird calls in the morning (with an angry cat thrown in); traffic noises on the way to work; typewriters at the office; Mary's scream, fading as she falls over the obviously *very* steep cliff; the noises of the carnival; and the kiss he plants on Mary at the end, which sounds almost vacuum-sealed. And there are two segments that are simply extraordinary: the first is his panicked phone call to Mary in which he's talking into the receiver, mimicking the high-pitched voice coming out of the other end and, almost simultaneous with both voices, making the sounds of his own rapid heartbeat. The second is at the carnival where he supplies the familiar auditory backdrop of carousel music: he rides on the merry-go-round, takes some shots in a shooting gallery, and tries the test of strength machine, providing sound effects for all of them—and *never stops* making the carousel music sounds as well. It's a virtuoso performance and almost has to be seen—or heard—to be believed. If there had been an award for Best Achievement in Comedic Sound by a Human Being, Sid would have walked away with it.

At the season-ender of the *Revue* on June 2, Caesar gave an emotional curtain-call speech, thanking the audience, cast, and staff and concluding with "Until next September." Sid and everyone connected with the show might have had every expectation of indeed being back. Liebman's Broadway-style revue concept was praised by *Life* as having "some of Broadway's best young talent," and Caesar had emerged as a TV comedy star, one critic calling him "one of the soundest arguments for buying a television set ... already widely regarded as the outstanding comedian developed thru video."[42] The show had received good reviews, it owned Friday nights, and usually placed second only to *The Texaco Star Theatre* in the ratings. Yet, despite its success, it was cancelled by Admiral—for reasons explicable only in the early days of television.

It was the usual practice for most major shows to have one sponsor, as in *Texaco Star Theatre* or *Ford Television Theatre*. There were obvious benefits for the sponsor which had a showcase for its products and could even exercise a degree of creative control through its advertising agency, which wanted to avoid anything controversial or considered even remotely detrimental to its client. The drawbacks for the cast and production staff were equally obvious. The sponsor could at any time pull the plug, which is what Admiral did. The usual reason given is the one Caesar himself provided in his autobiography: the president of Admiral told him that the sales of TV sets (which made up 65–70 percent of Admiral's gross) had skyrocketed.

The company had to either put more money into retooling factories to meet demand or continue funding the revue. The company chose the first option. As Sid pointed out, Revlon made a similar decision in cutting back on its advertising in favor of making more cosmetics.[43] However, some historians of early television take the story a bit too far in implying that Admiral put all their money into manufacturing sets instead of TV programming. The company would continue to sponsor programs, just less expensive ones than the *Revue*. Its production costs and talent budget exceeded $20,000 a week, making it costlier than either Texaco or Ford's sponsorship of their programs. After only four months on the air, the original budget estimates for the *Revue* had doubled before it went off the air in the spring.[44]

However, Max Liebman told Caesar, off to a summer-long booking into the Palmer House in Chicago, not to worry.[45] They would be back. And they were, thanks to Pat Weaver, the visionary programming chief at NBC who picked up the network's option for the old *Revue*. He implemented the "magazine method" of sponsorship for a new show. The network, not the sponsor, would own the program and sell advertising slots to a variety of individual sponsors, eliminating financial dependence on just one and theoretically making more money for NBC.[46] In hindsight it was just as important for the future of TV comedy, as it put creative control in the hands of the producers and staff (although it never completely eliminated individual sponsor watchdogging over content, one of the pitfalls of early, as well as subsequent, commercial television). So, a new show was planned, with Liebman as producer/director, the comedic principals of the *Revue*, minus Mary McCarty, who went back to Broadway (perhaps fortunately as Caesar and she had, in their few segments together, zero chemistry); and Tolkin, Kallen, and Brooks as the writers. It was to run for 90 minutes on Saturday nights under the title NBC gave it, *Your Show of Shows*. It debuted on February 25, 1950—and it would make television comedy history.

PART II

"Ladies and Gentlemen, the star of *Your Show of Shows*, Sid Caesar"

When *Your Show of Shows* debuted in February of 1950, it did so as the second part of *Saturday Night Revue*, NBC's ambitious attempt at dominating prime-time Saturday evening viewing from 8:00 to 10:30. *The Jack Carter Show* started with an hour from Chicago; *Your Show of Shows* finished with ninety minutes from New York. You might have predicted the future of both from Jack Gould's assessment of the premiere in the *New York Times*: "90 minutes of first-rate popular entertainment and only sixty minutes of mediocre stuff."[1] The "mediocre stuff" ended in June of 1951, as did *Saturday Night Revue*; *Your Show of Shows* would run for three more seasons. From its very beginning, it was something different from what viewers were accustomed to seeing in a comedy/variety show. Its star did neither stand-up nor old vaudeville or radio routines (he was too young for the former and had never done the latter). Rather, he excelled in sketch comedy, pantomime, and monologues of an impressive variety. Gould called Caesar "very much a rounded artist ... who must now be ranked with the genuine clowns of the day." The comedy sketches had no cream pies or powder puffs to the face, squirts with seltzer water, or dressing in women's clothes (that was left to Milton Berle and *Texaco Star Theatre*). The humor was witty and sophisticated with a bent toward satire and parody—Gould noted its "having an adult flavor throughout"—and was produced by a staff that included Mel Tolkin, Lucille Kallen, and Mel Brooks. Over the following seasons, it would add other great comedy writers, resulting in a team unequalled then or since.

Before beginning any analysis of that humor or the brilliance of Caesar and Company in performing it, it's necessary to know something about the setting in which it was produced and played. For those who remember what TV and TV comedy was like in the early to mid-'50s, consider what follows as a refresher course, points at which you can nod knowingly. For those too young, consider it an introduction to a very different time in television history. What did an audience see and hear? What were they not likely to? How was comedy programming then different from today's TV comedy programming? And how was *Your Show of Shows* like and—more importantly—different from other comedy shows of the time?

3

Brought to You in Living Black and White: Television in the '50s

Your Show of Shows was broadcast live, as most TV programs were then. Today, you can certainly see live network (as opposed to cable) programming—news, sports, awards shows—but drama and comedy, only occasionally. Both continuing drama and comedy shows have had live individual episodes and every now and then you can see one-shot dramas—and much is made of the daring of doing them live. However, a continuing live comedy show (taped before a live audience doesn't count) for 22-episode seasons is relatively rare. The obvious exception is *Saturday Night Live*, a direct descendant of *Your Show of Shows*.

Your Show of Shows was live for anywhere from 33 to 39 shows a season, and comedy segments generally made up roughly half of its 90-minute time slot. It was broadcast in real time—no delays, no edits—before a studio audience whose laughter was real, not canned or "sweetened." For TV audiences accustomed to today's taped shows, the concept of going live is sometimes difficult to grasp. Caesar was frequently asked how long it took to do an hour and a half show. His usual laconic reply was, "Oh, about ninety minutes."[2] And the timing had to be exact. How exact? One script for what was most likely the dress rehearsal of one episode lists times for all the sketches and notes by one of them "cut :10."[3] If a show ran short, a sketch would have to be stretched or the curtain call prolonged (sometimes awkwardly); if it was too long, it would be cut off, which meant the actors were often forced to, as Max Liebman put it, "edit on their feet."[4] Moreover, there were no teleprompters or cue cards. Both Caesar and Carl Reiner felt that they took actors out of a sketch. For Sid, with his immersion into a character and his skills in listening and reacting to the other actors, they would have been unthinkable: "If you're looking at someone, you can see what they're doing. You can feel what they're doing. If you're looking off at cue cards, you lose that connection."[5]

Live TV required experienced stagehands, seasoned cameramen, and dressers to assist actors. It might seem odd to include dressers in a list of indispensable staff, but it's easy to forget when most shows are now taped that costume changes—not just between sketches but *in* them—had to be quick. Frequently, they took place in the wings during musical numbers. One minor way of dealing with them can be seen in the first half season of *Your Show of Shows* when Caesar, after his introduction, would sometimes appear on stage in a dressing gown to welcome the guest host. One later critic, incredibly, described this as Sid appearing in a bathrobe at the beginning of every show (making you question his memory) in an attempt to appear humble and ingratiate himself with the audience.[6] Caesar was many things. Folksy was not among them. There was a good reason for that dressing gown. If he was in costume for the sketch that immediately followed, he had usually only a minute or so to get into it during the host's set-up. Being able to shed what was most certainly not a "bathrobe" to get into costume (or complete one) saved precious time. When Hickenlooper sketches, in which Charlie usually wore a business suit, began to be the first in the running order, the dressing gown made only infrequent appearances, and Caesar almost always wore a suit in subsequent introductions.

Changes could also be major, requiring a great deal of speed. Anyone who has seen the classic parody of *From Here to Eternity* (9/12/53) remembers the beach scene where Caesar and Coca are doused with water in the midst of their love-making. The one that precedes it is set in a bar where their characters first meet and she proposes a swim. Both exit rapidly— Coca practically sprinting up stairs and Caesar beginning to unbutton his shirt before he's even offstage. Because in 22 seconds, while Carl Reiner and Howie Morris are exchanging dialogue in the bar, they have to be on that beach, Imogene in a bathing suit (still wearing fishnet stockings) and Sid in swim trunks (still wearing his shoes and socks). Both unlikely accessories for a moonlight swim were kept on because at the scene's conclusion, both, this time in a more leisurely 32 seconds, had to reappear in the bar fully clothed (and still somewhat damp from their dousing).

There was always the potential for fiasco with costume changes, almost realized in an episode of January 2, 1954, because of miscommunication between Liebman and Caesar and his dresser. The running order of two sketches, the first set at a circus and the second in a bus station, was switched by Max at the last minute. Exactly who, Caesar or his dresser (or perhaps both), didn't get the message straight isn't clear, but Sid, wearing a strongman's leotard, open-toed boots, and leather wristbands, prepared to go on stage for the circus sketch. In what he later described as a surreal moment, he looked out, ready to go on, and saw the bus station set. Grabbing whatever clothing was available from the stagehands, he made his entrance in an ill-fitting jacket, a tie looped over rather than knotted, one end of a shirt sleeve unbuttoned—and still wearing the boots and one leather wristlet from the circus sketch.[7]

And there were always technical glitches. Although camera techniques could be relatively sophisticated for TV in its primitive stage (there were frequent close-ups, shots from overhead, superimposed imagery, even split-screen), cameramen could make mistakes: a camera tracks the wrong way and you can see it and its operator through another, or shots could occasionally include the overhead microphones. Sometimes stagehands are seen through a set window and thumps and bumps are heard from offstage. None of these could be edited out, including the aural accompaniment to practically every sketch—Caesar's cough, so omnipresent you could make a drinking game out of it if you watch several episodes in succession. He not only coughed during sketches, you can often hear him coughing *off*stage before he enters a set. His cigar smoking probably didn't help, but the primary reasons for it were the demands he put on his voice and, as he later admitted, sheer nervousness.

Technical errors (audiences almost expected them on live TV) and the Caesar Cough (you get used to hearing it) were relatively minor blips during telecasts. What really made for the working-without-a-net atmosphere of live television were the number of things that could—and did— go wrong in sketches. Any live comedy show needed actors who could either ignore them and carry on or adapt quickly, hopefully getting a laugh in the process. Caesar was a master at both. His saves were not only usually funny, on occasion they were brilliant.

In a parody of *The Seventh Veil* (3/21/53), Caesar is the tyrannical piano master who terrorizes his ward Coca into becoming a keyboard virtuoso. His methods include striking his cane on the top of the piano when she's reluctant to play—it's a funny bit, as are Imogene's reactions to it. But then, during one particularly vigorous thwack, the cane snaps in two. Sid looks deadpan at the piece he's left holding, at the camera, back at the cane stub, flips it in one hand several times, and then continues with the sketch. It got a big laugh from the audience, who probably assumed the whole thing was scripted. It wasn't.[8] However, the bit went over so well that when the sketch was repeated, the cane-breaking was purposely made part of it.

Caesar could not only react to the unpredictable, he could run with it for an entire scene, ad-libbing as he went. In "Emergency," a spoof of medical shows (4/24/54), Sid, as an idealistic doctor, is in the office of his superior (Carl Reiner) whose daughter he happens to be seeing. When the daughter, played by guest star Patricia Crowley, attempts to enter, the door sticks. Sid goes to the door and opens it, almost pulling that part of the set down in the process, and ad-libs, "This door never opens the same way."

And the door ad libs are on. On Crowley's way out, the door sticks again and Carl suggests Sid go with her. He responds, "I don't think she knows *which* way she's going." As they look at each other, both have to suppress a smile, but Caesar wasn't done yet. As Sid leaves the office, he asks Carl where the consultation room is, and, as he heads toward the door, inquires, "And the door opens that way?"

Caesar's most celebrated response to a potential sketch disaster was in an episode of *Caesar's Hour*. In a parody of *Pagliacci*, he is the tragic clown who has just found out his wife has betrayed him. But the show must go on. He enters the wagon his troupe uses as a make-up and changing room, seats himself at a table, and begins an aria in passionate faux Italian (to the tune of "Just One of Those Things"). As he plaintively sings, he begins to draw a tear on his cheek with a make-up pencil. The pencil point breaks. While he continues to sing, never missing a beat, he picks up a mascara brush and begins a one-player game of tic-tac-toe on his face. It is arguably one of the most brilliantly graceful saves in the history of live television and worth checking out on YouTube.

Sometimes mishaps were physical, but had to be ignored: in "Midnight Snack" (5/30/52), Caesar wields a cleaver a bit too enthusiastically in an attempt to cut through frozen butter and it glances off onto his other hand. He just briefly checks for the requisite number of fingers and continues his lines. On one occasion, a mishap was a little more dire. In a December 5, 1953, sketch where Sid is the operator of a newsstand and Imogene is a demanding customer, there's a running bit where a truck comes by and bales of newspapers are flung at him. On the first go-round, he doesn't duck his head quickly enough and takes one on the chin, opening a noticeable gash. Caesar stoically keeps blotting the blood with the back of his hand—and dodging more bales—until the end of the sketch (while Coca does a wonderful job of ignoring it).

But that was the nature of going live. An audience never knew what it was going to see (real blood, as noted, being among the possibilities); actors could never predict what might happen. And for everyone involved—cast, directors, writers, technicians—live productions, particularly for 39 weeks a season, could be nerve-wracking. Tony Webster, one of *Your Show of Shows*' writers, once compared it to the opening night of a play: "Your life is on the line. [But] we were doing that *every Saturday night*. 'Jesus, we're still alive!' You know? Like walking across Niagara Falls."[9] Fortunately for the show, Caesar seemed to thrive on the tension and adrenaline rush of live TV.

However, for the audience, live TV was a viewing experience like no other. There was an immediacy to it and a connection between actors and audience that's lost on tape. It was theatre in your living room—but

3. Brought to You in Living Black and White 43

with close-ups that let you see every expression on the actors' faces and shots that made you appreciate the physical nature of the comedy they performed. And it was up-close and very personal in a way that's almost inconceivable today: You can even see Caesar's sweat. And with the intensity of his performances, the physical energy he invested, and his habitual nervousness, there was a lot of it.

There was, however, something TV audiences of the '50s were accustomed to seeing on programming that they wouldn't have seen on *Your Show of Shows*: sponsors' insistent—and successful—attempts to integrate advertising and push product placement on shows. Although it occurs today, the frequency with which it appeared then can be somewhat startling. Both stars and hosts served as willing pitchmen (and pitchwomen) for products. Loretta Young does her signature entrance with a twirl, then sweeps into her "living room," where a box of Tide is prominently displayed on a table—and she segues into a pitch for it. The Ricardos decide to go on a diet; to quell their hunger pangs, Lucy and Desi puff away contentedly on Philip Morris cigarettes. On *The Burns and Allen Show*, Gracie discussed the virtues of Carnation Evaporated Milk with the announcer; on *The Jack Benny Show*, plugs for sponsor products were written into sketches.[10] Milton Berle sang a Pepsi jingle on *Texaco Star Theatre*, and any child of the '50s remembers Dinah Shore belting out "See the USA in your Chevrolet." Some hosts and stars could poke fun at sponsors' products: Arthur Godfrey and Alfred Hitchcock for example, and Jack Benny was a master at integrating humor into integrated advertising. But whatever form the pitch took, the message to the audience was the same: Buy.

Caesar was a notable exception. It wasn't as if *Your Show of Shows* suffered from a paucity of sponsors whose products he could have pushed. In 1952, the show had six; in its last season, fourteen. And sponsors had every financial incentive for encouraging stars to pitch them—the costs for ads on popular programs could be steep. In the show's second season, a half-hour sponsorship went for $55,000; a one-minute commercial after each half-hour segment cost $17,600.[11] The latter could bring in over half a million dollars for NBC per season. However, Sid refused to mix comedy with selling on *Your Show of Shows*. An almost amusing example comes from the last season, when the opening was changed from the usual production number to Sid and Imogene doing a brief intro. Camel was one of the show's major sponsors, and the initial shot was of a cigarette burning in an ashtray. The camera turns to Caesar and Coca, who then studiously ignore it as they engage in a bit of byplay before the show begins.

Sid did only one bit for a sponsor's product, a remarkable record in a TV era of rampant plug-ola—and even then, it wasn't really as "Sid Caesar." He and Coca did a stand-alone ad spot for Benrus watches, another major sponsor, but neither in person (it was filmed) nor as "themselves." They only supplied the voices for marionettes of the Professor and a student (which was as odd visually as it sounds). And in all of the sketches that can be seen, a brand product appeared only twice, when Ralph Bellamy and later Victor Jory, both guest hosts, pulled out packs of Camels. But both instances occurred in the sketches that incorporated guest hosts— that kind of plug was never engaged in by Caesar and the cast in the regular sketches. There were no close-ups of a Benrus on anyone's wrist and, if cigarettes were smoked, they were generic no-brands.[12] Sid's refusal to be a pitchman on the show as himself or acquiesce to product placement in regular sketches is understandable. Professional pride was probably a factor, but more likely was Caesar's approach to sketch comedy. He immersed himself totally in a sketch and wanted an audience to do the same—they were not to be distracted by recognition of a brand name in one.

These were some of the things audiences saw and heard. In the '50s however, there was a lot they wouldn't have seen—or heard. Like radio broadcasting, television operated under the authority of the FCC, which forbade the airing of obscene or indecent material (as defined by the always-slippery "community standards"). However, the television industry, as radio before it, generally followed a policy of self-regulation, i.e., pre-emptive censorship, to avoid Commission interference or scrutiny. NBC had its own code and a chief of the Department of Continuity and Acceptance (read censor). By 1951, there was actually a guidebook of topics to be avoided or handled sensitively.[13] Even comedy writers and performers had to abide by it, although some leeway was permitted. Some of the things prohibited seem today positively innocuous, particularly those regarding language. Forget George Carlin's Seven Words You Can Never Say on Television, codes back then expanded the number exponentially. You couldn't say, for example, the word "pregnant" or "pregnancy." "Expecting" or "with child" had to be substituted. "Sex" was obviously out; even euphemisms were scrutinized carefully. Any words or phrases that were deemed profane were deleted from programming, even "My God" or "What the hell." When Caesar, in a monologue, expresses something emphatically with "My Goodness" (coming from him, it's not only jarring, but somewhat quaint), that's why. He once transgressed, however. In a parody of *This Is Your Life*, overcome by the appearance of family members, Sid repeatedly cries (and it's one of the funniest bits) "Ah, jeez." That, too, was a no-no and would have been deleted from a script. Since it was ad-libbed live, the censor couldn't have wielded his blue pencil. Language considered vulgar *was* blue-penciled, as Lucille Kallen found out. She had written a sketch entitled "Pocahontas" for Imogene Coca and the dancers on *The Admiral Broadway Revue*. In it, the narrator uses the meter of "Hiawatha" (and it's cleverly done) as he provides background. He describes the mighty warrior whom Pocahontas will marry, Great Chief Birch Tree's eldest brave, descended of the noble birch. "He was fearless, he was strong/He was proud, this son of birch." A distinct pencil line (you almost wish it was in blue) is drawn across "son of birch" on the script and "stalwart birch" substituted—and that's how it aired.[14] Nothing had changed a year later: when the sketch was repeated on *Your Show of Shows*, it was with the same substitution.

Humorous treatments of drunkenness could be iffy. Fortunately, this was one of the areas comedy writers were granted leeway in—any kind of restriction would have eliminated a *lot* of *Your Show of Shows* sketches. That didn't mean that viewers couldn't occasionally object. On December 19, 1953, Caesar repeated a pantomime, "A Drunkard's Fate." The sketch was obviously a parody of the silent film trope depicting the Perils of Demon Rum, and Sid, in appropriately moralistic fashion, pays for his drinking (he loses his wife, daughter, and even, in a great bit of comedic piling-on, his dog and canary). Nonetheless, the network got angry letters because it was shown during the holiday season. The NBC censor, who could on occasion be relatively broadminded, dismissed them, pointing out that there were no objections the first time the sketch was aired.[15]

There was no broadmindedness, however, when it came to two topics in particular: sex and politics. Staples of TV comedy today, both were off-limits in the '50s.

As far as sex went—or didn't—standard vaudevillian reactions to beautiful women and the occasional eyebrow-raising comment were tolerated on NBC programming, but that was about it. The only even mildly suggestive sketch on *Your Show of Shows* was in a mini-parody of *Double Indemnity* (1/12/52), where Sid's insurance salesman is drawn into Imogene's plans to kill her husband. As he enters, she puts her hands on his shoulders and passionately declares, "Darling! Why don't you sit down and tell me all about your big, beautiful ... insurance policy." She pulls him down on a couch and he grasps her hands, telling her, "The minute I laid eyes on you, I knew you were meant for a twenty-year endowment policy." Kissing her hands, he murmurs, "Just think, honey, your dividends will accumulate, the interest will accrue to the principal—and you know what *that* means." She pulls him across the couch into her arms and says seductively, "You have such exciting ... statistics!" It's about as racy as anything on the show ever got. But the writers weren't likely to use off-color comedy of the Milton Berle or Jerry Lester variety in any event—those kind of jokes weren't the show's style.

They did have to contend with another of the NBC Code's directives: "The use of locations closely associated with sexual life ... must be governed by good taste and delicacy."[16] This was part of every network code, not just NBC's, and resulted in one of the depictions of '50s married life today's audiences find amusing. Couples always slept in twin beds. No exceptions were made even for real-life husbands and wives like Lucille Ball and Desi Arnaz.[17] Only three times in sketches did *Your Show of Shows* test the parameters of the Twin Bed Sleeping Rule. In "A Midnight Snack" (5/30/52), Charlie Hickenlooper makes himself a cornflake sandwich and goes off to eat it in bed. Doris promptly announces she's going to sleep in the living room, a decision explicable only if she didn't want to roll over into cornflake crumbs. In a pantomime about a couple on vacation (5/19/52), two chairs are put side by side to suggest a double bed both Sid and Imogene are sleeping in, obviously, as she spills a glass of water on him and they both wrestle for covers. Bizarrely, *that* depiction was acceptable. Obviously, more wiggle room was given to elements of mime, because in one of Sid's solos (9/26/53), he is in bed (a chair) after an argument with his wife; she enters ("Here she comes, the Big Conqueror!") and joins him there. Rolling over in the "bed," he tells her, still angry from their spat, "Don't get close to me, kid!" At least once, and who could blame him, Caesar appears to make fun of the twin bed arrangement in, as usual, an ad lib. In "The Sleep Sketch" (11/14/53), Charlie Hickenlooper has insomnia and asks Doris to talk to him. Because, as Sid says plaintively from his twin bed, "It gets lonesome at night."[18] The audience thought it was funny; the censor probably didn't, but since the line wasn't scripted, there was nothing he could do about it.

As for politics, the name Eisenhower is mentioned twice on the show and Truman once, but only in the context of being the presidents at the time. You could poke fun at politicians in general, but never specific ones.[19] Not that it was a huge handicap for the writers—*Your Show of Shows* was more about satirizing post-war America's middle-class society, not its political system. That, however, didn't mean that the political world couldn't intrude, both on-stage and off. This was the era of the post-war Red Scare, with its Communist witch-hunts, loyalty oaths, blacklisting, and security clearances. On an episode in March of 1950, the guest host was Melvyn Douglas who was married to Helen Gahagan, a progressive California congresswoman. After being introduced by Caesar as "the husband of Congresswoman Helen Gahagan," Douglas jokingly responded, "Just for that, I'll be happy to check your loyalty test anytime you want it." It's a somewhat jarring reminder of the political climate of the time. And eight months later, with the rise to prominence of Senator Joseph McCarthy and Gahagan's defeat in an election for a Senate seat, where she was smeared as the "Pink Lady" by the victor (one Richard M. Nixon), there wouldn't have been any jokes about loyalty oaths.

Caesar himself had little to worry about on that score. Although he appeared in a variety of benefits for charities and causes, some of which might be regarded as "liberal," they weren't leftist. According to his wife Florence, Sid was, if anything, apolitical in the '50s.[20] His writers were a different story. Joe Stein had been a member of the Party in his youth, when he was a social worker. He recalled that

> Every so often, some NBC functionary would call asking why no one had signed the loyalty oaths, and we'd say we lost them, so they'd send over another batch, and we'd immediately lose those.[21]

It almost sounds like the basis for a sketch. Pat Weaver's recollection of the period was different. He insisted that, while CBS required loyalty oaths, NBC did not. Technically, he was correct. However, since the mid-1940s, the network had required personal "loyalty statements" from all new hires, which is perhaps what Stein was referring to. Moreover, Carl Reiner says he was once visited by FBI agents inquiring if he knew any Communists, and McCarthyism and the threats it posed is a theme in the play "Laughter on the 23rd Floor," Neil Simon's (very) thinly disguised depiction of Caesar and the Writers' Room.[22]

Nonetheless, NBC had a financial ace in the hole if a sponsor or its ad agency rep objected to the political leanings of guest stars or production staff. According to Weaver:

> we simply told him ... we'd relieve him of his contract. We had so many hits on the air, sponsors were reluctant to back away from us. They knew that if they had a spot on *Your Show of Shows* ... and they decided to drop it, a dozen other clients would jump at the chance to pick it up.[23]

Certainly, blacklisting was totally ignored in the selection of guest hosts and performers for the show. Eddie Albert, Lena Horne, Jose Ferrer, Kim Hunter, and Burgess Meredith, all on the blacklist, appeared on programs, some more than once.

Although, like all TV comedy programs, *Your Show of Shows* had to abide by network standards regarding subjects deemed objectionable or controversial, it stood apart from the usual comedy fare of the '50s in one striking aspect: the sheer range of its humor. Viewers could see slapstick, witty and sophisticated parody, domestic comedy, and the truly off-beat or unexpected—frequently all in the same episode.

Most early comedy shows featured vaudevillian-style slapstick in which actors assault each other, usually with collateral damage to innocent bystanders. So did *Your Show of Shows*, but as usual, with a slightly different approach. There were no pratfalls or pie-throwing (Caesar's first Borscht Belt experience as a straight man getting a tomato to the face convinced him of the lack of humor in that sort of thing). Nor was the show's slapstick like that of The Three Stooges (what could be?)—there were no eye-pokes, face-slaps, or head-bops. Instead, the sketches usually had one or two characters setting upon another, leaving him generally in tatters at their conclusion. Howie Morris usually bore the brunt of such assaults and Caesar usually dished them out—picking him up, spinning him around, or tossing him about almost casually. And it could, and frequently did, go beyond that: in a bus station sketch (1/2/54), Sid and Imogene, in the course of an argument about which bus Howie should take, manhandle him to the point that his clothing is in shreds, and then continue to argue over his prostrate body. But Caesar could be a victim as well, suffering a similar fate when he is innocently drawn into a fight between Carl Reiner and Coca in a movie theatre (3/13/54).

And the assaults were equal-opportunity, as in Doris Hickenlooper's frequent elbowing of Charlie or launching projectiles in his general direction. Or most notably, in the versions of the old bit (and here they *did* go full-out vaudeville) "Slowly I Turned." For example, that of May 10, 1952, where Imogene's more than slightly demented character turns on a hapless Sid who always manages to provoke her by innocently saying the wrong thing. She swats him with a purse or his own hat, tears at his clothes, and finishes by improbably, but hilariously, wiping up the floor with him. As he finally sits, totally disheveled, with his shirt over his head, she continues to hit him with whatever she has at hand until she runs out of steam. Imogene may have been small, but she could throw herself into the action with enthusiasm—after one of these sketches, Sid's wife Florence wanted to know how he got all the bruises on his arms and shoulders.[24]

There is always an element of violence in slapstick, ranging from the mild to the cartoon-like. However, the show carried it to the point in some of the sketches like these (and in their repetition—you could always count on seeing at least two every season) that you can't help but wonder if a lot of writer—and Caesarean—anger and Id was being worked out in them. If so, it probably was more effective than the psychoanalysis many of the writers, and Caesar, were in. (Tony Webster would later ponder, if it was a cleansing process, "How come nobody got clean?")[25]

Mel Tolkin recollected that, besides free-floating anger, there were a lot of jokes about death and murder in the Writers' Room, and these too were reflected in sketches. People die, albeit comically, a lot in the sketches, whether by poisoning, shooting, or stabbing (a particular writer favorite). Granted, it's one way to end a sketch—definitively—but the body count at the end of many rivals that of Act V of your average Shakespearean tragedy. A silent film parody of November 7, 1950, ends with Sid accidentally shooting Imogene and Nanette Fabray, and finally his original target, Carl Reiner. He then shoots himself, but still manages to not only dispatch a man delivering a telegram but read the telegram before he joins the bodies littering the stage. And it *is* funny. However, not many comedy shows of the '50s played attempts at suicide for laughs. In the "Slowly I Turned" sketch, Sid's pummeling is brought on by a Good Samaritan act, his preventing Imogene from leaping from the top of the Empire State Building. After her exit, another woman enters in suicidal mode. Unable to face *that* again, he leaps off himself. In a parody of a French film (11/14/53), Sid as a Parisian baker talks Imogene out of flinging herself into the Seine. His attempt to help her by giving her a job in his bakery backfires when she flirts with his assistant Carl Reiner and he chases them both out of his shop. The sketch ends with him back by the river, where another woman threatens to jump—this time, he gives her a helping shove.

Yet, while the writers could generate endless knock-about sketches with occasionally dark humor (today's viewers might respond more to the latter than the former), they were also capable, as will be seen, of producing remarkably sophisticated sketch humor in parodies and satires. In that respect, which also set it apart from much of early '50s TV comedy, *Your Show of Shows* never played down to its audience. Coca said, some twenty years later, that they simply assumed that people understood what they were doing.[26] Certainly there was broad physical comedy and the zaniness of the Professor sketches, but there were also the parodies of opera and movies. What other show of the period spoofed foreign films? For that matter, what other show might have Coca, in a Strangers sketch that takes place on a cruise ship (11/10/51), observe its crows-nest ("four new baby crows!"), then begin to declaim a Shelleyan "Hail to thee, Blithe Spirit! Bird thou never wert"? Or have its actors, in a business sketch no less (12/27/52), trade lines from *The Merchant of Venice* and *Julius Caesar* and get laughs doing it? And at the same time, deflate any pretension by having Sid respond with a crazed parody of "The Boy Stood on the Burning Deck."[27] And audiences laughed at that, too.

And just when you think you've seen every possible genre of sketch, the show would throw in something from deep left field. For example, a Western movie sketch from March 22, 1952. But one performed entirely in German doubletalk—with the villain Carl Reiner commanding Howie Morris to "Tanz! Tanz!" as he shoots at his feet, and Sid, as the hero looking askance at a cowboy who helps saloon singer Imogene to adjust her garter, inquiring, "Was machen Sie hier, Buckaroo?" Some sketches presaged Monty Python by decades. In "The Butler and the Maid" (5/24/52), Carl is hosting a dinner party, served by maid Imogene and butler Sid, who begin to quarrel loudly offstage. As each enters to serve a course, they display evidence of the argument; he's wearing a salad on his shoulders, her uniform is soaked with ketchup. So far, so meh. Until they both burst from the kitchen with pistols, taking pot shots at each other while using the guests and the furniture as cover. This continues until Carl, getting up from behind the chair where he's been crouching, announces brightly, "I think we'll have coffee in the library." Or in just a simple one-liner: when Sid, as a doughboy in the trenches, hears news of the armistice, he exclaims in relief, "At last—World War I is over!"

4

The Writers' Room: Comedy in a Pressure Cooker

More than sixty years on, the range and diversity of the comedy of *Your Show of Shows* still impresses—as does its success in making viewers then and now laugh. And that comedy and those laughs were all produced in an office in City Center on W. 55th Street in Manhattan: the famous Writers' Room. Not many Writers' Rooms have plaques commemorating them. This one does, fixed on the wall of the W. 56th Street side of City Center. Not many Writers' Rooms have appeared in plays (*Laughter on the 23rd Floor*) and movies (*My Favorite Year*) in which its inhabitants appear in only thinly disguised fashion. This one has. For good reason—at one time this room was occupied by the best comedy writing team ever assembled.

It has become almost standard to list the accomplishments of the writers after *Your Show of Shows*. However, they bear repeating. Many of the writers continued with Sid on his own show, *Caesar's Hour*, which ended in 1957. One of them, Mel Tolkin, went on to write for Danny Kaye, and Tony Randall's *Love, Sidney*, and was the story editor for *All in the Family*. Lucille Kallen was a writer for Imogene Coca's short-lived series, as well as *The Bell Telephone Hour* and *The US Steel Hour* and went on to a successful career as a mystery novelist. Joe Stein wrote the book for *Fiddler on the Roof* (also adapting it for film), *Zorba*, and other plays and musicals. Tony Webster wrote for Victor Borge and Art Carney, *The Phil Silvers Show* and *Car 54, Where Are You?* Danny Simon was a writer for *The Carol Burnett Show* as well as for Phil Silvers. The stellar careers of Mel Brooks, Carl Reiner and Neil Simon are too well known to need exposition here. It was an amazing assembly of writing talent then, and at any time in TV history.

However, the names of two more writers in that Room should be added: Max Liebman, who was there frequently, and Sid Caesar, who was there always—his credit, appearing on the scrolling list of writers at the beginning of episodes, was more, as will be seen, than just star puffery.

The Writers' Room was on the sixth floor on the 56th Street side of the building, only a part of a suite in which Max Liebman had his office as well.[28] And it was not particularly large (only 14 × 20 feet), if you consider the number of people who might have been there at any one time—the writers, Liebman, Caesar, Imogene Coca, and Howie Morris. And of course among the number always taking up space were two very large men, Caesar and Carl Reiner. The décor was part zoo enclosure during and after feeding time, part undergraduate dorm room. Half-eaten sandwiches and Danishes, unfinished bottles of seltzer water and cups of coffee, crumpled paper cups, and cigar butts were strewn about. There was usually a miasma of smoke from those cigars; almost all of the male writers smoked them and the one window in the room was rarely open. There were splotches on the wall where Sid had flung sandwiches in anger and holes in the acoustic ceiling tile where writers had flung pencils in frustration. (Mel Tolkin once counted over 20 hanging from it.)

The noise level was generally high enough that Lucille Kallen would occasionally stand on a couch and wave a red sweater to get attention and make herself heard. Neil "Doc" Simon, shy and soft-spoken, had similar problems. They were solved when Carl Reiner, sitting next to him, would hear some muted contribution from Simon and loudly announce, "Doc's got it!" Ideas were flung out, lines shouted out, and sketches acted out. All of which might be interrupted by Mel Brooks, notoriously late for almost every writing session, making an entrance by sliding across the floor and then yelling "Safe!" There *were* quieter times—if a reporter, an outsider, or just two writers were there. Max Liebman's presence seems to have had a dampening effect as well. However, as Neil Simon recalled, when Max or Sid would leave the

The Room where it happened: City Center on W. 56th St. today. The Writers' Room was on the 6th floor, right corner.

room, "everyone would roll up paper and throw spitballs ... we were all very young."[29]

Mel Tolkin was the long-suffering philosophic head writer, usually the quieter voice in the midst of all the noise. Lauded by Caesar as a superb structure writer, he attempted to supply structure in the writing sessions as well. It was difficult. In later interviews, Tolkin remembered the euphoria of creating a great sketch and the frequent frustration while attempting to do so: "Nobody ever finished a sentence. Someone else would jump on it, competitively grab a sentence, a thought. It was absolutely the happiest and worst time of my life." Sid provided an indelible image of the latter when he described seeing "Mel Tolkin staring out the window like he wants to jump out."[30]

The din, freneticism, and angst were of course a reflection of the stress and tension involved in coming up with 5–6 sketches in only three days. And there was a variety of them to be written—almost always a Hickenloopers sketch and a parody of some sort, Sid's monologue, a sketch that had to accommodate a guest host, and maybe a Professor sketch or a pantomime. And no one came in with prepared scripts to be reviewed—there just wasn't enough time to write them. Sid could still say to a reporter, some fifty years later, "You don't realize the pressure."[31] He sometimes reacted to it in the expected Caesarean way: when a continually ringing phone kept interrupting a session, he eliminated the distraction by ripping it out of the wall and throwing it out of the room.

Writing for Saturday's show began on a Monday, when Caesar would enter the office and demand of the writers, "Show me the brilliance." On Mondays, there usually wasn't any (Sid would once refer to it as "bleeding to death day" on the show).[32] Then, Kallen and Tolkin might begin with an idea they had talked about on Sunday for a Hickenloopers sketch (Mel freely used situations from his own marriage, as would Sid from his), and others would throw out ideas based on things that had happened to them since the last show, or films they had seen or had ever seen. Both are good examples of what made the show's comedy so effective; for the most part, it was based on real-life, identifiable events, what people did and what they saw. The writers didn't write just jokes as such, they wrote characters and situations.

The process of creation, once an idea was agreed upon, was vividly described by Lucille Kallen:

> "It was like throwing a magnetized piece of a jigsaw puzzle in the middle of the room. All the other pieces would come racing towards it, each one adding another indispensable part, and then suddenly, there was the whole picture."[33]

The best of the lines and situations would be taken down by Kallen. Caesar would later comment that "she was the only one who could write and talk

Some of the writers in the Room. Left to right: Sid Caesar; head writers Mel Tolkin and Lucille Kallen; Mel Brooks (GettyImages).

at the same time…. The rest of us were all crazy…. 'Put it in!' 'Take it out!' 'You've got to put it back.' So it was a very frustrating job." On the other hand, she was hardly a subservient scribe: Carl Reiner claimed "she was the arbiter. If she didn't like a line, she wouldn't write it down."[34]

Of the writers for *Your Show of Shows*, Kallen deserves more attention than she usually gets—first, for her talents (she and Mel Tolkin were the workhorses on the staff) and second, for her situation. She was one of the few female comedy writers of the period. (Sid would later employ another of that select group, Selma Diamond, on *Caesar's Hour*.) Kallen's memories of the Writers' Room are understandably mixed, describing the joy of writing and collaboration while also feeling very keenly her position as the only woman in the room. She said she was the subject of "unconscious patronizing," but even though "there was a male phalanx and then there was me … when we were writing, there was no difference." She would also remember that Sid was "maybe a little careful with me." As well he might have been. Kallen, despite how she sometimes depicted herself, could be feisty (in a good way).[35]

The ideas and lines generated in the sessions were then put in sketch form by two or more writers (all of them might reassemble to work on the

4. The Writers' Room 55

more elaborate movie spoofs), and then turned into completed scripts by Wednesday night. That deadline was set for a reason almost inconceivable in a higher-tech age—there had to be enough time to copy, i.e., mimeograph, them, so they could be given to the production staff to begin their work on Thursday.

There was keen competition among the writers to get their lines in (and to gain Caesar's approval) but from all accounts, the writing was a communal effort. An examination of a number of completed scripts that were credited (and not all were) confirms what you might already expect: Tolkin and Kallen appear to have had most input for Hickenlooper sketches and parodies, Caesar and Brooks for Professor sketches, and Caesar, Tolkin, Brooks, and occasionally Liebman for the monologues. However, other writers' names appear as well, Tony Webster's for example, and both Joe Stein and Neil Simon, who was a major contributor to the parodies, had their names appearing occasionally along with those of the head writers in the credit crawl at the beginning of the show. Moreover, there was no gender split in the writing. Lucille Kallen insisted it was never a case of her writing specifically for Coca and the male writers for Caesar; everyone wrote for both of the stars. As Sid described it, it was truly writing by committee. The end result was that Simon once claimed that at dress rehearsal, it was often difficult to remember who had written what.

And Caesar's place in all of this? You will sometimes read that he never wrote a word. It depends on your definition of writing. Did he "write" in the sense of putting ideas into written or scripted form? Not really. Judging from the comments of those who were there as well as Sid himself, his contributions in the Writers' Room were verbal. He had written his own material in the Catskills and Coast Guard, but, as he began a television career, new material had to be developed every week and, as the comic actor he became, he depended on his writers (as did most comics then, even those who did stand-up).

Rather, he had three roles in the creative process on *Your Show of Shows*: as collaborator, idea man, and editor. In the first, he worked with all of the writers in contributing to, and frequently acting out, sketches in the Writers' Room and, with Tolkin, Brooks, and occasionally Liebman, developed the Professor sketches and his monologues. In the second, he came up with, among others, the ideas for the classic Bavarian Clock pantomime; the "Auto Smash-Up" sketch, in which Doris Hickenlooper demolishes the family car (as, apparently, did Florence Caesar, if not quite as humorously); and the monologue "A Day in the Life of a Fly" (the writers' initial response to the latter seems to have been a collective *eww*, but it resulted in one of his best solo bits). Above all, he was a superb editor; he decided what went in and what stayed out. What he did may not have been, technically, writing, although Max Liebman certainly regarded it as such, citing his "writing ability as well as creativeness."[36] However you define it, it was more than enough to justify his name on the credits.

In all three roles, he presented a very different image from the powder-keg-waiting-for-a-match, verging-on-the-out-of-control one that is usually ascribed to him. Yes, there was wall-punching and the occasional flinging of a bottle at Mel Brooks in exasperation (on the other hand, Max Liebman, a much calmer man, used to throw lighted cigars at Mel). And Lucille Kallen never quite forgave him for throwing a script on the floor.[37] However, Neil Simon remembered most not the famed Caesarean temper, but rather a weapon just as effective to show displeasure—"Sid could sarcastic you to death." (Caesar had learned one thing well from his father.) Nonetheless, Simon commented that he always followed the dictum: "Let sleeping large angry comedians lie." The writers were relatively tolerant and understanding about his reactions to pressure. After all, as Simon had one of them in *Laughter on the 23rd Floor* point out about the Caesar character, Max Prince: "We *write* comedy; Max *does* comedy. It's his ass out there in front of the cameras every week."[38]

Yet, Lucille Kallen, who certainly had the opportunity to observe Sid's temperament in Writers' Rooms dating back to *The Admiral Broadway Revue*, mentioned that different side of it in an interview from 1998.[39] She commented, as does practically everyone, that it was "volatile." Sometimes he was "broody," at other times he could be on an emotional high. But she then added an adjective—"businesslike"—one not always associated with Caesar, at least in articles and retrospectives (maybe because it was always more entertaining to describe the times when he wasn't).

It's an aspect of his personality that should perhaps be emphasized more. Because when it came to the actual process of creating comedy, Sid could be very serious, indeed businesslike, and far from volatile. He was a judicious and decisive editor: a nod of approval to a line and it would go in; a disapproval might be signaled by his pantomiming an anti-aircraft gun and shooting down the hapless line as it floated overhead. Joe Stein would later say that "Sid's instinct was infallible and he was immoveable about his opinion. We would write a sketch and he'd go 'Naah.'" ... It was dead. You can't argue with "Naah."[40] However, Caesar, in this instance not living up to his name, was not a total autocrat. He listened to everyone's ideas and the writers were given free rein with no potential subject for a sketch dismissed out of hand. He had control; they had, as Tolkin put it, total permissiveness.

Only Max Liebman could overrule him, and the situations in which he did can be a bit murky. Although Liebman had been a sketch writer in a variety of venues (vaudeville, Tamiment, USO shows, and Broadway) before *Your Show of Shows*, and occasionally had his name on scripts—and

4. The Writers' Room

Sid and Max. Their remarkably productive association would begin in 1944 in the Coast Guard revue *Tars and Spars* and end with the finale of *Your Show of Shows* in 1954. In between, Liebman would work with Caesar in developing his first nightclub act, direct him in the Broadway revue *Make Mine Manhattan* (1948), and star him in *The Admiral Broadway Revue* (1949) (GettyImages).

credit on the writers' crawl—he liked to think of himself more as an editor, albeit a flexible one. As he told Pat Weaver, "Very often I would say 'I don't think this will work' but even then I would say, 'Well, okay, do it."[41] Nanette Fabray would once refer to him as "Sid's editor," telling him when he was going "too far." Unfortunately, she, or anyone else for that matter, never defined exactly what "too far" was. Certainly, it wasn't anything controversial in a sketch; neither NBC's censor nor Sid's style of humor would make that a plausible definition. The need to tone down parts of a performance? Maybe. Drawing out a sketch that was far too long or over-elaborating aspects of one? Perhaps. Whatever it was, Caesar acknowledged later that "everybody needs an editor" and that he missed Max in that regard when he went out on his own in *Caesar's Hour*.[42]

There are definitely specific instances in which Liebman overruled Caesar, and when he did, it usually took the form of cutting minutes from sketches to accommodate musical numbers (Sid wasn't happy about it, but respected Liebman immensely and went along). When it came to the content—rather than the timing or length—of comedy sketches, however, Caesar appears to have almost always got his way. Carl Reiner recalled that Sid was adamant about doing the Bavarian Clock pantomime when Max initially was lukewarm to the idea.[43] Imogene Coca remembered two instances, both of which involved her directly. When Max dismissed her idea for a sketch in which Sid, Carl, Howie, and Imogene entered and sat in long silence before any action took place (the germ for The Four Englishmen sketches in which they did just that), Sid's response was "Let's try it. Let's try it." When Liebman was reluctant to do a parody of the movie *A Place in the Sun*, Caesar, when told it had a great part for Imogene (it did), immediately said, "Then why don't we do it?"[44] The two sketches made their appearance on the show. In the case of the parody, it would prove to be one of the show's best. Both instances are a reflection not only of Sid's respect for Imogene's instincts and talent, but his absolute certainty about what would work. It was also a reflection, perhaps, of something else: his growing independence from his mentor in his conception of what the comedy on *Your Show of Shows* should be like.[45] If so, it would have been bolstered by another factor: how much time Liebman had to devote to writing sessions isn't clear. His producing and directing roles (and those are the ones emphasized in most contemporary articles) must surely have limited his time in the Writers' Room, further reinforcing Caesar's control over content.

One of television's best comedy sketch ensembles, clockwise from left: Sid Caesar, Carl Reiner, Howard Morris and Imogene Coca (Getty Images).

Caesar's relations with his writers differed in a number of respects from those of many of his contemporaries and their writing staffs. He was always in the Writers' Room and worked extensively with his writers; Jackie Gleason preferred that scripts be slid under his door and never even met with some of his staff (nor, although he could be unpredictable and difficult at times, was Caesar outright abusive to his writers, as Gleason often was).[46] Employment with Sid was not the revolving-door for writers that it was with Red Skelton, notorious for his frequent firing of his staff; many of Caesar's stayed with him for most of his television career. He supported his writers, unlike George Gobel, who lost one of his most valuable because he wouldn't increase his salary.[47] *Your Show of Shows* paid its writers well ($2500 a week as the show became a hit), and Sid could be personally generous to them, helping Mel Tolkin weather financially the hiatus between *The Admiral Broadway Revue* and *Your Show of Shows*, and paying Mel Brooks out of his own pocket when Liebman initially refused to put him on salary for the *Revue* and the first half-season of *Your Show of Shows*.[48] Caesar's head writers, as well as some of the others, also got screen credit. This was in marked contrast to Milton Berle, whose *Texaco Star Theatre* never had a writers crawl. Berle's rationale? "The audience wants to think I'm making this shit up by myself."[49] The relationship between Sid and his writers might best be described as one of mutual respect and an almost perfect comic symbiosis: he wanted, and needed, the best material; they could provide it and knew he could perform what they wrote better than anyone else.

5

Scripts Versus Performance: Whose Line Is It Anyway?

That was the writing process in all its pressure-cooker, frenetic glory. But were the contents of the scripts completed on Wednesday always what an audience saw on Saturday night? It's a long-standing debate about the comedy of *Your Show of Shows*: How much was tightly scripted, how much of the live performance deviated from or added to the scripts, and how much was ad-libbed, particularly by Caesar? It's also been framed another way in evaluating the often brilliant comedy of the sketches—as Jane Klain, the manager of research services at the Paley Center for Media in New York, put it, "Some have credited Sid Caesar's comic genius with their success, while others have portrayed the writers as the creators, making Sid and the actors merely the vessels for their genius."[50]

The only way to even begin to settle the issue is to compare a script with what was performed live—and the opportunity is there to do so, from two different sources. It was front-page news in the *New York Times* in November of 2000 when 47 boxes of material from *Your Show of Shows* as well as *The Admiral Broadway Revue* and other early TV productions were found in a long-forgotten locked closet off the Writers' Room during renovations at City Center. Preserved and stored by Max Liebman, who kept his offices there until his death in 1981, they contained 137 scripts of *Your Show of Shows*, which were subsequently donated to the Library of Congress by Liebman's heir. Their discovery, after they had remained untouched for over two decades, made for a great story,[51] and for historians of early TV comedy, it was a real treasure-trove. However, it wasn't the only one. Buried in the *Times* article was a brief mention that Sid Caesar had deposited part of his "non-video collection" to the LOC as well. If the writer of the article had just been a little more explicit in his definition of that deposit, it would have added to the Saga of the Scripts, if in a less dramatic way. In 1987 Sid donated his papers to the Library; in the 20 boxes of material from *Your Show of Shows* were *his* copies of 141 scripts. Today, then, you can look at

5. Scripts Versus Performance

both collections, Caesar's in the Manuscript Division and Liebman's in the Moving Image section. Fortuitously, what Sid didn't have, Max often did, so that close to 150 of the 160 scripts for the show are available to look at.

So what do they reveal? Was the comedy tightly scripted or more free-form and freewheeling? A comparison of some 40 scripts with their live performance provides an at least tentative answer: It was both. And which predominated depended almost entirely on the type of sketch.

Almost always, additional bits of business were added, or more often deleted (sometimes entire endings were scrapped), before the live performance. These major changes took place during rehearsal. However, that time was limited: most sketch rehearsal took place on Wednesdays and Thursdays in Studio 6, a floor below the Writers' Room. Changes even on Thursday could be worrisome. Imogene Coca told of rehearsing a sketch with Caesar during which, using their usual almost wordless, we-know-what-each-other-is-thinking, communication, it became apparent that neither was particularly happy with the way it was developing. Sid asked Max Liebman, who was directing the rehearsal, why they were doing it that way. Max's understandably harried response was, "Because it's Thursday *and the show is Saturday!*" Nonetheless, Caesar stubbornly insisted it wasn't a good idea—and changes were ultimately made.[52] Friday was the dry run on the main stage at the International Theatre in Columbus Circle with no costumes or scenery; further adjustments to sketches might be made, which meant more pressure on both writers and actors. After noon on Friday, the show was essentially frozen. Saturday was "on camera" day where final tracking, timing, and marking was made. There was a dress rehearsal from 5:30 to 7:00 and the show aired live at 9:00.[53] Over three days then not only did 5–6 sketches have to be rehearsed but Caesar and Coca would have needed additional rehearsal time, Imogene for her comedy song and dance routines (James Starbuck, the choreographer, wouldn't even see her until Wednesday), Sid for his monologues.

What a Saturday night audience saw, however, could still differ from what emerged after rehearsal. The Hickenlooper sketches were tightly scripted; so too the movie parodies. There was little alteration before their live performance. However, even here, Sid and Imogene generally added unscripted physical comedy or vocal interjections. Working with Caesar daily allowed the writers to use a form of shorthand for many of these unscripted bits of physical comedy on his part; there are frequent notations like [Sid—business] or [Sid does routine]. Moreover, Caesar almost always inserted an ad-lib here or there—and he was the only one who consistently did it.

Pantomime scripts were literally outlines, describing just the sequence of events. In the ones that Caesar and Coca did together, it was up to them to fill them in, which makes you marvel at what Sid and Imogene could do with little rehearsal time or on the fly during live performance. The terse script descriptions are almost humorous when compared with the physical comedy and mime an audience saw. For example, Sid's impressive choreography of hand movements in his solo "Boy at First Dance" (4/22/50) is scripted as [has trouble with hands]. The brilliant pantomime of "In a Shoe Store" (1/10/53) where Imogene is directing Sid in threading a needle with which he then sews up a rip in her stocking is simply [business with needle].[54] In "A Drunkard's Fate" (12/19/53), the script calls for Sid to enter a bar and walk in backwards. What appeared in live performance was Caesar miming being pulled into the bar as if by a magnet. In a later scene, instead of [Goes straight to bar and buys a drink], he does an almost thirty-second drunk stagger trying desperately to reach it, and in the process, bends and twists his legs into positions most human limbs don't normally go.[55]

Probably the best-known of the group pantomimes with Caesar, Coca, Carl Reiner, and Howie Morris is "The Clock" (9/26/53). In it, they are mechanical figures striking the hours in a gigantic Bavarian clock. They enter: Sid strikes an anvil with a hammer, Carl follows with a mallet, Howie applies a bellows, and Imogene finishes by dipping a ladle into a bucket of water and pouring it on the anvil. Then, the clock begins to malfunction, as do the figures. They slow down, and then their movements get out of sync. You know eventually Sid's figure is going to get Imogene's ladle of water in the face. He does, repeatedly, as the figures' movements speed up, go totally and hilariously out of control, and finally grind to a halt. The miming of the figures' movements is impressive, particularly on Caesar and Coca's part, as is the timing. That's what an audience saw.

Minus an announcer's voice-over at the beginning and end of the sketch, here in its entirety is the script for all the action[56]:

[figures appear and disappear]
[hour strikes, figures appear. Go thru business of striking and disappear]
[sound of mechanical difficulty]
[figures appear. Go thru motions a little off.]
[figures come out. Go thru business of striking. They strike three times. On the fourth they slow down. As Coca brings up ladle, they stop. Sound of clock being wound six times. Coca throws water. Figures exit.]
[figures appear. Go through their routine very fast many times. Sound effect of clock going to pieces. They end up in static pose.]

A better example of the physical comedy supplied by the actors to an outline script would be hard to come by.

Genuine and purposeful ad-libbing occurs most frequently in the

5. Scripts Versus Performance

Professor sketches with Caesar and Reiner and in the foreign-language film parodies where doubletalk, which couldn't be scripted, was used, primarily by Sid and Carl. Like the pantomimes, these film parodies had scripts in outline form, to be filled in by the actors. You can almost always detect when Caesar is ad-libbing in both genres: it seems to have been one of Sid's missions in these sketches to get Carl to break up, and Reiner had a tell when this happened, tucking his chin into his chest to avoid laughing. Caesar and Coca also were occasionally called on to do extensive filling-in; for example, one of the "Strangers" sketches is also in just outline form.[57]

And Caesar's monologues? Scripted, some more tightly than others, and hardly surprising as they could run anywhere from 6–8 minutes. But there were instances in which Sid was expected to come up with bits on his own; for example, embedded in script dialogue would be [tells him story]. One script for a monologue done on *The Admiral Broadway Revue* actually has [adlibs] embedded in it.[58] Moreover, although he generally stuck to the script (or at least its outline), Sid rarely followed it to the letter. In performance, he would add or extend bits, delete others, and sometimes run segments of the sketches out of sequence, probably with great confidence as he had a hand in writing them. If you watch monologues that were repeated, each one is still slightly different. And of course, little of the facial expressions or physical comedy was scripted. For example, Sid did a memorable monologue (10/18/52) depicting a day in the life of a housefly (as previously mentioned, he came up with the idea, a good illustration of how his comedic mind worked). The sketch was tightly scripted. But some of the funniest parts weren't. How *could* you script CaesarFly landing vertically on a wall—and doing a remarkable impression of clinging to it? You couldn't—it doesn't appear in the script for the monologue.[59]

Ultimately, trying to divvy up credit for *Your Show of Shows*' comedy is fruitless and beside the point. Actors need great material to work with; writers need superb performers to deliver it. Fortunately for TV comedy, this pioneering show had brilliance in both parts of that equation.

Having said that, however, there were notable instances in which the performances could transcend the writing, brilliant though it could be. The cast, including Caesar, didn't usually do extended improv, but when they did, the results were worth it; and the writers, far from resenting it, generally applauded it. The best example is a parody of *This Is Your Life*, a program where unsuspecting celebrities as well as ordinary folk were lured into a studio and seated on a couch where they were to be interviewed, they thought, about some innocuous issue. They were then surprised by the show's MC ("This is your life!") with a review of their past, replete with old photographs and reunions, always emotional and usually tearful, with important people in their lives. It was as schmaltzy as it sounds and *Your*

Show of Shows absolutely eviscerated it in their take, "This Is Your Story" (4/3/54).

This classic sketch is one for which we have not just the original script to compare with the live performance but also the recollections of the three major participants in it, Caesar, Reiner, and Morris.[60] And the difference between the script and what aired is jaw-dropping. Many of the sketch scripts are funny even on paper. This, however, wasn't one of them. Despite the brilliance of the concept for the sketch—what might happen if you had a guest who really didn't want to participate and whose reunions with people from his past almost completely derail the show—the script is just, well, flat. It's "This Is Your Story" in some alternate (and not particularly funny) comedy universe. By the time the actors were done with it, about the only things left from the script were the original idea, the characters, and some—but not all—of the action. With the addition of their unscripted physical comedy and improvisation, it was now hilarious. Every cast member in it shone: Caesar as the unsuspecting "honoree" Al Duncey who is seated in the studio audience; informed that This Is *His* Story, he attempts to flee the theater, with ushers in hot pursuit, by running up and down the aisles, across the stage, and back into the aisles before he's tackled by them and carried up on stage. Reiner as the relentlessly smarmy MC who cheerfully attempts to keep the show on track even as it descends into chaos. Morris as Al's Uncle Goopy, who, once reunited with his nephew, can't—*really* can't—be separated from him.

The physical comedy of the sketch is excruciatingly funny: Sid and Howie embracing each other, crying and roaring in over-the-top emotion, with Sid punctuating every reunion with people from his past with "Ah, jeez!" Howie attaching himself to Sid like a crazed limpet (when he's not either embracing him or jumping on him) and Carl trying to separate them; as he's being dragged away in one sequence, Sid, sprawled on the guest couch, grabs his feet and Howie catapults himself into his arms for one final embrace. The scrums of Al, his aunt Mildred, Uncle Goopy, and Mr. Torch, the kindly fireman who rescued a young Al from a burning building. And the final segment where, surrounded by the Northern New Jersey Drum and Bugle Corps of which Al was a member, Sid and Howie jump up and down on the couch, with Caesar reaching out one long arm to grab Carl to pull him into the group. It's the funniest eleven minutes ever shown on TV and the audience laughs non-stop. As Dick Cavett once commented, "It's been known to lift people from the blues. Treat yourself to it."[61] It's excellent advice.

Carl Reiner said that much of the sketch wasn't rehearsed; certainly the opening wasn't because it required a live studio audience for Caesar to be sitting among and to some extent interacting with. Nor was the chase in

5. Scripts Versus Performance

the theater—Sid corroborated this, pointing out that it would have been too physically exhausting to run through in its entirety in rehearsal. And when you see it as aired, he was right. Minutes into it, he's drenched in sweat from all the running and scuffling with the ushers; by the end, having been climbed and jumped on by Morris repeatedly and carrying Howie at least three times, he looks like (for probably the only time in the show's run) he's almost out of gas.

Reiner and Morris are brilliant in the sketch, but, as usual, you have to come back to Caesar. He was, in this sketch as in so many others, far more than a "vessel for the writers' genius." Some of the funniest parts of it came from the inventive mind of Sid. He didn't like the opening where Al's reaction to finding out he was the guest was expressed in corny gee-whiz dialogue, so he scrubbed it and substituted fainting bits whenever Reiner said the magic words "This is your story." Where the script directed [Carl draws Sid out into the aisle], then [Sid runs up aisle], Caesar changed the action substantially. Carl now tugs repeatedly at Sid's arm as Caesar keeps pulling it away, punctuating the action with "No!" and "Get outta here!" And when Carl does get him into the aisle, Sid hits him over the head with his topcoat, flooring him, before he takes off. The script specified where the ushers were to enter and the route Caesar was to take in his flight, but *how* he did it was up to him. Fending off the ushers by hitting them with his topcoat and flinging it at a camera at the beginning of his run up onto the stage wasn't scripted. Reiner would comment that "Sid committed to it so deeply—we didn't rehearse that—he would've kept going out of the theater if they didn't catch him." At the beginning of his attempted escape from the ushers, he actually attempts to punch one of them, something he didn't even remember doing. You can't help but wonder if the usher appreciated Sid's level of commitment.

And there was Caesar's willingness to play straight man if someone else, in this case Howie Morris, was on a roll. Parts of the funniest physical comedy involving the two weren't scripted or rehearsed. When Howie hilariously prolongs the uncle-nephew joyous reunion, Sid, recognizing how well it was going over with the audience, played along with it. You can see him, after a nanosecond, adjusting and continuing the bit. He does the same with Morris' inspired improvisation when Uncle Goopy refuses to be separated from his nephew. The first time their embrace is broken up, Howie jumps up and clings to Caesar's shoulder as Sid carries him back to the guest chairs. That was obviously planned. The second time it happens, Howie took it upon himself to latch on to Caesar's leg. Both Sid and Carl pause for a moment (*that* was obviously neither scripted nor rehearsed), then Caesar gives Reiner the briefest of "I've got this" looks, turns, and walks back to the chair with roughly 140 pounds clinging to his left leg. It got one of the biggest laughs of the sketch.

And some of the dialogue and action was obviously Caesarized. At one point, a guest from Al's past, a beautiful woman, enters and he looks blank for a moment as she asks, "Don't you remember me?" The script runs as follows: Sid: "Oh, honey! [Throws his arms around her. Gives her a big kiss] Hold me tight. I'm so glad to see you." When Reiner as the MC asks Al to tell the audience who she is, he responds "I don't know, but Oh, Boy!" Carl says there must be some mistake: "Thank you very much, Miss." [Girl exits]. The writers might just as well have added [Crickets]. The whole bit just wasn't very funny. On air, however, the sequence went like this: Sid: "Honey, Baby!" He bends her over backwards for a series of passionate kisses, coming up occasionally for air. When Carl asks who the young lady is, his response is "I don't know who she is, but it's all right with me!" When Reiner tries to interrupt the kissing, Caesar, again prolonging a bit that was going over well, twice pushes him away, telling him to "Get outta here" before resuming the task at hand. Finally, it's determined that she's next week's guest and Carl leads her off stage. Trailing after her, Sid exclaims, "But I want her now!" and then moves to the guest chairs where Howie once again launches himself into his arms. *Now* it was funny.

There were very few occasions, and "This Is Your Story" was certainly not among them, in which the cast's occasional improvisation and Sid's additions, deviations from script, and ad-libs didn't enhance the final sketch as aired. Danny Simon, recalling them some fifty years later, said that "it was exciting to know that someone can do your material even funnier than you wrote it."[62]

6

The Sketches: "Show Me the Brilliance"

Your Show of Shows didn't originate sketch comedy on television, but in the sharpness, wit, and sophistication of its writing and playing, it was sketch comedy unlike anything before and would influence and shape TV comedy after it. The program explored—and exploited—its almost infinite adaptability. It lent itself to the domestic satire of the Hickenloopers, the interview format of the Professor bits, and, especially, the parodies of movies that both writers and cast excelled in. The sketches were usually short, 6–8 minutes for Hickenlooper ones (although they could be longer, particularly in the show's last two seasons) as well as the Professor and Strangers bits. The film sendups were generally the longest, as they required treatment of at least some plot points or genre clichés an audience would know or expect. The number of characters—and cast—could range from the standard two, Caesar and Coca, for the Hickenloopers (although they were often joined by Reiner and Morris, especially Reiner), and Caesar and Reiner for the Professor interviews, to everyone on board, including the stock company singers, for the film parodies. The format of sketch comedy didn't leave much time for character development (although Caesar could do a surprising amount in some of the longer movie spoofs), but the sketches on *Your Show of Shows* had arguably more narrative than most—they generally had some kind of set-up and development, and some kind of resolution, no matter how absurd.

Besides sharp writing, good sketch comedy requires good ensemble playing and in Caesar, Coca, Reiner, and Morris, *Your Show of Shows* had some of the best in early TV. All had at least some experience with the demands of live television, even if not those of a 33 to 39-week season in a 90-minute show. As previously discussed, Caesar, Coca, and Morris had been on *The Admiral Broadway Revue*, and from 1948 to 1949, Carl Reiner had been a regular on two short-lived programs, ABC's *The Fashion Show*, in which he provided comic relief as a photographer, and then CBS's *The*

The Hickenloopers: Charlie and Doris in mid-"discussion" (courtesy Barry Jacobsen).

54th Street Revue. But what made them so good at ensemble acting? Even on the *Revue*, Caesar, Coca, and Morris were never all together in a sketch. What were their experiences and backgrounds that developed the talents that made it possible for them to perform so well together on *Your Show of Shows*?

Three members of the quartet had a great deal in common. They were relative newcomers; when *Your Show of Shows* began, Caesar and Reiner were 27, Morris only three years older. All were from the New York area—Caesar from Yonkers, Reiner and Morris from the Bronx. Two, Caesar and Reiner, had been *tummlers* in the Catskills, although Reiner had far less experience there (only one summer) than Caesar. All three had been in service revues during World War II: Caesar in the Coast Guard, Reiner and Morris in the Army. In the Small New York World Department, Reiner and Morris were in the same entertainment unit in the Pacific, but they already knew each other from participating in a WPA-sponsored Public Radio Workshop in 1941.[63] Like many in their cohort of post-war aspiring comedians and actors, they gravitated toward Manhattan (Caesar, of course, making a short Hollywood detour), vying for roles in Broadway plays and revues. You will hopefully be familiar at this point with Caesar's Broadway experience. What were Reiner's and Morris's? Like Caesar's, not particularly extensive. Morris was Rosencrantz in Mike Todd's 1946 production of *Hamlet* that featured returning servicemen[64] and, after his stint on *The Admiral Broadway Revue*, landed a role in *Gentlemen Prefer Blondes*, which ran from December of 1949 to September of 1951—and prevented him from becoming a regular on *Your Show of Shows* until its second full season. Reiner had been in several short-run Broadway productions and the national touring company of *Call Me Mister* before he was tapped by Max Liebman to become Caesar's Second Banana in the first full season of the program.

The fourth member of the quartet was, in many ways, the odd person out, and not just because of her gender. Born in 1908, Imogene Coca was fourteen years older than Caesar and Reiner and came from a different generation of performers. She was the only member of the group who had been in vaudeville, albeit at a relatively young age, and had had a great deal more experience in Broadway plays and revues. Coca was the only non–New Yorker of the quartet, born in Philadelphia. And, although she left it at age 12, she never entirely escaped its distinctive accent, which pops up occasionally on *Your Show of Shows* (in "The Scented Letter" [3/22/52], she talks about the Staten Island "furry" in genuine Philadelphia-ese). Unlike the other three, she came from a show business family; her mother was an actress and magician's assistant, her father a musician. She also began her career as a dancer, with an emphasis on ballet. She started in New York as a Broadway gypsy, working her way up from dancing in the chorus to roles in plays and revues. Although she usually received good notices for her developing comedy style, they were in plays whose runs were generally short. Up to 1940, her biggest successes were in revues, *New Faces of 1934* and *New Faces of 1936*. To make ends meet, she frequently played nightclubs (an experience the shy Coca enjoyed about as much as the shy Caesar did in his early career, even though both received good reviews).[65] However, her revue and Broadway performances led to an invitation from Max Liebman to come to Tamiment to perform in its productions and she spent several summers there, which led to a prominent role in *The Straw Hat Revue*, a collection of Tamiment sketches that had a 10-week Broadway run in 1939. After that, she appeared on Broadway only twice in very short-run plays and her New York engagements were primarily in nightclubs until 1949. It was then that, familiar with and appreciative of her dancing and comedic skills, Liebman cast her in *The Admiral Broadway Revue* and *Your Show of Shows*.

All four then had some degree of success up to 1949 (Caesar with arguably the most, with two supporting film roles, nightclub engagements, and a year-long run on Broadway in *Make Mine Manhattan*), but they were hardly household names. It would be television and *Your Show of Shows* that would provide them a venue to fully display their talents and, for

Caesar and Coca, give them almost instant name recognition. What did each bring to ensemble playing? Caesar's skills as a comic actor will be discussed in greater detail later. Suffice to say here that he was one of the finest sketch comedians in television history and he always acted well and seamlessly with others.

Reiner was television's best Second Banana. He was a superb straight man in sketches, excelling as the unflappable interviewer of the Professor (for a straight man, keeping a straight face was a skill of its own when acting with Caesar). But he was also a gifted comedian and actor in his own right. He appeared frequently as a friend of the Hickenloopers or, memorably, as a number of snooty restaurant waiters who intimidate them. He performed physical comedy very well—his "death" scenes were epic—and his skills at doubletalk were second only to Sid's. And he had an amazing ability, unfortunately not always on display in the sketches that can be seen widely today, at reeling off complicated chunks of dialogue at top speed—and getting laughs doing it.

Morris was the only member of the quartet with acting training (he had been a drama major at NYU), as well as experience in comedy and he put both to use in the sketches, playing a notable variety of characters—trusty doctors, stage managers, and the like—and specializing in elderly, fussy, and sometimes manic men (near-hysteria was a Morris specialty). Like Reiner, he was excellent at physical comedy—and had to be. His small stature guaranteed exercising it frequently as he was flung and tossed about by Caesar on a regular basis. It's an indication of the comic talent on *Your Show of Shows* that only on that program would Morris be regarded as a Third Banana.

Coca's physical talents were extraordinary and not just as a dancer. Her large eyes could convey any emotion and her arched eyebrow could speak volumes. She could mold her features into almost any expression (and in one memorable pantomime from May 10, 1952, "The Photographer," Caesar molds them for her—and she makes them stay that way). And the former dancer had developed into a formidable comic actor—whether luring Sid to his doom with vampish come-hither looks in silent film parodies or making Doris Hickenlooper feisty enough to stand up to the bluster of Caesar's Charlie. And her acting range could encompass the sexy dance hall girl from the spoof of *From Here to Eternity*, who attracts both Sid and Carl, as well as the frumpy girlfriend with a whiny monotone that drives Caesar's characters to distraction—and attempted homicide—in takeoffs of *Golden Boy* and *A Place in the Sun*.

But what made them so good together? It's perhaps self-evident but bears repeating: These were not stand-up comics (and would not have been as good as they were if they had been primarily that) thrown together and suddenly required to develop ensemble skills. No matter the length of their experience or whether they had formal acting training or not, they were comic actors from a theatrical background, used to the give-and-take and requisite cooperation of ensemble work. And it was Max Liebman who recognized the largely untapped talent of Coca, and the potential of Morris and Reiner, and assembled them around his star Caesar, who was, despite being always the first among equals, skilled—and generous—in playing ensemble sketch comedy. And Liebman's instincts about how the four would mesh were correct. They were possibly the most talented comic ensemble in television history—only Gleason, Art Carney, and Audrey Meadows on *The Honeymooners* and Carol Burnett, Harvey Corman, and Tim Conway, on her eponymous show, were in their league.

What follows are descriptions of the kinds of sketches an audience would have consistently seen them in—some are known well today, others hardly at all. Within genres will be analyses, subjective of course, of what worked and what didn't in terms of writing and playing. Caesar could on occasion be very straightforward as well as discerning about both the show and his work on it; he once commented that "75% of the stuff is still good today. The rest is not so good."[66] But what a 75 percent. Much of it did indeed deliver the "brilliance" Sid expected of his writers.

The Hickenloopers: Marriage *Your Show of Shows* Style

One of the staples of modern TV comedy that can be traced back to *Your Show of Shows* is the sitcom. "The Hickenloopers" was television's first recurring domestic sitcom in revue format.[67] Many might assume it was "The Honeymooners," but Ralph and Alice Kramden came later. The Kramdens made their first appearance on DuMont's *Cavalcade of Stars* in a sketch in October of 1951. However, Alice was originally played by Pert Kelton and Art Carney's inimitable Norton would not make his appearance until several episodes into the season. The ensemble every classic TV fan knows would be completed only in 1952, when Audrey Meadows assumed the role of Alice on CBS's *The Jackie Gleason Show*. However, it would not be until 1955 that the Classic 39 episodes aired as a half-hour series. Charles and Doris Hickenlooper, always played by Caesar and Coca, made their debut on *Your Show of Shows* in 1950 during its first full season. From then until the very end of the program in 1954, a Hickenloopers sketch would be a regular part of almost every episode.

"The Hickenloopers" was observational comedy; in it, the quotidian was made a source, and a highly successful one, of laughter. The majority of the sketches used the sorts of situations in which real married couples find themselves as a springboard to comedy: Charlie telling a joke Doris doesn't find funny, Doris cleaning out a closet, or their making Sunday breakfast. And they were very much situation, rather than character, driven. You never know as much about the middle-class Hickenloopers as you do, for example, about the blue-collar Kramdens. Charlie works somewhere, doing something unspecified, but it always involves taking a lot of inventory. He wears a business suit doing whatever it is he does and he has a secretary. Doris is primarily a housewife, although she occasionally seeks work both inside and outside the home. Their parents are still around and presumably close by, although they exist only as unheard voices in telephone conversations. Beyond these few bits of biographical information, things could get murky, not to mention ambiguous. The couple are childless—until they aren't. In one episode (1/19/52), they show up in a park with a baby boy and a mere five months later (5/17/52) there is a reference in a sketch to the boy (or at least *a* boy)—who is now 5. Neither he nor any other offspring is ever seen or heard of again. The Hickenloopers live in an apartment on West 23rd Street in Manhattan—for the most part. However, Charlie takes the Staten Island ferry in one sketch (3/22/52), and in several others, he and Doris seem to have a house on Long Island. As you have no doubt surmised by now, character development and continuity frequently took second place to opportunities for good lines or comic situations. Charlie and Doris suddenly appear with that baby in the park so that their smothering attention to it can be contrasted with the extreme laissez-faire child-rearing approach of another couple with a baby ("Open your yap," commands the father, as he tosses bits of hot dog into its carriage—to eyebrow-raised double takes from both Hickenloopers). Charlie takes that ferry so he can help a beautiful woman who doesn't have the fare; and, when she returns it to him in a scented letter, Doris' suspicions can immediately be aroused ("You have to get up prett-ty early in the morning to pull the wool over my eyes!").

Although the Hickenloopers and the Kramdens shared some similarities—in their bickering and in Caesar and Gleason's bellowing and slow burns—their differences are more noticeable, as they also were from the early sitcom couples that would follow, including Lucy and Ricky Ricardo (who would make their TV debut in 1951). Part of the difference, of course, lay in the comic actors portraying them, but also in the characters' relationships. When Ralph Kramden yelled at and insulted his wife, Alice responded with magnificent eye-rolling silence, then squelched him with a cutting comment. The Hickenloopers were equal opportunity arguers and were far more verbal. Doris gave as good as she got, sometimes more so, and never suffered in silence. And watching their arguments is like watching a tennis match with skilled volleyers, who return sarcasm and put-downs instead of balls. While Lucy Ricardo's funny and generally hare-brained schemes to break into show business or get more of a household allowance were usually dashed on the rock of her disapproving husband Ricky, Doris generally got her way. There was often a steely shrewdness in Coca's playing of Doris, and her dogged persistence usually resulted in Charlie's capitulation out of sheer frustration or exhaustion ("You have won your battle—I am in your iron hand in your velvet glove"). And Caesar and Coca would do noticeable trade-offs in characterizations: Doris could be ditzy at times and Charlie the relative voice of reason, but just as often Charlie played the buffoon and Doris the more commonsensical—and deflating—partner.

Any comparison of these classic couples is a stunning reminder of what, if you were in the mood for sitcom in 1952, you could have watched on your 19-inch screen (once the set warmed up and you adjusted the vertical hold knob to prevent picture-rolling): three of the greatest TV comedians ever in Caesar, Gleason, and Ball. Add Imogene Coca and Art Carney, and you realize that The Golden Age of Television Comedy is neither a misnomer nor an exaggeration. So what did Caesar and Coca bring to this illustrious sitcom table that made the Hickenloopers distinctive?

Besides the usual sharp writing, the humor in the Hickenlooper sketches was largely due to the comedic skills of Sid and Imogene in back-and-forth dialogue, timing, and delivery. The variety of their put-downs and insults was truly impressive and were always timed perfectly. They could toss off the casual put-down in absentia, as Doris, in a panic, telephones her mother: "Something terrible's happened! No, nothing's happened to Charles ... this is serious!" Or Charlie could deliver a face-to-face brief, but devastating, zinger (3/31/51):

> DORIS [trying to convince Charlie to purge their closet of outdated items]: Don't you think it's silly to hang on to something that once you might have been madly in love with but that today has lost its glamor and is now an old relic?
> CHARLIE [long pause while looking down at her]: Yeah.

Imogene Coca could specialize in sharpness like no other female comedian of her time. Her Doris could be comically brutal when Charlie got on her last nerve. In a sketch where he comes home with a toothache (1/2/52), sympathy is the last thing he's greeted with: "You ate candy! I warned you. Suffer! I have no sympathy for you at all! At all! At all! [Caesar wincing in pain with each 'all']. Suffer! ... and stop that moaning." And bedroom talk with the Hickenloopers could be in a class by itself. When Charlie can't sleep and continually wakes up the soundly sleeping Doris so she can share his misery, she finally explodes with "Shut up and let me get some sleep, will ya!" (11/14/53)

The writers made good use of Coca's talents in playing the side of Doris who was expert in the twin arts of being both irritating and persistent in one of the best of the Hickenlooper sketches, "The Point Killer" (5/17/52). The sketch is also a good illustration of the writers' and Caesar and Coca's ability to make hilarious the occasions in any marriage that lead to stray thoughts of spousal homicide. In it, Doris not only succeeds in reducing Charlie to silence, a notable feat, she almost crushes his spirit in the process. At a party with friends, he's trying to tell a convoluted story involving a package delivered in error, the involvement of a gardener in the mix-up, and the arrival of a next-door neighbor in the middle of all of it. But he can't complete more than a sentence without Doris interrupting and contradicting him. Charlie goes through stages of toleration, increasing exasperation, and then outright anger, particularly when she stands in back of him, mouthing and miming her corrections. Sensing what she's doing, he finally explodes and tells her to keep quiet. Of course, when he resumes, he's so discombobulated that he starts forgetting elements of his own story, including the name of the gardener. Pathetically, he appeals to the others, "Please, don't you know his name?—you've got to know his name!" He's reduced to turning to Doris for help, who refuses to tell him: "You told me to keep quiet." But she then proceeds to correct his story, point by excruciating point, down to the color of the paper the package was wrapped in. Throughout, Caesar remains absolutely motionless, with a thousand-yard stare straight ahead, giving a marvelous impression of a man whose soul is quietly shriveling inside. Coca finally runs down, concluding with a brilliantly disgusted "Mercy!" One of the friends, trying to throw a lifeline to Charlie to get him back into telling the story, asks whether this was when the next-door neighbor arrived. Charlie, utterly defeated, says softly with bewilderment, "I don't know." You can almost sympathize with him in a sketch where the Hickenloopers are volunteers for a magician's act. When the magician makes Doris disappear, then announces he will make her reappear, Charlie asks, "You're gonna make her come back? ... Can I see you for a second?"

But when they got down to serious arguments, they were unmatched by any other sitcom couple. Their arguments were not only epic—they could take up an entire sketch—they approached argument as art form. And their style of argumentation, although funny, had a bite that was remarkable and an intensity that was at times almost unnerving. There was never any of the Kramdenesque "One of these days, Alice. Bang, Zoom! To the moon!" But given Caesar's rather alarming skill in portraying rage, there are nanoseconds in which you wonder if Doris might not be headed in that direction—even though you know that Charlie, like Ralph, would never act on his anger.

For example, in a sketch from November 11, 1950, they enter as an argument is already in full swing. Doris announces, "This is the end!" To which Charlie responds, "So, what do you want—a divorce?" (No other early TV sitcom spouse that I know of would come up with *that* line, particularly in 1950.) She narrows her eyes, he flashes his, and as he's changing clothes in mid-argument, he rips off his unknotted tie with such violence you expect to see a tie burn on his neck. As the quarrel progresses, her cooking becomes a bone of contention. Charlie complains that, besides boiling bread ("What other woman *does* that?!"), she serves everything with carrots. Doris: "This may come as a surprise to you, but carrots are good for the eyesight!" Charlie: "Big deal! So I can see a hundred miles in the dark. But I still can't look at your face." As the argument reaches its climax, Doris takes it up a final notch:

> You know what I want? Can I tell you?
> I'd like to know.
> I'll tell you what I want. I want you to go to that door, open it. Go out, close it behind you, go out into the night, keep going.
> Fine! Fine! Fine! But just remember you were the one who said get lost. You were the one who started it! You said open the door, go out into the night....
> I didn't say "get lost," but it's a good idea! I said it and I'll say it again. Open the door, go out into the night....

As he finally reaches that door, Charlie turns, looks around, and, for once, gets the last word: "Goodbye! It's been miserable. Let me take one last look at the torture chamber." The rawness of Caesar and Coca's "anger," along with her implacability and his exasperation make the sketch—and the edgy argument—a memorable one.

But Charlie and Doris were not all arguments and edginess. If they had been, they would have ended up as tiresome and one-dimensional as The Bickersons. Mismatched though they were, underneath the domestic combativeness were two people who did love each other. The couple could always team up to face a challenge together, whether coping with an unexpected overnight visitor or a snooty waiter in an exclusive restaurant. Doris could be solicitous about Charlie—she *does* eventually help him with his toothache and insomnia in those sketches. And their detentes when the arguments ended could be charming: In "The Birthday Present" (9/19/53), Charlie has seemingly forgotten Doris' birthday. Another epic argument ensues, but ends when he whips out a small box and asks, "So what do you think this is?" She snaps, "Probably a pack of gum!" But no, it contains the diamond earrings she has always wanted and he's saved a whole year for. Still in anger mode, Doris declares "Fine way to give a birthday present" as she puts them on. Checking herself in her compact mirror, she admits gruffly, "They're beautiful!" Then she smiles at Charlie; he smiles back and says softly, "Happy Birthday, Doris." He puts his arm around her and they go off to have dinner.

There could also be a playfulness in Caesar and Coca's depiction of the Hickenloopers, even in argument mode, that the audience picked up on and responded to. In "Get It Off Your Chest" (10/17/53), Doris decides (for some reason she obviously hasn't thought through) that their marriage would be improved if they shared what they found most irritating in each other. Charlie is reluctant as he, and we, know how this will end. He finally comes up with "You always squinch the toothpaste from the bottom, then [growing more exasperated in the telling] I gotta even it up!" She retaliates by accusing him of being a sloppy eater ("Why don't you just eat in a stall with a bag around your neck?"), then delivers the *coup de grace*—he slurps his soup. He indignantly denies it and stumbles over the tongue-twister—he is not a "slurp souper," or a "sloop surper." Realizing how silly their argument has become, Charlie laughs, which turns into a genuine Caesar laugh at the absurdity. Coca responds with a wide grin of her own. As the two look at each other, obviously having a good time, the audience laughs, no longer at the tongue-twister, but at Sid and Imogene enjoying themselves.

Caesar and Coca were also expert in capturing naturalistic rhythms of speech, whether in an argument or just having, for the Hickenloopers, a calm discussion. It was never just a matter of delivering a line and waiting for a laugh (in fact, Caesar sometimes cut audience laughter short by continuing, as his character would have, to talk). They actually listened to each other and provided the ordinary filler of everyday speech. The main dialogue of the Hickenlooper sketches was tightly scripted (which didn't mean that Caesar didn't occasionally ad lib—he did), but the filler was not. It was provided by Sid and Imogene on their own, especially Sid. To listen to Charlie's responses to Doris as she's telling him a story ("Yeah.... Then what? ... Think I should?") is to listen to real conversation. This is how people talk and, if they're really good at it, how they argue.

In fact, they were so good in their portrayal of the Hickenloopers that many viewers in the '50s assumed Sid and Imogene were husband and wife. And not just in the '50s—I once overheard a woman watching a Hickenloopers sketch with her husband confidently inform him, "They were married, you know." Well, yes, they were, but not to each other. There was another reason why audiences might have made that assumption and it's one that's understandable only if you see episodes of *Your Show of Shows* in their entirety. Beyond their immense talent, Caesar and Coca had little in common, other than their shyness (in that, Imogene's was almost a match for Sid's). They socialized with different sets of friends, and on the set, they rarely engaged in long conversations, instead relying on their remarkable ability to anticipate what the other would do. Yet, they had developed a natural rapport which was reflected not only in the sketches but also in their unscripted interaction when they appeared together as themselves. The

6. The Sketches 77

normally undemonstrative Caesar would hug her or bend down to kiss the top of her head; Coca would frequently reach up to touch his face as they talked or, if they were not already holding hands as they stood together for the cast curtain call, would always reach for his. In sketches, when she would affectionately hug him, it was to the accompaniment of "*aww*"s from women in the audience. Of their "marriage," Imogene once joked that she was the only socially acceptable bigamist in America. That assumption that they were married could also have its amusing downside: when Sid was at parties or restaurants with his model-attractive real wife Florence, he would sometimes get glares from people who assumed he was cheating on Imogene.[68]

Watching the Hickenlooper sketches some 60 years on is like being teleported back to the early '50s. Charlie and Doris are members of the increasingly well-off middle class of the post-war period, and the writers humorously as well as thoroughly satirized their aspirations, pretentions, and consumerism. (And they knew whereof they satirized: most of them had just joined it, moving from lower or lower-middle class Brooklyn, the Bronx, and Yonkers to The City. Of course, once there, Sid's Manhattan trajectory was a bit more pronounced—from furnished apartments in the West 50s and 60s to one on Park Avenue). The Hickenloopers can afford new furniture (although Charlie grumbles about the expense and modernistic design), buy new cars on occasion, take a flyer in the stock market (which promptly goes through minute-by-minute boom-bust cycles) and, briefly, have a maid. Doris in particular wants to be upwardly mobile and not just in the financial sense. She is constantly dragging Charlie to cultural events, for example a symphony performance which he neither likes nor understands or taking him to faddish new restaurants where he is either defeated by incomprehensible menus or intimidated by snooty waiters. On one episode (11/21/53), they go to the Vitality Health Food Restaurant which is vegetarian with a vengeance. After gamely trying a flower hors d'oeuvre, he rebels: "Next time, I'll go to Pepito's. You can go to the Botanical Gardens."

In sitcoms of the '50s, middle-class women didn't work. It was a reflection—and popular reinforcement—of a societal norm: the man was the breadwinner, the woman was a housewife and mother (someone had to take full-time care of all those baby boomers) who didn't pursue a career outside the home. Of course, the reality fell far short of the ideal. Women continued to make up a significant portion of the work force after the war, and middle-class women were among their numbers. But on television, it was definitely the standard. Margaret Anderson of *Father Knows Best* and Harriet Nelson of *The Adventures of Ozzie and Harriet* embodied it. Lucy Ricardo tried to break free from it, but when she did, disaster was usually the result (as in the classic Lucy and Ethel get a job as candy factory inspectors episode). The writers of "The Hickenloopers" (primarily Mel Tolkin and Lucille Kallen) would play with that norm—both reinforcing it and undercutting it—in ways that, although always funny, flirted with the subversive.

In "The Wife Works" (10/16/51), Charlie enters the kitchen for breakfast. But there's no Doris at the stove and nothing on the table save a basket of eggs, lurking in a Chekhovian sort of way. Doris appears, wearing a business suit, to announce that he'll have to get his own breakfast: "I've got a job." Charlie at first laughs dismissively, then declares, "You're not going to work! Don't I support the house?" She responds with what amounts to a manifesto: "A person has a right to do things, to accomplish things, to earn self-respect and dignity. A person has that right." He responds with a manifesto of his own that begins as sexist and ends as ludicrous in its itemization of household drudgery: "A person, yes, but not a woman! Maintain your dignity? Being married to me—that has no dignity? Preparing meals for me, taking care of the house, washing the dishes, cleaning the floors, making the beds, throwing out the garbage. That's dignity!" But Doris stands her ground in a symbolic showdown—over those eggs no less.

As the argument escalates, Charlie picks up an egg and commands, "Boil it!" She responds, "Boil it yourself!" After a back and forth of "I said you boil this egg!" and "You boil it!" he hits the table for emphasis, with of course the hand he's holding the egg in. And she laughs. Wiping his hand on a towel, he insists, "No woman I'm married to, including you, is ever going to work! I'll be the laughingstock of the office. I can see Harry, Jim, and Pete. What will they think?" And in a twist you have to suspect Lucille Kallen supplied, Charlie goes on: "My boss—what would *she* think?" Doris seizes the moment to remind him that 'Your boss is a woman and *she* works.'" He shoots back (hardly making his case but not realizing it), "She doesn't work. She owns the place—it was left to her by her mother."

As Doris begins to leave, Charlie yells, "Come back here!" and insists she sit down to continue the discussion, and she does so, but mutters rebelliously "It's the Dark Ages." She finally explains the reason for her job: she needs money to get a new car, because she's crashed the old one—and he's going to be sued by the drivers of the car and truck she ran into. At this point, we seem to be returning to '50s "Oh those crazy women!" stereotypes and we expect Charlie to explode. But instead the writers throw in one of the almost surreal touches they were expert at. Instead of exploding, Charlie reaches into the basket of eggs and picks one up while calmly saying, "No sense of your going to work for that—it's just an accident." With an easy overhand lob, he tosses it against the wall in back of Doris. "The main thing is to keep your wits about you. [another toss, another splatter]

You just feel better about it [toss, splatter]." She just as calmly asks, "Do you mind saving two eggs for breakfast?" (And here, Coca almost loses her straight face, understandably so, as her hair is now adorned with bits of eggshell.) And the sketch ends—without resolution.

Doris may make that breakfast but gives no indication that she isn't then going off to her job (where in the early '50s, she would have made one-third of the salary of a male counterpart). With the writers' usual blithe disregard for continuity, you never find out in subsequent Hickenlooper episodes. It's hardly early consciousness-raising, but in Doris' manifesto, her persistence, and her assertiveness, it's striking—and you wouldn't have seen it on any other sitcom in 1951.[69]

Today, some of the subjects of the Hickenlooper sketches—a disastrous first dinner, the wife wrecks the car—can seem hackneyed (although they were fresh then). And the sketches are very much of their time in their frequent reliance on what were considered female foibles, even with Lucille Kallen writing them. Nor did Charlie and Doris always travel well outside of their home theater of battle (some of the weaker sketches took place far afield of their usual New York haunts). However, considering that almost every episode of *Your Show of Shows* featured the couple, it's a tribute to the writers' inventiveness and skill that the hits far outweighed the misses.

It seems appropriate to leave Charlie and Doris with a bit from a sketch "It's Only a Movie" (9/18/51). In the rhythm of the dialogue, the back-and-forth between them, their timing, and a silly but funny ad-lib from Sid, it's quintessential Hickenloopers. They have just returned from a movie. She's crying and he's laughing; she thought it was tragic, he thought it was funny. Doris begins in exasperation:

> The trouble with you is you can't understand suffering because you've never suffered in your *life*!
> I never *suffered*?
> Never!
> In my life I never suffered?
> Not once!
> I *suffered* in my life!
> *When* did you suffer?
> You want to know when I suffered?
> I'd like to know when you suffered!
> All right! They used to call me Suffer Boy! I worked very hard in school....
> That's not suffering!
> Wait! Will you wait? Then I got a job in an office....
> That's not suffering!
> Wait! I didn't *come* to the suffering yet! Then I started going out ... parties ... dances
> That's not....
> Wait! This is on the *way* to suffering!
> Well, where is the suffering?

I'm *coming* to it! And when I *get* to it, boy will I suffer!
Go on. Get to the suffering.
I met a girl.
Proceed.
We started going steady.
Continue.
We got engaged.
Go on.
We got married!
[After a pause—Doris screams][70]

Jim and Margaret Anderson they weren't, but Caesar and Coca made them an unforgettable comedic couple. For the final three episodes of *Your Show of Shows*, NBC invited viewers to write or call in to request seeing their favorite sketches one last time. The Hickenloopers appeared on all three.

The Professor: Caesar's Clown Persona

Among the most popular recurring bits on *Your Show of Shows* were the Professor sketches, in which Caesar played a zany authority on everything. "The Professor" is a standard comic figure and can be seen in a variety of venues: Irwin Corey's "World's Foremost Authority" in nightclubs (he did the Professor only rarely on TV until the late 1950s) and earlier vaudeville incarnations. But the character is a lot older than that. *Il Dottore* ("Professor" as well as "Doctor" in Italian) was a familiar figure of *commedia dell'arte*: a pompous know-it-all (who really doesn't) whose costume is an exaggerated version of academic garb. Move *Il Dottore* several hundred miles across the Alps and four centuries forward in time and you have Sid's Viennese professor, clad in slightly more "modern" academic dress—an oversized tailcoat and vest and a battered top hat—and still a self-proclaimed expert in everything.

The Professor is one of the roles people seem to remember Caesar in best, rather ironically because he was atypical of the characters Sid played in other sketch genres far more often. As Mel Tolkin observed, he was Caesar's clown persona, plain and (very) simple. But he was a bit different from the other 20th-century professors: pompous, yes, but also irrepressible in his enthusiasm about sharing his "knowledge," and easily and somewhat pathetically wounded if his expertise was challenged. Above all, he was adapted for a television dialog format. The sketches were always in the form of an interview—and always began the same way. Carl Reiner would appear onstage and brightly announce, "Hello there! This is your roving reporter Carl Reiner here at LaGuardia Airport where a planeload of eminent visitors has

6. The Sketches

The Professor: Caesar in clown persona in a publicity shot with Coca. A slightly misleading one, because she appeared in only one sketch of this kind with Sid—as a mini-Professor.

just arrived, among them the distinguished Viennese authority on [insert topic], Professor [insert silly Germanic name], who has just written a book on the subject [insert even sillier title]." The possibilities for ludicrous names, topics, and book titles were endless: Ludwig von Pablum, expert in child psychology: "Children Are People—Only Smaller"; Filthy von Lucre, financial expert: "Money Talks, So Listen!"; Lapse von Memory, memory expert: "I Remember Mama, But I Forget Papa"; Ludwig von Fossil, expert on archaeology: "Archaeology Made Easy—Don't Lift Heavy Rocks." Caesar would then stride, amble, shuffle, however the spirit seemed to move him, on stage and the interview would begin, with Sid employing the thickest German accent of which he was capable. (You will thank me, if you've ever seen a Professor sketch or especially if you hasven't, for not attempting to reproduce it in phonetic dialog here—it's almost impossible to do it justice, particularly Sid's impeccably back-of-the-throat Germanic 'r.')

How much you like, or laugh at, the Professor sketches will be in direct correlation to how funny you find Mel Brooks, because these were the ones into which he seems to have had most input (and may have been the earliest he provided material for before he officially joined the writing staff during the show's second season). The Professor's names and titles of his books should certainly have provided a clue. And you need look no further for a Brooksian imprint than a sketch in which the Professor is an expert on royal procedure and ceremony (5/2/53). When Carl asks him who the worst ruler in history was, Sid describes a nonsensically-named tyrant, who nonetheless redeemed himself in the eyes of his people when his kingdom was attacked—by winning the famous Battle of Yells and Screams. You can also detect a heavy dose of Brooks in the "if that line didn't work, here's another—and yet another" rhythm of the sketches.

Because of his limited writing (and credits) during *Your Show of Shows*' first season and a half, Brooks was very much invested in the sketches. Both he and Sid told a story about just how much. In a sketch about the Professor as an animal psychiatrist, Mel wanted to use a joke about a snake who didn't think he was one and refused to share a cage with his fellow reptiles. Caesar thought it distinctly unfunny and rejected it. Brooks was however insistent and continued his campaign for its inclusion outside the Writers' Room as the two walked down 54th Street, arguing as they went. Finally, Mel halted and risking limb, if not life, jabbed his fingers into Sid's chest, insisting, "You've got to use this joke!" Caesar looked down at him and after a long pause said, "I'll let you live." And used the bit.[71] After all of Brooks' insistence, however, Sid's instincts were correct; if you watch the sketch, aired on January 27, 1951, the joke fell flat (the audience response was underwhelming), something Caesar still remembered vividly and sardonically some thirty years later.[72] Obviously, Mel would go on to write better ones.

The Professor sketches are an acquired taste. The humor wasn't always sustained, and it was far broader (as was Caesar's playing) than in most of the other sketches. They also relied more on straight jokes than in any of the other genres. But the Professor grows on you and the sketches almost always had their funny moments in their sheer silliness or absurdity. For example, when Professor von Bloodhound, an expert in criminology and criminal disguise, consults his notebook and suddenly demands of Carl Reiner, "Are you sure you were never a tall, beautiful blonde? It's been done, you know." Or when Rudolph von Rudder explains his theory of flying: "It's like the birds. What keeps the birds in the air? Courage. If that bird ever looked down...."

However, they could occasionally go far beyond the broad jokiness to toy with the boundaries of logic, cheerfully and repeatedly crossing them to the point of surrealism. Only on *Your Show of Shows* could a Professor sketch, "Mind over Matter" (9/23/50), turn into a demented discourse on the subjective nature of reality. As Professor Sigmund Shock, Sid explains his mind/brain theory to Carl:

> CAESAR: The mind directs the brain. I tell the mind; the mind tells the brain. If I don't want to see something, I tell the brain there's nothing there. The brain believes me—it's very naïve. The only one who knows you are here is me. I tell my brain "He's not here." [Poof] "He's not here."
> REINER: Does this really mean I'm not here?
> CAESAR: [looking through Reiner] I wonder where he went?

6. The Sketches

REINER: Who?
CAESAR: You.

Reiner, not giving up easily, asks, "If you can imagine someone who's here not being here, can you imagine someone who's not here being here?" Of course the Professor can—he summons up an invisible "Hilda," with whom he has a conversation in fractured German ending in an argument. He then causes her, somewhat paradoxically, to disappear. (It's best not to contemplate the metaphysics of any of this for very long.) Finally, Shock insists that just because Carl shows him his hand, it doesn't mean that one is there if he doesn't want it to be: "There's nothing there." When Reiner protests that there is indeed a hand attached to his arm, Shock invites him to hit him with it and he won't feel a thing. After repeated punches, the Professor exclaims, "That's plenty of nothing!" and reels offstage, rethinking his theory. The entire sketch is inspired absurdity and it's difficult to imagine it being played on any other early '50s TV show.

The Professor sketches were also among those in which Caesar ad-libbed the most—not just to get laughs from the audience but also, and it's obvious, to try to make Carl Reiner break character and laugh. As Professor Hans von Bulldozer, Sid is an expert in architecture (3/31/51). Among his prize pupils was one who wanted to build a 116-story skyscraper. The Professor pointed out he was building on quicksand but was dismissed as old-fashioned and construction proceeded. The result? "It was the shortest skyscraper in the world. I used to pass by it every day and look down at the observation tower. [Walking around an imaginary building with hand at waist level] It was about this high." As Reiner began to move on to another question, Sid ad-libbed, "Poor fellow. It was very sad. He committed suicide. Leaped off the building." The desired result was achieved: the audience laughs and Carl breaks up, as Sid looks off to one side with the slightest of smiles.

You can also detect some ad-libbing in what is one of the funniest (if not *the* funniest), Professor sketches in which he is an expert on mountain climbing. There are two versions of the mountain climbing sketch; *Your Show of Shows* would repeat many sketches, although always with variations. The one to watch is with Professor Ludwig von Snowcap (1/30/54); in its description of his expedition to Mount Everest and advice on what to do if your rope breaks, it's the Professor at his best. It begins with Sid doing a little skip-dance over to Carl, yodeling as he goes (in an example of the amazing things he could do with his voice, he yodels and says "Good Evening" simultaneously). He's wearing a mountain climbing rope around his waist, which is frayed at one end. Carl asks quietly, "There was somebody on the other end of that rope, wasn't there?" Sid replies, "There *was* somebody at the other end of that rope," as he twirls it and looks pensive. Carl asks, "I imagine you're wearing that in sentimental memory of this person?" "No," shrugs Sid, "it just holds my pants up."

The frayed rope is soon employed by the Professor to flog Reiner when Carl asks why he never attempted to climb Mount Everest. Highly indignant that the reporter has never heard of it, he launches into a description of the expedition he mounted: he collected five of the greatest mountain climbers in the world, purchased special equipment, and prepared to leave New York.

> SID: And on that fateful day of October 18, 1935, we left New York City to conquer Mount Everest!
> CARL: What happened?
> SID: Well, as you know, it's an old story, but we didn't reach the peak. You should see—those men were gallant—they tried and they tried. It was to no avail.
> CARL: How far did they get?
> SID: Well, we got as far as 23rd St. and Broadway. Crosstown traffic was horrible! The fellows were honking their horns—please get out of the way, we have to conquer Mount Everest. No, they wouldn't move. One lousy bus driver was changing a transfer—he stopped the whole expedition.

In an aside/ad-lib, he continues ruefully. "And we brought so much stuff." And then shifts the Professor from Vienna to the Lower East Side, making it difficult for Carl to refrain from laughing: "We had corned beef sandwiches, some pastrami. We were well-prepared—we had a gallon of tea and everything [sigh]."

Recovering, Carl moves on to a question everyone has asked himself at one time or another: When you're climbing a mountain and the rope you're attached to breaks, is there anything you can do to save yourself?

> SID: Didn't you read my book on rope-breaking? [Of course, the Professor has written one.] It's my famous theory. When you're on the top of a mountain and all of a sudden you see that your rope is gonna snap and you have two seconds to act: You start to scream—and you keep screaming all the way down. So they'll know where to find you. It doesn't look right if they don't find you.
> CARL (appalled): Isn't there any other method you can use?
> SID: Yes, there is an alternative. If you see your rope is breaking and again you have two seconds to act. Immediately, the alternative is you spread your arms full and start to fly as hard as you can! [flapping arms vigorously]
> CARL: People just can't fly!
> SID: How do you know? You may be the first one. You got nothing to lose. You can always go back to screaming—that's always working for you.
> CARL: I hate to bring this up, but your friend Hans [the unfortunate on the other end of Sid's frayed rope]—was he a flyer or a screamer?
> SID: Hans was a flying screamer—and what a bouncer!

Some segments of the sketches are notable for their superb timing as well as amusingly unexpected twists. The Professor on Space Travel and

Jet Propulsion (9/12/53) is a good example. Carl asks an incredibly complex, gibberish-laden question (and he does the scientific word salad marvelously) about "interstellar gravitational relations," involving "the gaseous layer between the ionosphere and the stratosphere," relative with "the terrestrial pull of any of the 12 orbits," and on and on. Throughout, Sid nods knowingly. Deep in thought, he looks at his hands which he holds in front of him, in apparent intense concentration. Carl finally runs down: "Is this because of the ionic gaseous pressures that build up in the ionosphere?" Continuing to look at his hands, Sid is silent for 8 seconds, an eternity in sketch comedy. But he was a master at timing, and it works—the audience begins to laugh in anticipation. Finally, he holds up his thumb, which he has been looking at in a particularly intent way, and asks: "You think this is infected here?" As Carl stands there nonplussed, as well he might, Sid announces in a wonderfully professorial way, "But—we go on, Ja?"

There have been occasional attempts to analyze the Professor sketches: They puncture the persona of the "all-knowing intellectual" (something Americans have always been all too good at). Well, yes, to some extent. Or the Professor is a parody of a central European (read Jewish) intellectual. Maybe. But ultimately, trying to come up with a profound analysis of the Professor is like trying to pin down a slightly crazed butterfly and dissecting it to see what makes it fly erratically. Better, perhaps, just to surrender to the amiable lunacy of the sketches.

Hits and Misses: Nobody Bats a Thousand

Among the less successful recurring sketches were the "Strangers Meet and Converse in Fluent Cliché" ones. In them, Caesar and Coca were real out-of-towners: he was from Peoples Creek, Idaho, she from Twin Falls, Iowa. Encountering each other in a variety of places and situations, they discover some kind of tenuous (at times, *very* tenuous) connection, and one of them invariably exclaims, "Isn't it a small world?" With great enthusiasm, they would exchange clichéd and trite observations about wherever they were (a New York cocktail party, a pet shop, a department store) and what they were doing. No matter how clichéd the comment ("Well, you can't tell a book by its cover!" "Money can't buy happiness!"), one would declare "You can say that again"—and the other always does.

The premise was initially humorous (it was a great concept) and the earliest "Strangers" sketches were the best, or at least the freshest. They had their moments, usually based on absurdity or a twist on a cliché. In one from May 5, 1952, Caesar and Coca are parents seeing their kids, his son and her daughter, off to their usual summer camps, and as it turns out, they're on opposite sides of the same lake. Sid enthuses about the boys' camp that has themed programs (in a nice touch, one summer's was knife-throwing—"bullies don't bother Herbert any more"), and as he notes, last summer's featured a Hopalong Cassidy theme: the children got Hopalong Cassidy hats, boots, and guns.

> SID [excitedly]: And do you know who they got to show up on the last day of camp?
> IMOGENE [just as excited]: Hopalong Cassidy?
> SID [still excited]: No! Gloria Swanson!

In another (12/9/50), they meet at a wedding reception and engage in rhapsodic clichés about how the happy couple got together:

> IMOGENE: Did you hear how they met?
> SID: Wasn't that something?
> IMOGENE: Like a fairy tale!
> SID: Like Cinderella or Romeo and Juliet!
> IMOGENE: If you read it in a book, you wouldn't believe it.
> SID: If you saw it on the screen, you'd say—
> TOGETHER: Hollywood!
> SID: So romantic, so beautiful—it was something! [Beat] Picked her up on the street....

In a somewhat old bit—but funny when Caesar and Coca did it—the two strangers meet at the top of the Empire State Building (10/3/52). After trite observations about Manhattan and the building, Imogene peers from the viewing area and exclaims, "Look at the people rushing helter and skelter." "Yeah," says Sid, glancing down, "they look just like ants. [Pause] That's what they *are*!" [Stomping vigorously].

However, even though the sketches seemed popular with the audience at the time ("Isn't it a small world" became even more of a catchphrase), the taglines got old, as taglines always do, the premise creakier, and the situations and dialogue sillier. Looking back at them over 60 years later (particularly if you have seen a number of Caesar-Coca sketches), there was another reason why they were among the weaker sketches on *Your Show of Shows*: two intelligent comic actors were playing inane and vapid characters and even their skill at spirited ping-pong conversation wasn't always enough to overcome that. Both Sid and Imogene got through the "Strangers" sketches gamely and often humorously, but they are among the few in which Sid at times looks almost uncomfortable.

Another hit-or-miss series of sketches were those featuring "The Four Englishmen." Even more of a concept type of sketch than "The Strangers," their plots were very simple: Four Englishmen (Caesar, Coca, Reiner, and Morris), with upper lips so stiff their conversation is often unintelligible, enter, one by one, a hall in an English manor or a box at the Ascot races and then sit stone-faced for an interminable amount of time. Then some mishap occurs—they're drenched by rain dripping, then pouring, through the roof of the manor hall; or they're splattered by mud thrown up by the racehorses as they gallop past. Rather than reacting as any sane, presumably non-English, folk would, they stoically ignore it, and then they leave. And that's it.

You have to give props to the writers for their daring: making an audience wait for a long time, at least as measured in sketch minutes, for something to happen and then providing a pay-off worth the wait was not your usual fare in '50s television comedy. Sometimes it worked: the manor hall sketch (5/30/53) was amusing, as the rain first drips and then turns into a torrent of water, while the four sit there expressionless as they're inundated (it also featured one of the rare times Sid almost breaks character and laughs when he glances at a sodden Carl Reiner). So too is their imperturbability as they become increasingly mud-coated in the Ascot sketch (9/19/53). Sometimes it didn't work: the sketch that ends with a genteel food fight (5/23/53) is distinctly unfunny. Even the successful ones took a very long time to set up as each character makes a separate entrance, and a later one with Muggs the Chimpanzee (10/17/53) would be a minor disaster.[73] The writers should have known better than to violate the W.C. Fields Rule: Never Work with Children or Animals. In rehearsal, Muggs was hilarious, climbing over everyone, even biting Caesar's ear. It would certainly be funny to see the imperturbable Englishmen coping with a lively chimpanzee, right? Except when the sketch was broadcast live, despite the lure of bananas strewn over the couch where they sat, the chimp just drank from teacups, then stood on Sid's leg and put his arms around his neck, looking at him. Actually, that part *was* funny—two primates almost appear to be communing. However, when Muggs refused to do anything more than that, the sketch had to be cut short. It probably was not a coincidence that it was the last of the "Englishmen" sketches.

However, the writers didn't give up on the concept. After the Chimp Incident, it would appear again, although in slightly changed format. This time, Caesar, Coca, Reiner, and Morris are musicians playing in a concert hall, and the sketch is genuinely funny throughout. Perhaps because it still has the characters' imperturbability under pressure bit, but there's less of a wait for the sketch to develop. In "The String Quartet" (11/14/53) said quartet enters, they seat themselves, and begin to play. Then a fire breaks out somewhere offstage. Three firemen enter with hoses, which they drag across the stage, then disappear (all of this while the quartet continues to play, without even glancing at them). Soon, sprays of water from those hoses begin to hit the four musicians—and continue until they are drenched. Nonetheless, they play on, much as you imagine the band on the *Titanic* did as the ship slowly sank, and the quartet gets almost as wet. They continue until the piece is finished, stand, take a very soggy bow, and exit. The sketch may have violated the standard "Four Englishmen" format—but as a whole it was a lot funnier.[74]

Guest Hosts: There Were Guest Hosts?

A little-known genre of sketches, only a few of which can be seen widely today, were those involving guest hosts. Because complete episodes that can be viewed outside the Paley Center, UCLA, or the Library of Congress are extremely rare, it's easy to overlook, or not even realize, that *Your Show of Shows* followed a variety show format; guest hosts were a standard feature of it. Caesar would briefly introduce them and beat a hasty and relieved retreat to get into character for the first sketch; the host would then introduce the sketches and acts that followed. For the most part, hosts were actresses and actors, with the occasional opera star or dancer. As Max Liebman noted in 1953, "None of them comes equipped. Most are aliens in the revue world."[75] Nonetheless, they were expected to do something useful in the sketches and to be congenial and deliver introductions adequately. Jose Ferrer, for example, was adept at all of these tasks and appeared frequently in the first two seasons.

Some guest hosts were unfortunately unable to do any of the above well—even introductions. A few were simply unused to live television, looking into the wrong camera and appearing alternately ill at ease or deer-in-the-headlights frozen (even though they could rely on cue cards). Their introductions made Sid's look almost polished and animated. Nevertheless, even these hosts were almost always put into sketches with Caesar and Coca, who did most of the comedic heavy lifting if necessary.

And you can occasionally sense writer fatigue in trying to come up with guest-host turns for actresses that weren't particularly suited for them, because they relied on one sketch a number of times: a glamorous turn-of-the-century city girl visits the sticks where her affections are vied for by two unsophisticated country boys, Caesar and Reiner. Sid and Carl were manifestly neither, despite their acting talents, and the sketch in any of its variations just didn't work. About the only humor in it came from Sid's physical comedy. (There was one exception to the Urban-Comedians-Shouldn't-Do-Hick-Humor Rule: in an early Interview sketch [4/15/50], Caesar appears as folk-singer Lemuel T. Cornball and proceeds to reel off a string of countrified sayings, topped by a mile-a-minute rendition of a Mel Brooks ditty, "The Cry of Crazy Crow," complete with caws. It's so unexpected and bizarre that it's hilarious. Nonetheless, you're sort of glad Sid never attempted to repeat it.)

6. The Sketches 89

Other guest-hosts were excellent however and contributed to some memorable sketches: for example, Jackie Cooper as a testy drummer seated all-too-close to Sid and Imogene at a dinner theatre (2/14/53), or Rex Harrison as a cut-rate and fast-talking haberdasher trying to make a sale to an overwhelmed Caesar (3/11/50). Dennis King had a first-rate turn as a judge trying to arbitrate between Sid, a building super, and Imogene, a tenant who insists on throwing garbage out her window (5/31/52). Marguerite Piazza was a superb sexy applicant for a job as Charlie Hickenlooper's secretary (5/3/52). Betty Furness and Binnie Barnes were fine Stellas in *Your Show of Shows*' two parodies of *A Streetcar Named Desire* (4/5/52, 1/26/52). And Nanette Fabray was an excellent pantomimist in two silent movie parodies (10/7/50, 1/27/51)—which obviously did not go unnoticed by Sid, who would sign her for two seasons of the later *Caesar's Hour*.

Almost all of the good guest hosts, and Arlene Francis and Faye Emerson can be included in this category, had had some TV experience (even the non-human ones: Kukla and Ollie, along with Fran, were charmingly funny in their two episodes). However, that didn't always guarantee success. For example, Jack Carson was overbearing in sketches and abysmal at hosting (how *do* you omit Imogene Coca in your listing of the cast?).

For good or bad (and some truly fit the latter description), guest hosts were part of the format Max Liebman had devised and both writers and regular cast accommodated them. However, there was a limit to Max's accommodation—and patience. You will sometimes see ventriloquist Paul Winchell's name in episode guides as the host for the December 23, 1950, show. Yet, if you watch the episode, he and his dummy Jerry Mahoney are MIA. With good reason. All had gone well until after the dress rehearsal. Standard procedure was for Liebman to then give notes or make last-minute adjustments. No one questioned them, not even Caesar; there wasn't enough time to. After this particular rehearsal, Max said that cuts had to be made to the sketches because otherwise the show would run over. Bill Hayes, one of the regular singers, was there to watch what followed. Winchell and his manager objected, Max quietly observed that as director it was his call, and the manager then upped the ante by announcing that they would walk out if Winchell's bits didn't remain intact (they seemed oblivious or didn't care that the star of the show, without objecting, was going to have some of *his* sketches reduced as well). Liebman looked down at his notes, calmly announced "Winchell is out," and instantly rearranged the show: Marguerite Piazza, an opera singer who was then a regular, would be the host; an additional song would cover one of Winchell's sketches; and Sid would do two monologues instead of his usual one to cover another. And that's the way the episode aired—less than 90 minutes later.[76]

That, however, was the exception. Generally, Liebman was gentle in his handling of guest-hosts and Caesar could be very accommodating to them. In an episode from September 1950, actor Lee Bowman went so far as to give an impromptu speech before introducing a sketch, thanking Sid for being so solicitous of the hosts and generous to them (no doubt causing considerable consternation in the control room—there went the careful timing for the show). He later explained why he had done it: "Other comedians upstage guest artists and push them all over the place."[77] Even when hosts were less than stellar in sketches, they were never upstaged by Caesar or Coca, and when they were good, Sid, Imogene, Carl, and Howie were willing to turn themselves into a supporting cast (Dennis King's sketch is a good example). Caesar often said that it didn't matter who got the laugh as long as there was one. And Sid and company were always willing to let a guest host who could do a sketch well take the spotlight.

Song and Dance: Caesar and Coca Together Again—and Solo!

Every episode of *Your Show of Shows* featured musical numbers—songs, dances, and big production finales—performed by a stock company of dancers and singers. Although little of it can be seen today, two other permanent cast members sang and danced in sketches and solo routines: Coca and Caesar.

Coca was, of course, a professional dancer. She started lessons in dance, with an emphasis on ballet, at age 10 and five years later embarked on a show business career. Her ability to make an audience laugh (also developed early) led her to combine dancing and comedy in nightclub and cabaret acts, as well as in a number of Broadway productions. Max Liebman, well-acquainted with her talents from her summer stock routines at Tamiment, signed her for *The Admiral Broadway Revue* in 1949 and her first television comedy song and dance routines were a feature on the show. Imogene would then follow Caesar and Howard Morris to Liebman's next, even more successful, foray into variety shows a year later.

On *Your Show of Shows*, she did musical numbers weekly, usually right before Caesar's monologue unless she was featured in the final production number.[78] They were a showcase for both her dancing and comedic skills, and her versatility was amazing. She spoofed opera singers, '20s Charleston-dancing flappers, and notably, in "Mon Amour Americaine" (written by Mel Tolkin), a French Apache dance-hall singer (3/25/50). Striking a Marlene Dietrich pose, one leg on a chair, she laments her inability to attract a GI with flirting: "I tried a different approach. Dance? Shyly, he lunged at me...." Perhaps the funniest of these spoofs were of torch singers—her throaty rendition of "Jim," in which we discover just what an undesirable rat he is, is a classic satire of the genre (4/22/50). It's also a good example of her combination of song and comedy:

> [Spoken over music] Jim. You should have seen Jim ten years ago ... he was just as repulsive then. I'll never forget the first time I saw Jim ... he was passing by and stopped to pick up a cigar (pause) but he picked me up instead. I must have been lying there for a good hour.... It was love at first sight ... he looked at me. I looked at him.... And we both shuddered.
> [Song] Jim doesn't send me pretty flowers. Jim never helps to cheer my lonely hours—Gone all the years I've wasted on him—Jim.

Coca could also introduce a touch of pathos in her Chaplinesque Little Tramp sketches, where no matter the hardships or adversity, she met them with a touching optimism in songs such as "Life is Just a Bowl of Cherries." She joined the production company singers and dancers for parodies of operettas (*Die Fledermaus*) and operas (*Tales of Hoffman*). In top hat, white tie, and tails, she was accompanied by a male chorus in music-hall songs like "Harrigan" and "I've Got a Lovely Bunch of Coconuts."

Among the most memorable of her numbers were the ballet parodies. She and the show's choreographer, James Starbuck, were faithful to the original ballet at least in terms of plot and choreography, then added Coca's comedy. In *Swan Lake* (10/11/52), she molts feathers as she dances and employs her wings like a burlesque dancer's fans; in *Sleeping Beauty* (5/17/52), despite the Prince's ardent wooing, all her Beauty wants to do is go back to bed. At the end of one ballet spoof, she's left clinging to the proscenium after a particularly energetic lift by her partner. Perhaps the best parody, in terms of sheer cleverness, was of *Afternoon of a Faun* (4/29/50). Far from the shy nymphs of the original, Imogene is a flirtatious nymph on the prowl who attempts to arouse the interest of the Faun with a complete repertoire of vamps, winks, and come-hither looks. When that doesn't work, she sprinkles salt on his tail. However, she discovers to her dismay that he is far more interested in the veils she wears around her waist than in her. (An in-joke for ballet buffs, who would recall the sexually graphic ending of the original in which the faun gratifies himself on the nymph's veil.)

Coca and Caesar did their first brief comedy dance bit on the *Revue* and would continue and expand them on *Your Show of Shows*. They would sometimes appear at the end of production numbers, and a surprising number of sketches have them doing at least a few dance steps, whether it's to swing, slow dance music, or a jitterbug. Despite their height difference (Sid usually bent down toward her just a bit to reduce it), they danced well together when they were being serious and when they weren't, the Mutt and Jeff contrast was always good for a laugh. A good example of both is in one of the many Hickenlooper sketches in which Charlie can't get to sleep (11/17/51). Doris suggests a dance might tire him out and she puts a record on. Her unlikely choice: a polka. The contrast between Sid's extra-long legs (looking even longer in the pajamas he's wearing) and Imogene's much-shorter ones makes for an effective sight-gag as they begin their dance. But then it turns out they can do a pretty mean polka together, and the audience's initial laughter turns to applause.

Sid and Imogene did only two full-scale song and dance numbers: "Lily of Laguna" (2/9/52), a music-hall/vaudeville turn, and "Over a Bottle of Wine" (9/8/51), which had them singing a scat song together and dancing to Latin music. Both were good enough to make you wonder why they didn't do more. Perhaps because of the additional rehearsal time that might have been required? (On the other hand, they did pretty well on, at best, two rehearsals of the numbers.) Or because it would have meant one less pantomime or Hickenlooper sketch? Who knows.

How did they do in the "song" component of the sketches? Opinions of Coca's singing vary. Although she had had vocal training and her range was impressive, she didn't have a spectacular singing voice. However, her ability to imitate a variety of singing voices and use them, as well as her own, comedically was more important. And she could convey emotion in song superbly. As Max Liebman observed, she was "a great singer in the way that Fred Astaire is a great singer."[79] Opinions of Caesar's voice don't vary. Rather surprisingly, considering his facility with sound effects and the other amazing things he could do vocally, singing was one of the very few things he didn't do all that well. He could imitate singing voices, and when he needed volume would adopt a Jolson or Jessel-esque delivery. He's also rather good in the scat song with Coca in "Over a Bottle of Wine." However, neither is exactly straight singing and his natural voice, a light baritone, was serviceable—he could stay on key and harmonize well—but not particularly noteworthy. He fared far better in the talk-sing of patter songs.

The "dance" component was another matter. He had done a bit of song and dance in *Tars and Spars* as well as *Make Mine Manhattan* on Broadway; he would also do a vaudeville number with Mary McCarty on *The Admiral Broadway Revue* in which the pair, in an amusing reversal, periodically halt their song and dance routine to break into dialogue. You don't usually think of Caesar as any kind of dancer and he was certainly no Harry Ritz (perhaps the best dancer among 20th-century comedians, and someone Sid greatly admired). And in the dancing he did do there was always more emphasis on comedy than on dance, but within these parameters, he could surprise. For example, he could do more than passable swing moves. Whether with Imogene or, on rare occasions, with another female partner, it usually brought applause from the audience. Maybe because it was unexpected. But he was, after all, skilled in the body control needed for physical comedy (at which he was superb) and for a big man, was agile and light on his feet—and given his strength, lifting or swinging his partner across his back was easy for him. He demonstrated this in one sketch set in a French jazz club (11/3/51) where, among other things, he plays the sax, sings a patter song in rapid-fire faux French, and, oh yes, does a pretty good jitterbug in between. In the Latin dance from "Over a Bottle of Wine," he was capable of executing some fairly intricate steps in unison with Coca and did some solo moves, which were not only funny but demonstrated conclusively that he was loose-hipped as well as loose-limbed.

Nonetheless, the premise for "Lily of Laguna" also serves as a good example of Caesar and Coca's real-life dance relationship. The vaudeville partners in the routine, also sweethearts, begin their routine lovingly enough, but it then turns into an anything-you-can-do-I-can-do-better contest—one which Sid loses. In their dance sketches together, Imogene was the professional; he was not. Yet, he could generally keep up his end of the game. In "Lily," he does choreographed steps well, manages some impressively high leg kicks, and in the course of a tap dance (of course he could convincingly mime one to the sound of taps) fake-kicks himself in the chest. Which is even harder than it looks.

One of the most memorable dance bits Sid and Imogene did together came at the end of a "Hobo Ballet" (3/11/50). Set in a railroad yard, two "hobo" dancers perform their version of a *pas de deux* for their fellow tramps. It was originally done on *The Admiral Broadway Revue*, minus Caesar and Coca. *Your Show of Shows* would reprise the number on an early episode from 1950. In this version, the two dancers, who emerge from a boxcar, were Sid and Imogene—to the surprise of the audience. The dance that follows is obviously a parody done for laughs—low culture imitating high—and Caesar and Coca reproduce perfectly the comic awkwardness of the hobo dancers in the original, while adding their own comedy touches. But they also add something else, as they adapt the bit to their individual physical talents: her gamin-like agility and his combination of strength and delicacy (he executes the hand and arm movements of ballet with surprising grace).

In the end movement of their sequence, following the *Revue* version, Sid lifts Imogene onto his shoulder (she plants her foot on his leg for a comic boost) and she slides down his back and comes up between his legs. Then, in a departure from the original, Sid lifts her from between his legs to his shoulder, and she drapes herself like a scarf across his opposite shoulder. She then half-slithers, half-climbs headfirst down his shoulder, arm, and leg, as Sid supports her full weight on just one side of his body. Lying on the floor, she props up her chin with her hand and looks up at him with a smile. It's an impressive illustration of her agility and his strength. He offers his hand, lifts her up, then escorts her back into the boxcar and the doors close—the dance is over. It's a reminder, if you ever needed one, of how good they were together in any genre.

The Parodies: Satire Is What Didn't Close on Saturday Night

Arguably, no set of sketches holds up better or shows the wit of the writers more than the parodies of films. Other TV comedy shows parodied movies, but none to the extent *Your Show of Shows* did. Film spoofs were featured in 108 of its 160 episodes. Remarkably, close to 90 were performed only once (including some of the classics), and of the ones that were repeated, it was usually with some degree of change to the original (sometimes there were entirely different endings or alterations of major plot points).

Occasionally, attempts have been made at analyzing the attraction of movies as a source of parody on *Your Show of Shows*, particularly for Caesar. One writer suggested that Sid was so attracted to and brilliant at doing movie takeoffs because he could respond, through satire, to the gap between the glamour of film images and the reality of his immigrant ethnic heritage. He could make ludicrous the movies' artificiality and melodrama in contrast to real life.[80] This seems a somewhat involuted analysis (you almost wish you could have known Sid's reaction if he had read it). Comedians and writers can produce movie parodies without using them as a form of socio-psychological catharsis. Sometimes a spoof is just a spoof. Albert Goldman was on somewhat firmer ground in describing Caesar and the writers sending up, almost subversively, the stereotypes of American folk consciousness by exaggerating them and turning them into their own satiric myths.[81] To be sure, there is an element of subversion in all parody and the writers delighted, as will be seen, in their takeoffs on the Western hero.

Nonetheless, there's also a simpler reason for the attraction of movies as objects of parody, one that Caesar himself talked about: he and his writers were always on the lookout for material. Film—or any other aspect of popular culture at the time—was a good source. As well, it was an appealing one because Caesar and his writers, yes, loved movies. (Which didn't mean that they lacked discrimination about what they were going to spoof: "The better a movie, the more material ... we would never do a satire of a bad movie, because bad is bad."[82]) And it was a source that audiences could identify with; it's sometimes difficult to appreciate today how popular, and dominant, an entertainment form movies were in the early '50s. Of course, ironically enough, the medium that so effectively spoofed them would soon undercut that dominance. Whatever the underlying motivation for them, the sketches were indeed satiric, but rarely scathingly so, nor did they ever descend into outright farce; rather they were genuine parodies in their occasionally subversive but always comic, and at times almost affectionate, imitation of their targets.

They opened as actual movies would, with titles that poked fun at the real ones (Cecil B. DeMille's lengthy circus epic *The Greatest Show on Earth* became "The Longest Show on Earth") and credits that ran over the opening frame. One of the most imaginative visuals appeared in "Dark Noon," a spoof of *High Noon*, aired on October 18, 1952. Caesar, as the beleaguered sheriff, is walking slowly down a road, while a man sings a song à la Frankie Laine with endless variations on "You're gonna die." An expository crawl begins: "In the state of Montana back in 1886..." and continues for a good six seconds in print so tiny you'd need 20-10 vision to read it, and then, in readable font, concludes with ... "and this is their story." Cast names in the credits frequently numbered far more than those of any possible real cast and were always an occasion for a quick joke—"Prison Walls," for example, stars Prisoner 678905432175689025, played by 3274; and the credits for "The Longest Show on Earth" include "Lions Tamed by the Late George Pierce." For some reason, perhaps because Sid and the writers thought it humorous to use a white-bread name, the movies were invariably produced by "Jim Richardson," or in the case of British film parodies, "Sir James Richardson." The endings? Nostalgia-inducing, if you've seen a lot of old movies, and funny in any case: if they were happy ones, they usually featured Sid and Imogene in the classic "man puts arm around woman and both smile with heads slightly tilted toward camera" close-up as THE END appears.

As with Caesar and Coca's pantomimes or the Hickenlooper sketches, it's difficult to choose a "best of"—or even a top 5—in part because every kind of film imaginable was parodied. The selection here is based on, I freely admit, my own preferences. Some are described in more detail than others, either because they can't be seen widely today or just because they represent the best in each genre (frequently, and unfortunately, these are often overlapping categories). What made them effective and, above all, funny?

First, the parodies featured genuine ensemble acting. Other shows' parodies at the time tended to feature the star. When Jack Benny did a spoof of *Gaslight* on his show, in which he was the husband trying to drive his wife insane, he was funny—but you were always aware, particularly when he did his patented "look" toward the audience, that he was, well, Jack Benny. Caesar and Coca played characters, never stepping out of them to briefly be themselves. Nor did the cast imitate the actors in the films they parodied. Sid didn't do Charlton Heston in *The Greatest Show on Earth* (although it would have been fun to watch) nor did Imogene imitate Barbara Stanwyck in *Double Indemnity*. That would have been humorous for maybe a minute, tops, at the beginning of the sketch. Rather, in the usual *Your Show of Shows*-type of humor, the writers and actors used situations and characters as springboards to comedy. A hilarious parody of *A Place in the Sun* uses the famous scene where Montgomery Clift is going to dispose of Shelley Winters in a rowboat on a lake—but without imitations of either actor. Rather, the sketch envisions what might happen if a bumbling Sid just *can't* kill his annoying wife-to-be Imogene, despite his best efforts. Exaggerating aspects of the characters could also get laughs. In a spoof of *A Streetcar Named Desire* (4/5/52), Sid takes Stanley Kowalski's slobbiness to a memorable extreme: he stuffs an amazing amount of chicken in his mouth (and continues to talk while chewing it), then uses his little finger to dislodge a troublesome piece—the same finger he's just had in his ear to scratch an itch (the audience reaction was an interesting mixture of laughter and *ewws*). Imogene makes the discontent and extremely alluring wife in a parody of *Double Indemnity* so ludicrously sexy that she can immediately, as in 15 seconds flat, seduce Sid's insurance salesman to enlist his help in killing her husband.

Second, Caesar and the writers had an unerring instinct for homing in on characters, conventions, and situations ripe for parody and reducing them to the ridiculously funny. Their eye—and ear—for cliché was uncanny and they generally picked exactly the right ones to poke fun at: The romantic moment in *Now, Voyager* when Paul Henreid puts two cigarettes in his mouth, lights both, and then passes one to Bette Davis? In a sketch set in a casbah, Sid, as a French gangster, gives his spitfire lover Imogene a smoldering look, puts two cigarettes in his mouth, lights them, and then puffs contentedly away on both. That sheriff in *High Noon* who is forced to face killers coming to town with no help from the cowardly townsfolk? In "Dark Noon," when Sid's sheriff is confronted by his new bride Imogene who demands to know why he's staying to face certain death, he replies with irrefutable logic, "Cause I'm stupid, Mary Ellen." As the last example illustrates, nowhere is this instinct more evident than in their takeoffs on Westerns, where there is a complete deflation of every oater trope, particularly that of the hero figure, whether he be a wagon master or a gunfighter standing up for oppressed homesteaders.

A sketch of January 17, 1953, "Westward, Whoa!" (a Jim Richardson Production "filmed in glorious black and white"), depicts the perils encountered by a wagon train on its way to California, one of them being its less than intrepid leader. Sid is Curly, the wagon master, and Imogene his sweetheart Sally. Riding together in a covered wagon, with Sid controlling the reins, they attempt the stock chaste kiss. Which isn't remotely consummated—because the jolting of the wagon, which they mime perfectly, prevents their lips from ever locking. A further disruption comes in the form of Howie Morris, a Gabby Hayes-like character, who pokes his head through the wagon cover behind them. He begins a hysterical rant (a Morris specialty): "We're never going to get there. We're going to run out of water, we're going to starve. The horse is going to die, you're going to die, I'm going to die, we're all going to die." Caesar, after a pause: "That's the spirit that's going to build the West."

The reason for Morris' hysteria is well-founded: Curly is perhaps the West's most inept wagon master. Facing a revolt by the party, Sally attempts to defend his leadership. So he forgot to plug up the water barrels and we're running out; he forgot to get covers for the covered wagons; he was the one who said let's go around the Mississippi to get to Dodge City—by way of Montreal. But, as Curly points out, "We can't go back now. After all those nice going-away presents?"

Further trouble arises when Curly listens to the advice offered by a shady stranger (Carl Reiner) who suggests an alternate route. They promptly come under Indian attack. Fighting against overwhelming odds, deliverance seems at hand as you see a clip of galloping horsemen and hear the bugle call for a charge. Morris cries, "It's the U.S. Cavalry. We're saved!" Sid peers at the horsemen and delivers a line that should be enshrined in any pantheon of parody: "Nah. Those are just Indians with bugles." Betrayed by Reiner who is in cahoots with the attackers, Sid and Imogene are captured and tied to a tree to await their fate. Sid declares, "If we're going to die, Sally, we'll die for a good cause." Imogene asks, "I'm not afraid to die, are you?" The stalwart wagon master responds, "No, I'm not afraid to die." (Pause while thinking it over) "I ain't against *living*, you understand...." The real cavalry does, of course, show up to rescue the wagon train, and it can proceed (maybe, considering Curly's leadership skills) to California.

The most impressive dismantling of a heroic Western figure, however, is in a parody of the classic Western *Shane* (1953). The plot in a nutshell for those who may be unfamiliar with it: Shane is a gunfighter attempting to escape his past by settling down with a homesteader couple and their young tow-head son Joey (who soon comes down with a severe case of hero-worship). Complications arise when he finds himself in the middle of a conflict between the homesteaders and a cattle baron who wants to drive them out. Initially resisting provocation by the cattlemen, Shane is forced into action when one of them kills a sodbuster. In a showdown in the town saloon, he shoots the cattle baron and his henchmen, making the valley safe for the homesteaders. In the iconic final scene, he then rides away, knowing there's no place for him in this new West, as Joey cries, his voice echoing, "Shane! Come back!"

Your Show of Shows' version of all of this, aired on September 9, 1953, was entitled "Strange" (first name Very, but you can just call him Strange). And you know immediately what you're in for when it begins with a clip showing a horse and rider approaching, then moves to a close-up of Sid as the gunfighter, moving up and down in his saddle trying to look heroic— and also trying to find a comfortable position, as he winces from obvious saddle sores. The utter demolition of the Western gunfighter hero trope is on. The scene shifts to the farm of a homesteader (Howie Morris) and his wife where Imogene Coca (in a blonde wig) is the Joey-character and is shooting everything in sight with an imaginary gun. When the real gunman arrives and introduces himself to the family, Joey is the most annoying hero-worshipping kid ever: "I *like* you, Strange! You're *nice*! I like your belt! I like your boots! I like your hat!" His understandable response: "Get outta here, kid, or I'll blast ya."

Enter Carl Reiner menacingly, as Barton the cattle baron with his gang. He threatens the homesteaders, but the farmer stoutly informs him they're all staying. When they leave, Joey asks, "You gonna kill him?" Strange responds, "My shooting days are over—that's why I'm hanging up my gun [as it keeps falling off the peg he's trying to hang it on]. Killing's no good, sonny. If you kill a man, you're in trouble because somebody'll come to get you. Maybe his brother, a half-sister, an aunt—somebody."

When a member of Barton's gang, obviously undeterred by the homesteaders' putative protector, kills one of them, the farmers rally at the ranch and debate whether they should go or stay. Joey enthusiastically advises (and here Imogene's look of maniacal glee is priceless as she upends the oater cliché of resistance against overwhelming odds), "We should stay here and *fight*, so we can all stay here and get *killed*!" Her father decides to go into town and Strange, knowing he doesn't stand a chance against Barton, prevents him—by thoroughly beating him up. "I don't (punch to the head) want you (slug to the stomach) to get (throwing him to the ground) *hurt*!" Glancing at the father's prostrate body ("he'll be up and limping around in about a month or two"), he snaps an order to Joey: "Sonny, get me my gun—I'm going into town!"

Inside the bar, Barton and his men hear the usual ominous boot steps on a boardwalk approaching the saloon. Strange enters dramatically, but the boot steps continue—as he turns to yell out the door, "So long, Willie." Barton yells, "Draw!" and Strange reaches for his holster, only to discover he's forgotten his gun. (Sid claps his hands together and looks heavenward with an expression comprised of equal parts of surprise, chagrin, and sheer goofiness.) He's ultimately saved by Joey, who *has* remembered to bring the gun and tosses it to him. Strange then shoots six of Barton's henchmen, but the villain points out, "6 shots, 6 bullets—you're empty!" Then, to Barton's surprise and demise, Strange shoots him. "Only 7-shooter in the West," he declares. Joey predictably gushes, "You're a *hero*, Strange! I *like* you, Strange!" The hero muses, "Sometimes I wish it was an 8-shooter."

And that iconic scene as the gunman rides away? In this version, Joey cries, "Come back, Strange (echo) Strange, (echo) Strange!" And the response comes, "Go home, you rotten kid (echo) rotten kid, (echo) rotten kid!" TV critics of the '50s often remarked about the difficulty of watching the real film without laughing after seeing the *Your Show of Shows* parody of it. The same holds true over 60 years later. Long intervals between viewing both are recommended.

Another genre the writers enjoyed spoofing was that of films involving secret agents or foreign intrigue. In the former, you can clearly see the genesis of *Get Smart*, a '60s TV secret agent satire, not surprisingly because it was created by Mel Brooks along with Buck Henry. Like Don Adams' Agent 86, Sid's secret agent was frequently bumbling, but like 86, always enthusiastic, albeit ludicrously so, about his spy trade. In "Foreign Agent" (12/27/52), as Agent B-59, he is summoned by his "Chief," played by Carl Reiner, for a dangerous mission:

> CARL: I have a tough assignment for you.
> SID: Trouble is my hobby!
> CARL: I'm sending you to the trouble spot of the world.
> SID: Danger is my meat!
> CARL: Where you're going, it's crawling with murderers. You may even be killed.
> SID: Dying is my business!

After finally reaching that assignment in "Jargonia" [insert clips of trains, ships, rickshaws, camel trains, and dog sleds], he attempts to meet his contact in the Hotel Mahal, which is filled with spies. Unfortunately, his carefully established cover is immediately blown when the desk clerk unhelpfully keeps calling for "Thomas J. Gordon, USA."

"A Stranger in Danger" (1/6/54) is set in "occupied Europe," where we discover, somewhat unnervingly, that the fate of the Free World depends on the chance meeting of a singing spy (Coca) and a facial tissue salesman from Milwaukee (Caesar). Every cliché of the innocent abroad who becomes entangled in espionage is mined for laughs, from the unlikelihood of the two main characters who barely know each other falling in love to the "we have ways of making you talk" interrogation scene. After Sid is enlisted by Imogene in her mission for the good guys, which involves a roll of microfilm, he's roughed up by the bad guys, knocked unconscious, and comes to in a room alone with Imogene. By this time, they're attracted to each other—in a *Your Show of Shows* sort of way. As they embrace, Sid declares, "I've only known you one day ... but it's the lousiest day I've ever spent." No time for any of that however, as the enemy spies enter and their leader demands to know from Imogene where the microfilm is. Getting nowhere, he grabs Sid—"What do *you* know?" Sid bleats, non-heroically, "Me? I don't know *much*." Nonetheless, he's dragged off for the obligatory torture scene—with a writers' we're-not-taking-this-cliché-seriously twist. From offstage, you hear his increasingly agonized cries: "No! Don't! Don't do it! [Imogene reacts to each with horrified faces] Don't do it! No! Oh, don't do THAT! [Imogene's raised eyebrows meet her bangs]." When he's tossed back into the room, she anxiously asks "What did they *do* to you?" He calmly responds, "Nothing. I told them not to do it and they didn't. You have to know how to talk to these guys—loud." They, and the Free World, are saved (and here you can really see the *Get Smart* to come) when Imogene detonates a proto-neutron bomb which only kills bad guys.

Film noir and crime stories, with their melodrama, interior voice-overs, and *femmes fatales*, (not to mention bodies strewn on the set at their end—after all, the wages of noir is death) were fertile fields to plow for parody. Two of *Your Show of Shows*' best—and funniest—sketches spoof the genre superbly. One of the most daring, considering the material, was of *A Place in the Sun*. In the film, a poor factory worker (Montgomery Clift) seems on the verge of climbing the socio-economic ladder and marrying a rich, beautiful woman (Elizabeth Taylor) to boot. However, he has gotten his old girlfriend (Shelley Winters) pregnant, and she demands he marry her or she will reveal all. Knowing she can't swim, he takes her out in a rowboat on a deserted lake; the boat capsizes and she drowns, as he makes no attempt to save her. He is convicted of murder and dies in the electric chair.

Well. How *do* you make a laugh-out-loud parody of a film that is, let's face it, dreadfully grim? First, you poke fun at the title, in one of the writers' best forays into black humor, by calling yours "A Place at the Bottom of the Lake" (4/19/52). Then, you focus on the dramatic scene of the rowboat on the lake, with Caesar as "Montgomery" and Coca as "Mildred" (who is *not* pregnant—you simply couldn't include that detail on TV in 1951). Next, you have Carl Reiner voice Sid's interior thoughts, to such an intrusive and hectoring degree that Sid begins arguing with "himself." Finally, you use Imogene's brilliance to create a character so comically obnoxious that you actually begin to root for the man who wants to eliminate her.

The sketch opens as Caesar and Coca arrive lakeside to rent a boat. Sid looks grim and carries a sack over one shoulder. It contains, as we soon find out, a rope, a gun, chains, and a knife ("if the gun don't work"). Holding on to his arm like a limpet, Imogene utters her first words—and we start to understand why he brought them. In an incredibly annoying but hilarious mix of monotone and whine, she begins, "You're so good to me,

Montgomery. I can't believe I ever thought you'd want to get rid of me so you could marry that rich, beautiful, gorgeous society girl Gloria." Sid says, "Yeah. That rich, beautiful, wonderful Gloria" [almost breaks into a sob].

As he rows to the middle of the lake, Caesar begins his interior monologue. Voice: "What are you waiting for?" Sid: "I can't kill her—she loves me." [Imogene helpfully says, "I love you, Montgomery."] Sid to Voice: "See?" But then Imogene disastrously whines on: "When are we going to get married, Montgomery? Why can't we get married today? It'll be real nice, you'll see. We'll get a real nice apartment with real nice curtains at the window and real nice carpets. We'll have real nice meals. It'll be real nice. I'll take real good care of you. I'll take you to work every day, call you every hour, pick you up after work.... I'll never let you out of my sight." Contemplating the marital equivalent of being buried alive, Sid declares to himself, "I've *got* to kill this girl!"

Voice: "All right—now's your chance! Take out the gun—get the gun! Take out the cartridges, put them in the gun. You dropped them—pick 'em up. You're putting them in backwards! You don't want the rope, you want the cartridges. No, not the chain—the gun!" [At this point, Caesar is practically juggling all of them.]

Sid (in exasperation): "I only got two hands, will ya!"

The Voice reminds him of the past he could leave behind if he could only kill this woman: "You grew up in the slums, never had roller-skates, never had an orange." Imogene breaks in and, to Sid's look of horror, asks: "Want an orange? Oranges are real nice. Not as nice as pomegranates, but they're real nice."

Abandoning his prepared weapons of destruction, Caesar tries another stratagem. He tells Coca to put her head on his shoulder; she does and he applies a headlock, attempting to strangle her [close-up of Sid's comic faces of superhuman exertion]—but with a total lack of success ("She's like an ox!"). The Voice is by this time somewhat irritated: "Just push her over the side of the boat. Make her stand up." She does, to the accompaniment of dramatic music. Then sits down, then stands up, and sits down, as the music swells and Sid is in an agony of frustration. Finally, the call of "All boats in" echoes across the lake. The Voice helpfully points out, "You've lost your chance, you fool!"

But Sid makes one final try: He suggests enthusiastically, "Tell you what. We'll go into New York City tomorrow to the Empire State Building—look over the edge, see that wonderful view from the top." However, the Woman Who Cannot Be Murdered dashes that scheme: "I don't like it there. I fell off once.... I still have a little scratch."

The writers didn't always stick an ending to a sketch, but here they scored a perfect 10. All of his homicidal plans having gone for naught, Sid, with a look of utter resignation, says to Imogene as he begins to row back to shore, "We'll get married tomorrow. It'll be real nice, you'll see."

A parody of *Double Indemnity*, titled "The Final Payment" (4/25/53), takes the basic outline of the original and then takes several detours down a road to the ridiculous. Imogene is the *femme fatale*; Sid is the insurance salesman who becomes involved with her and her plans for murdering her husband, Carl Reiner. When Sid arrives at their house to pick up Carl's insurance payment, the bored wife not only finds him more attractive than her husband, she realizes he might be the key to escaping her humdrum life. After some preliminary flirting, she cuts to the chase: "Stay a while. Don't you like me? I like you. Let's kill my husband!" "Comin' through," says Sid, as he attempts to flee. But he's intercepted by a passionate kiss. When he comes up for air, he declares, "I've *got* to kill this man!"

But how to do it and make it look like an accident? Rejecting several ludicrous options, they hit on switching insect poison that's in a brown bottle with the brown bottle of Carl's headache medicine. When the husband arrives home, the two plotters, in a gem of a sequence, try to talk him into signing a policy for $100,000. He's not sure, so the insurance agent convinces him:

> SID: "Think of your wife. You're taking a walk down the street, strolling along, the sun is shining, the birds are singing. Then a car jumps the curb. Blam!" [Sid hits Carl along his shoulder blades, knocking him to the floor] Shielding Imogene from the sight of her prostrate husband, "Don't look!"
> IMOGENE: "He didn't have any insurance!"
> SID: "We'll have to take the house!"
> IMOGENE: "Where can I go? What will I do?" [Carl gets up, dazed, but still not convinced.]
> SID: "You're taking a walk down the street, strolling along, singing a vagabond song, the sun is shining, the flowers are blooming. A 10-ton truck! Blam!" [Carl goes down again] "No, don't look! Yes, he is—he's gone!"
> IMOGENE: "He didn't leave me anything!" [Carl struggles to his feet.]
> SID: "A fire engine!"
> CARL (flinching): "I'LL SIGN!"

After all of this, Carl has developed—of course—a headache. He downs the poison he thinks is medicine and promptly goes into an epic paroxysm, so epic he loses his shoes. It's not only funny, it's a reminder of how good Reiner was at physical comedy. However, as Sid and Imogene are congratulating themselves, he pops back up with a gun. (You can't always assume in a *Your Show of Shows* sketch that someone is really most sincerely dead until at least 5 seconds have elapsed.) Imogene pulls out another, and each manages, juggling their guns, to shoot themselves. Picking up her gun, Sid has had enough—"I don't want it any more"—and decides to call the police. He puts the gun on the table and dials the number. And then, as

6. The Sketches

anyone would, picks up the gun instead of the receiver, and puts it to his head....

Some movies were parodied in a downright affectionate way, none more so than "Broadway Rhapsody" (2/14/53), a spoof of *42nd Street* with a bit of *Gold Diggers of 1933* thrown in for good measure. The cast and writers obviously enjoyed themselves, gently kidding all of the clichés of the "harried director puts on Broadway show, making a star of the kid in the chorus" '30s musicals. One of *Your Show of Shows*' most elaborate sketches, it makes you appreciate what could be done on TV in 1953 with skilled stagehands and good camera work—scenes, all on one stage of course, take place in a rehearsal hall, a city sidewalk, back to a rehearsal hall, backstage, and then a full stage for the final production number. It also had two original songs, most likely written by Mel Tolkin, who, along with Caesar, composed most of the musical comedy snippets for the show.

Sid is Larry Crane, the Broadway director trying to put on a musical in the midst of financial and production troubles ("All I want to do is put a smile on the face of America. No, they won't let me!"). The last straw comes when he loses his spoiled leading lady. As he complains to his stage manager, Howie Morris, "After all I did for that kid? When I found her, she was nothing but a star!" All seems lost until Morris points out the talented "kid in the chorus" Mary Stumbler, played by Imogene. When she's told to audition, she's reluctant—at first: "Sing for Mr. Crane? I'm just a chorus girl. My voice will crack. I couldn't. I'll forget the lyrics.... [beat] Key of C, please, and not too fast." She launches into song, as the camera pans over the reactions of the company: chorus girls look awed, a stagehand eating a sandwich freezes in mid-bite, and Nipper, the RCA dog, listens attentively with cocked ear. She's a hit and moves into the star's dressing room, and, of course, Larry's heart.

However, Crane's financial troubles continue until he gets the backing of "J.J. Worcestershire, the Mayonnaise King." But it's only at the cost of making the wealthy magnate's "tomato" the star of the show. (Many mayonnaise, lettuce, cabbage and tomato jokes follow, which sound suspiciously Mel Brooksian.) The girlfriend is patently unsuitable—her audition number is "The Road to Mandalay," sung in a startling basso profundo. Sid's poleaxed expression is followed by a "Great!"—he needs the money. On a date, he tactfully breaks the news to Mary ("By the way, you're out of the show"). However, love wins out; he fires the "tomato," and brings back Mary.

With his major backing gone, he tells the assembled company the show is in danger of cancellation. The aged doorman offers help: his life savings of 37 cents. Crane is reluctant: "Pop, I can't take this. You've been saving up for an operation." But then everyone joins in, stuffing money in his hand. Touched, he says, "Gee, you kids, chipping in like this? It's ... it's (looking into his hand) not enough." $9.37 rarely is. Just at that unlikely moment, another of the backers arrives, demanding payment for costuming. Conveniently, he's J.R. Stumbler, Mary's father, who seems to have been totally unaware that she was in a Broadway musical. After their reunion ("Father!" "Daughter!"), he agrees to back the entire show. And Mary is ready: ripping off the raincoat she's been wearing, she's in costume ("I've had it on for three weeks").

Crane exults, "At last! I can put a smile on the face of America!" But not quite yet. There's one more cliché to rib. Backstage, as the overture begins, he tells Mary that in a few minutes, she'll be a star. However, she gets stage fright. Larry tells her, "I'm sorry. I have to make you a star." And instead of the usual snap-out-of-it slap, he delivers a right uppercut that temporarily rearranges her dental work. Somehow, that works. She makes her entrance and the big production number ensues ("97th Street, New York, New York. The street of streets—and we don't mean 42nd") with Imogene and the entire company. Grabbing a top hat and cane, Sid joins her for the final chorus. If any of the many parodies of *Your Show of Shows* can be described as charming, this one can.

Your Show of Shows spoofed boxing movies, doctor movies, circus movies, newspaper movies, test-pilot movies, movies about making movies—the inventiveness of the writers seemed endless. If you are a classic film buff, to watch a number of them is nirvana; even if you aren't, they're still enjoyable as stand-alone comedy sketches. With only a few exceptions (for example, an Agatha Christie–like "Invitation to Murder" that is stretched out for far too long), these parodies, perhaps more than any other sketch genre, were consistently funny and clever. They were enjoyed by both audiences and critics—and by at least some of the movie-makers who had provided their targets. George Stephens, producer/director of *Shane*, enthused over "Strange," the show's parody: "I thought it was wonderful. It was great publicity for the picture. I hope it happens to all my films."[83]

Columbia Pictures, and presumably its irascible head Harry Cohn, took a dimmer view of the show's parodies. After the September 12, 1954, airing of "From Here to Obscurity," a takeoff on Columbia's *From Here to Eternity*, the studio filed suit claiming copyright infringement. By the early '50s, the film industry was somewhat belatedly recognizing the economic threat posed by the growing popularity of TV. One of the implicit issues cited in the suit was a potentially negative impact on box-office returns, even though in this case it would appear to have been moot: the parody was some six months after the film's release and certainly didn't diminish its economic value or its critical standing, then or now.

It *did* however very effectively play dramatic situations and characters for laughs, as all good parodies should: from Sid, in the Montgomery

6. *The Sketches* 105

It's all fun and games until someone sues: The beach scene from "From Here to Obscurity," the 1954 parody of *From Here to Eternity* (right after the first bucket of water thrown by stagehands). Columbia Pictures filed suit for copyright infringement. They lost.

Clift role, employing his best semi-doofus voice as "Montgomery Bugle," who refuses to box for the regiment ("Listen here, Sarge, I didn't join this army to fight, I joined it to bugle!"); to the slapstick "treatment" he receives from his sergeant for his refusal; and Imogene's hilariously sultry turn as the dance hall girl with whom he falls in love (as the GIs clamor for a dance with her, she declares, "Take it easy, boys. There's enough for everybody."). Above all, it scored a parodic 10 in its treatment of the iconic scene in the film where Burt Lancaster and Deborah Kerr in swimsuits make love lying on a beach, as gentle waves wash over them. *Your Show of Shows* came up with an iconic version of its own, starting with the logical premise that, if you have a romantic interlude on a beach, you're going to get wet—very wet. The scene begins auspiciously enough with Imogene by the water calling "Montgomery? Where are you?" and Sid making an entrance wearing an inner tube the size of a truck tire around his waist. They sit on a pile of sand, nestled close to each other, and begin to declare their love. However, their romantic dialogue is interrupted by periodic deluges of water by the bucketsful thrown by the off-camera stagehands: "I love you, Monty!" [Splat] "I've been waiting an eternity to hear those words from you, Duchess" [Splosh]. And on for four more dousings. It's blissfully silly, the audience laughs throughout, and Coca has to hide her face in Caesar's shoulder to keep from laughing herself. Critics at the time noted that it was difficult for audiences (as it still is) to see the original without remembering the parody.

But was the parody a violation of copyright? In *Columbia Pictures Corp. v. National Broadcasting Co.* (known in legal circles as the Sid Caesar Case, a distinction he probably could have done without), the District Judge for the Ninth Circuit didn't think so. He ruled, basically, that if an audience can't figure out *what* is being parodied, it's a pointless exercise. So long as the minimum of material, situations, roles, etc., is taken from the original to identify the object of parody, it's permissible under the fair use doctrine.[84]

The decision was handed down in 1955, by which time Sid and most of the *Your Show of Shows* writers had moved on to *Caesar's Hour*. Sid claimed that he and the writers were always careful in parodies on both shows not to take too much, particularly verbatim, from the originals, and the claim is borne out if you see enough of them. They happily continued to parody films on *Caesar's Hour*, including another Columbia release, *On the Waterfront*. No lawsuit ensued over "On the Docks," in which Sid reprised the superb Marlon Brando impression he had done on *Your Show of Shows* (although Sam Spiegel, *Waterfront*'s producer, threatened one before coming around to the George Stephens school of thought on parodies).[85]

Your Show of Shows didn't limit its parodies to just American or British films. In their quest for material, Caesar and the writers would go to New York arthouse theatres to view foreign films, both old and post-war. Spoofs naturally followed—of French noir, Italian *neorealismo*, and German *weltschmerz*. The French ones featured passionate love triangles, with all points of them usually dead by the film's end; the German ones variations on *The Blue Angel* and *The Last Laugh* (obviously Emil Jannings was a favorite). The focus on everyday life in Italian *neorealismo* was reflected in the parodies: DeSica's *The Bicycle Thief* became "Who Stole My Bicycle?" and there were various sketches on coping with both modernity and tradition, whether getting a telephone or arranging a marriage. Along with Caesar and Reiner, and occasionally Morris, they included a tempestuous Coca in an Anna Magnani–like haystack of a wig, always an effective sight gag. Of course, the sketches were comedy versions of the originals and frequently used only a basic outline or situation. However, the concept of using foreign films for parodies at all was somewhat daring in the early '50s, when they would have been known primarily to an urban or collegiate audience and even that would have been a small one. It's yet another example of the writers doing what pleased or amused them and trusting the viewers to respond to the comedy of the sketches even if they were unfamiliar with the genre.

One last form of parody, in a kind of biting-the-medium-that-feeds-you, was of other TV programs. And in TV programming of the early '50s, there was a lot to make fun of (it wasn't all the comedy brilliance of Lucy and Jackie Gleason or excellent live drama; there was a lot of dreck as well). *Your Show of Shows* parodied at least two other TV shows, both of which were, in their different ways, sitting ducks. The uber-schmaltzy *This Is Your Life* was memorably spoofed in "This is Your Story," described earlier.

The second was a wicked takeoff on one of the TV vehicles of Arthur Godfrey, the first television "personality." He was extremely popular in the '50s, for reasons that are pretty much unfathomable today. Basically a host for his programs, he traded on a cloying folksiness and artificial geniality. *Arthur Godfrey's Talent Scouts*, whose format was exactly what the name implies, was kidded, and not very gently, by Caesar and Company in the form of a talent scout show run by his Russian counterpart. The entire sketch (9/19/53) was in faux Russian, with Sid as the genial host, pushing Tchaikovsky Borscht (Lipton Tea was one of Godfrey's sponsors) and plucking a balalaika (Godfrey played the ukulele). The sketch is memorable, first for Carl Reiner's brilliant turn as a contestant who does imitations; his Russian Lionel Barrymore and Jimmy Durante are to be savored. Second, for Sid's impression of Godfrey—which was devastating. He absolutely nailed all of Godfrey's most irritating characteristics, from his folksiness to his annoying shoulder-lifting chuckle ("heh-heh-heh"). After several of the latter, he gives the cut-off sign of the hand across the throat with an expression of faint disdain. Today, you have to see a bit of Godfrey on old film to appreciate what Caesar was doing, but the audience at the time knew very well.

Sid didn't do impressions of specific personalities or actors all that often (nor were they ever as biting as his Godfrey); rather, as discussed earlier, he played character types in parodies. But when he did, they were impressions rather than outright imitations. If you're expecting to hear their voices being mimicked, Caesar isn't going to do it for you. In his stellar Marlon Brando impression in the parodies of *A Streetcar Named Desire*, he didn't rely on just the shtick of imitating Brando's mumble. Instead, he reproduced the halting speech patterns of Brando's Kowalski as well (and it's all the funnier for it) and used his face and body to suggest the hulking Stanley. In one shot, he even managed to look like Brando. It's another reminder that Sid was really a comic actor; in this instance, it was one actor not imitating another but *playing* the other's character.

7

Jewishness and *Your Show of Shows*: White Bread or Rye?

One of the aspects of *Your Show of Shows* that was largely unremarked upon in the '50s was that most of the cast and writers were Jewish. Not until a generation later was the program discussed—and celebrated—as a showcase for the comedy of American-born children of Jewish immigrants.[86] From the '70s onward, books on Jewish humor almost invariably have an entry for Sid Caesar and *Your Show of Shows*. After Caesar's death, a number of magazine articles focused on "the deep Jewish roots" of Sid and the show; one went so far as to term him "the ultimate mid-century Jew," whose career paralleled the emergence of Jews as influences on American popular culture.[87] Given this particular focus and emphasis on the show, it's a legitimate question to explore: was Jewishness an integral part of it and, if so, how was it manifested?

There's no question about the cultural identity of *Your Show of Shows*' cast or its writers. Caesar, Carl Reiner, and Howard Morris were Jews (Imogene Coca was not); of the writers, so were Mel Tolkin, Lucille Kallen, Mel Brooks, Danny and Neil Simon, and Joe Stein. So was Max Liebman, its producer and director. And none made any particular attempt to downplay or conceal it. In fact, Sid, in an interview from 1950, casually discussed learning Hebrew for his bar mitzvah, a reflection perhaps of the confidence of a new generation of Jewish comedians. (It's difficult to imagine Jack Benny, George Burns, or even Danny Kaye mentioning their Jewish upbringing to a reporter in that time period.)[88]

However, is Jewishness reflected in the sketches or in Caesar's solo routines? Yiddishness certainly is. In foreign film parodies, particularly those in faux German, Yiddish words are tossed in, most often by Sid, but also by Carl Reiner (although most of the examples usually cited from sketches are from *Caesar's Hour* not *Your Show of Shows*). In a Western

7. Jewishness and Your Show of Shows   109

parody done in German doubletalk that features a gunfight of sorts, Caesar as the white-hatted hero counts to 21—in Yiddish—before he and the villain Carl Reiner draw. The knowledgeable listener can also pick up Yiddish in Sid's speech patterns: when he exclaims, in both statement and question, "What kind of a thing is this?" or asks Doris Hickenlooper as she's spring cleaning, "Why are you starting with the throwing?" His sentence structure and phrasing often reflects that of Yiddish: putting a direct object as a subject, as in "The bread bring in!" or "A match I gotta have!" or in listing a pet dog's accouterments, including a coat "so he shouldn't get wet." And, at least once, he utters "Oy" in describing a lamentable situation.

But, beyond this, are there *representations* of Jews in the sketches? If you're looking for anything like *The Goldbergs*, you're not going to find it on *Your Show of Shows*. There are no identifiable Jewish characters, and none of the sketches features any aspect of a Jewish lifestyle or culture, unless you want to count the humorous dietary incongruence in "Business Lunch," where Sid orders a bacon and raisin sandwich and when he doesn't get it, looks covetously at Carl Reiner's ham hock concoction. The battling couple played by Caesar and Coca are not The Steins or The Cohens, but The Hickenloopers, whose name came from a decidedly non–Jewish Midwestern senator of the time.

You also have to wonder if even the few examples of Yiddishness were picked up on by much of the viewing audience. The writers were well aware that a significant portion of the early TV viewing audience was urban and Jewish (Carl Reiner recalled Mel Tolkin rallying them: "Gentlemen, we've got to get something done! Jews all over America will be watching Saturday night!"[89]). However, there was a large segment that was not. Did the Yiddish ad-libs, which were usually embedded in faux German to begin with, register with non–Jewish audiences of the '50s outside urban areas— or even in them? To state the obvious, you had to *know* some Yiddish to identify or appreciate them. It's hard to avoid the conclusion that its use was very much of an inside joke, shared only with themselves and Jews in the audience. Even here, Carl Reiner claimed that every time they used a Yiddish word, "we always had another joke that everybody who didn't understand the word would be watching at the same time that joke was happening."[90] And while the writers might have amused themselves by thinking of the Hickenloopers, played by the Jewish Sid and the Gentile Imogene, as TV's first mixed marriage, the non–Jewish audience probably regarded them as just the mismatched Charlie and Doris. As well, for that audience, Sid's inflection could easily have come across as "urban New York," not necessarily "Jewish."

And what of Caesar himself? Albert Goldman once commented that "Sid bore plainly the stamp of the urban Jewish scene."[91] To a Jewish audience, probably. To a non-Jewish one, not necessarily—there wasn't always an immediate identification of Sid as a Jew. One woman, writing in to a TV question and answer column, inquired if he was Italian. The confusion of a non-Jew might have been understandable; "Caesar" as a surname wasn't particularly Jewish and there's always the automatic mental association of Caesar with Roman emperors. But Mel Tolkin? When he first met the hazel-eyed Caesar, whose hair still bore traces of the blond he had been up to his mid-20s, Mel decided Sid was "Christian—a Greek." Until the day Max Liebman mentioned to Tolkin and Caesar that he thought the critics would be particularly rough on that Saturday's show and "this Greek" responded—in Hebrew—"Why is this night different from all other nights?" (one of the questions from the Passover Seder). The penny then dropped for Tolkin.[92] It never did for many of those I've talked to in non-urban areas who saw *Your Show of Shows* or *Caesar's Hour* live. Most didn't know Sid was Jewish or had never considered it—they just thought he was very funny.

Moreover, if you define a Jewish comedian as one who uses his or her religion or ethnicity as a basis for humor, Caesar wasn't one. Rather, he was a comedian who happened to be Jewish. He was above all a comic *actor* who assumed roles and characters, never playing himself, nor did he do stand-up comedy with its necessary self-identification. Consequently, there was no reason for audiences of the '50s to have associated him with whatever stereotypes of Jewish comedians they happened to have or were aware of. In his subdued and serious introductions to each episode of *Your Show of Shows*, he suggested none of the brashness and verbal aggression of Milton Berle or the klutziness of the early Danny Kaye or Jerry Lewis. He may have played *characters* like them, but they weren't identifiable as distinctively "Sid Caesar." If anything, he fit a stereotype very different from these and one with which most non-Jewish audiences would not have been familiar: the *shtarker*, a big, strong guy. And in watching many of his monologues, you are struck by the universality of the situations he depicts—a man coming down with a cold, a man watching his son graduate from college, or trying to work up enough courage to propose to his girl, or awaiting the birth of a child. In them, he is, brilliantly, an Everyman, not a particularly Jewish Everyman. On *Your Show of Shows*, Sid never used his Jewishness as an overt subject of comedy in his performances; decades later, he would state simply, "I didn't want to make fun of being Jewish."[93]

Am I suggesting that there are no traces of Jewish humor or sensibility in *Your Show of Shows* or, for that matter, Caesar's comedy? Not really. It's there, but in less obvious ways than just tossing Yiddish into a sketch, which the show did, or employing characters with Jewish names, which it didn't. Lucille Kallen maintained that the essence of the show was in "that

7. Jewishness and Your Show of Shows   111

particular comic point of view that was born at the wailing wall ... the we-must-look-at-life-as-being-ridiculous-or-we'll-never-get-through-it philosophy."[94] She saw it reflected in the sketches which comically exaggerated human experiences that are timeless, and you can see it too in Charlie Hickenlooper's kvetching to, and about, Doris, and in Sid's characters hilariously trying to cope with life's problems, whether they were big, small, or of his own making. That underlying theme was one that audiences, whatever their background, could identify with: life is not always good or fair and there's little you can do about it. Everyone else is in the same boat, so you might as well look at an absurd world and kvetch—and laugh. You can also argue that *Your Show of Shows* reflected Jewish humor in the sophistication of its comedy writing and in the zany anarchy and wordplay of Mel Brooks' writing and Caesar's playing of The Professor. And in Caesar and Company's poking constant fun at authority figures inflated by their own self-importance (Cf. any Marx Brothers movie for the latter two illustrations).

However, as the Marx Brothers comparison shows, American humor from the early 20th century onward has always had an infusion of Jewish humor. And it appeared first on television with Milton Berle's *Texaco Star Theater*; unfortunately, in vaudevillian style, Berle tended to beat the viewer over the head with it, for example referring to his secretary as "Miss Shugana of 1953."[95] Reiner once said, "We were very aware that we were Jewish and we wanted to make sure that America understood our humor."[96] What Caesar and *Your Show of Shows* did was to introduce that humor in a more sophisticated and witty (and ultimately subtle) way, one fashioned for that much wider TV audience. And they did so in a post-war America more receptive to, and increasingly more appreciative, of it.

PART III

Rendering Unto Caesar

More than anyone else, it was Sid. He was from another planet.
—Mel Brooks[1]

Perhaps the tribute most appropriate to render to this particular Caesar is that, once you've seen a number of sketches and monologues from *Your Show of Shows*, it's almost impossible to imagine anyone else but Sid doing them. He was Comedian As Utility Tool: sketch comedy, monologues, mime, sound-effects, language mimicry—the range of his skills leaves you not just marveling at what he could do, but wondering if there was anything he *couldn't* do. Joe Stein, one of *Your Show of Shows*' writers, had worked with Jackie Gleason, Phil Silvers, and Jerry Lewis, and would later say, "they all had their areas, but Sid had no limits."[2] Caesar simply operated on a different level, in fact several different levels, from other TV comedians of the '50s. He was at times indeed, as Brooks suggests, from another comedic planet. In physical comedy, he was superb; in comic acting, he was unmatched.

8

Caesar as Physical Comedian

Sid was born with the ability to write physical poetry.
—Steve Allen[3]

Physical comedy is more than just simple slip-on-a-banana-peel slapstick; gestures and movements, double-takes, expressions, and mime are also components. Caesar's talents in all of them, including slapstick (although it was beneath him to slip on a banana peel), deserve an extended analysis and description. Although Sid is perhaps remembered best for his verbal skills in sketches, he was a master of all aspects of this genre of comedy as well.

At first glance, Steve Allen's choice of words to describe Caesar's ability seems somewhat incongruous. "Poetry" suggests a kind of balance and delicacy not always associated with someone who was literally outsize in terms of stature and strength. "Physical" certainly suits: Caesar's sheer physicality set him apart from other comedians of the '50s. Tall and powerfully built, with broad shoulders and extra-long arms and legs, he dominated the stage. In the curtain-calls that usually ended an episode of *Your Show of Shows*, there were sometimes taller members of the line-up than Sid—but rarely were there any who were bigger.

Richard Corliss, in an appreciative essay on Caesar in *Time*,[4] referred to the impression he gave of barely controllable strength. It was far more than an impression; he actually had it, and when he was angry, it was not always under his complete control. How strong was he? Mel Brooks' stories of Caesarean feats of strength are legion, and it has sometimes been suggested that they are exaggerated. If you want to trust and verify, you can find other contemporaries' accounts of them. Brooks has embellished, but he didn't really have to. Amazingly—and sometimes appallingly—most of the stories seem to be true.[5] Caesar did rip offending inanimate objects from walls or off hinges. And punch holes in walls and doors. Or punctuate his displeasure with a writing session by picking up a massive wooden desk and then letting it drop, usually a surefire way of focusing everyone's

The Tango—One of many examples of the writers extracting comedy from the height difference between Caesar and Coca—and Sid's strength.

attention. Sometimes the offending objects were animate. He did, provoked beyond endurance by Brooks, dangle him out that 18th-story hotel room window. (Sid would later remark that "we had a relationship that was based on trust, affection and his relentless attempts to piss me off.")[6]

Both Brooks and Carl Reiner were among those with Caesar one day when a taxi driver almost ran into him and the group on a New York street. Sid unsurprisingly took issue at this, and a shouting match ensued. The cabbie either didn't recognize Caesar or perhaps he harbored a secret death wish, because as the situation escalated, he called him a crazy son-of-a-bitch. Sid then asked him if he remembered what it felt like when he was being born, and announced, "Well, you're about to reenact it." Reaching into the cab, he grabbed the driver by the collar, and attempted to pull him out through the narrow opening in the wing window. Cooler heads, Sid's not among them, prevailed and he was pulled away from the cab.[7] Could he have completed this rather novel form of defenestration? Probably not. But note that his friends assumed he was *capable* of doing it. After all, this was a man who once, on a riding path, brought a horse to its knees with a single punch.[8] In his defense, it had thrown his wife, and he couldn't get the spooked animal away from her. But still. When recounting all of these episodes, you almost feel the need to provide the classic disclaimer that no humans or animals were seriously harmed in their making. Although you have to wonder about the cabbie if Caesar had been given more time.

This strength was frequently on display in the sketches and could be employed to comedic effect. For example, a song and dance number with Imogene Coca, in which he swoops her up into his arms and does a passionate tango across the stage—with her legs dangling two feet off the floor. Sid and Imogene's dances together usually featured bits like these. You can imagine the writers exploring the possibilities for dances and sketches: Let's have Sid pick Imogene up by the waist with one arm and twirl her around. Or how about he scoops her up and puts her on his shoulder so she can perch there? One of their more imaginative uses occurs in "Buzz and Bubbles" (5/17/52), where two vaudeville partners, Sid and Imogene, are approached by Florenz Ziegfeld; unfortunately, he wants "the girl, not the boy." But Imogene refuses to break up the act. Sid tries to convince her to go on to a career in the Follies without him. When words don't work, what better methods of persuasion than a series of wrestling moves? When an arm twist, a full Nelson, and a headlock don't do the trick, he lowers his shoulder, picks her up, slings her across both shoulders and does an airplane spin with her.

Not only was Sid's strength featured in many sketches, the writers obviously enjoyed poking fun at it as well, using the diminutive Howie

Morris in sometimes unexpected role reversals. One of the best of these—very funny in its own right—is about a disastrous community theatre production. In a semi-parody of *The Heiress* (9/6/52), a penniless Sid and the heiress Imogene plan to elope because her father (Carl Reiner) wants her to marry a suitor with means (Howie Morris). Why disastrous? Unfortunately for the amateur actors, the stage door used for both entrances and exits begins to stick. Intermittently. Everyone in the sketch adopts a British accent—except under door-duress. At one point, Sid, after tugging at the door with all his might (and rocking the set in the process) finally gets it open. He yells offstage as he exits, "Why don'tcha fix the door, Charlie?" in accents of purest Yonkers. As the lovers plot their elopement, she anxiously announces that her rich suitor is going to be coming through the door (pause for wordless Caesarean take of "Yeah, right"). The door then opens easily to admit Morris. Sid feels his own bicep, then Howie's with a look of astonishment. At times, the action is worthy of a Feydeau farce—and just as funny. After Carl tells Imogene for a final time that he forbids her to marry Sid, he announces he's leaving for his club—and of course the door sticks. Sid enters (easily for a change) and asks, "Has your father gone?" Imogene rather desperately responds, "Oh, he's left some time ago," as Carl pulls his coat over his head and tries—with a remarkable degree of success—to become part of an adjacent wall. Then ducks out under Sid's arm. Finally the door becomes well and truly stuck (cue backstage sounds of hammers and chisels). The two lovers have to get out somehow and the writers resort to the usual display of Caesarean strength-moves: With the realization that ordinary means will no longer suffice, Sid picks up Imogene, flops her into a head-first horizontal position and prepares to use her as a battering ram.

In "The Sewing Machine Girl" (5/16/53), a silent film recreation included in *Ten from Your Show of Shows*, Caesar and Coca are two ill-fated sweethearts, she with an obviously tubercular condition, who work in a garment sweatshop. After Imogene collapses in an operatic (and hilarious) fit, Sid climbs over a bench, bends down from the waist and picks her up in a deadlift, using just arm strength. And then, still holding her, has a tug of war over her limp body with Carl Reiner, the lascivious shop boss—while Howie Morris, as another worker, is tugging on one of his arms.

Of course, it was child's play for Caesar to demolish Howie Morris. Morris could assist in being bounced up and down, which happened frequently, not so much with being picked up bodily by Sid, which also happened frequently. In a sketch from October 11, 1952, "Parlor Games," where Charlie Hickenlooper is playing musical chairs with a group of friends, Morris's character has the temerity to try to grab the chair Charlie has his eye on. Caesar picks him up by his collar and jacket and actually *throws* him up in the air and away from it. Morris once commented about being used as a human ragdoll: "It got laughs. The most interesting morning was Sunday morning when I would look at my body and find the various bruises and great clumps of hair missing."[9] Granted, Coca and Morris were small people, easily manipulated by someone with great strength. Carl Reiner was not small; a big man in his own right, he was taller than Caesar. Nonetheless, in a sketch set in a restaurant (1/3/53), they're arguing over who will get the tab, which naturally degenerates into a wrestling match. Sid lowers his shoulder, picks up Carl in a fireman's carry, and deposits him on top of the bar—with ease. But he could do better than that. In "The Long, Long Voyage" (3/6/54), where Reiner and Morris are trying to prevent Caesar from going into a bar, Carl leaps on his back—and is joined by Howie, who leaps on top of him. Sid walks offstage, with no discernible effort, carrying about 300 pounds of Second and Third Bananas on his back.

Yet, Caesar's size and strength were accompanied by an amazing agility and delicacy of movement that he could use to convey emotion and feeling, whether his character was human—or an inanimate object. Very few comic actors can make you not only "see" but feel sorry for a crooked slot machine about to be demolished in a police raid or an old, discarded whitewall tire. Sid could. In the varieties of physical comedy in which he excelled, he could indeed, as Allen suggests, write physical poetry.

Nowhere was this ability more striking than in pantomime. Caesar's miming could be broad, subtle, and almost every gradation in between. It could also be, as Chaplin's was, funny or sad, or simultaneously both. One of the best examples comes from a silent movie parody, "The Foundling, or I Want My Child." (10/28/50). Carl Reiner and Virginia Curtis are the doting parents of a little girl (Imogene Coca, with blond curls and a frilly short dress) whom they shower with gifts and affection. Trouble, however, intrudes in the form of Sid, who as the titles tell us, is the real father and wants his daughter back. He mimes their past history: his marriage; the birth of their little girl; the death of her mother; his raising the child on his own, rocking her cradle, and, as she grows, playing patty-cake and taking her for walks. Then, he loses his laborer's job, becomes destitute, and is forced to beg for money. After poignantly reaching toward a superimposed picture of his wife, he takes his daughter to Carl and Virginia so that she may have a better life. You "see" clearly every part of the story and it's done with both humor and pathos—all in less than a minute. Caesar always maintained that Chaplin was one of his comedic idols. And in Sid's reunion with the little girl there is a stunning moment when he *becomes* him, putting his hands to his mouth in nervous expectation in a perfect imitation of Charlie in "City Lights" when The Little Tramp waits for The Flower Girl to recognize him. Homage or comedic audacity? Whatever the intent, as well as being touching, it's funny—as Imogene, licking her lollipop, executes a perfect "Who *is* this guy?" look. All ends well nonetheless when Carl discovers a birthmark on Sid's arm that is identical with his—and his wife's, and the butler's, even a messenger boy's. Everyone goes into silent film-style paroxysms of delight as they realize, improbably but humorously, they're all related.

Caesar almost always employed some degree of mime in his monologues and sometimes in sketches where he was either a Tin Pan Alley music writer or a composer, which required "playing" a piano. He could play the saxophone and the clarinet; whether he could play piano is hard to tell. Lucille Kallen insisted he couldn't; on the other hand, there are a number of photos of him with them, including one taken in his King's Point, Long Island house seated at a piano, and you don't normally keep a Steinway in your living room as an accent piece. Regardless, he could certainly mime playing one convincingly. His finger and hand movements were in perfect time with the music. (He could also use other extremities. In one sketch where he is composing a symphony, he plays the "keyboard" with his foot—announcing, "footnote!") However, his most skilled piano miming would come on the later *Caesar's Hour*. Earl Wild, the renowned concert pianist, was brought on board the show by Sid, who admired both his sense of humor and his musical improv skills. Wild provided music for silent-film sketches, helped to develop opera parodies, and composed incidental music. He would stay with *Caesar's Hour* for its full run—he enjoyed the musical parodies and liked Sid.[10] Together they concocted the brilliant pantomime "Grieg's Piano Concerto," in which Sid is a concert pianist making his debut, seated at a piano stool in front of an invisible piano and orchestra. Much is of course played for laughs: He accidentally slams the fallboard on his hands, gets dizzy from the complicated back-and-forth (and multiple) jumps and has to take a break, and, after repeatedly hitting a wrong note, is forced by the conductor to practice scales before resuming the piece. However, the "serious" playing is truly impressive. Wild was offstage, playing a real piano with the real orchestra while watching Sid's miming on a monitor. The synchronization is astounding, as is Caesar's mime. During the cadenza, with its rapid chords alternating up and down the keyboard, he just as rapidly moves his head in the opposite direction of his hands—the way real pianists have to play it, looking one chord ahead. It's perhaps the best collaboration ever of mime and pianist and it's a marvel to watch.

Sid also did occasional full-blown pantomime in solo sketches. For example, "Boy at First Dance" and two pantomimes of a man and a woman getting up in the morning. He also did a lengthy number that opened the final season of *Your Show of Shows*, in which, to the music of *The Sorcerer's*

8. Caesar as Physical Comedian 121

Apprentice, he mimed the misadventures of a dentist's apprentice. But most of his pantomime was with other cast-members, particularly in the silent movie parodies. And, most notably, paired with Imogene Coca. There was simply no better duo at pantomime. Ever.

Caesar and Coca did pantomimes on 68 episodes of *Your Show of Shows*, and they would bookend the show's run: they did one on the very first program and on the very last (the audience-requested "1812 Overture"). The skill with which they performed mime was extraordinary, given that there was relatively little rehearsal time. However, the two had developed an amazing comedic connection that made it possible—and their performances together were unforgettable. The scenarios were unceasingly inventive as well as funny: Sid as a performing seal who *really* doesn't want to balance a ball on his nose and Imogene as his insistent trainer. On a date at Coney Island where the roller coaster is impossibly high and a terrified Sid puts a finger under his nose to try to prevent a nosebleed. Trying to hail a cab, in a rain so heavy it bends Sid's hand as he tests it, and none of their stratagems work, including Sid's lying down in front of one and Imogene's showing a bit of leg. Sid as an inept magician and Imogene as his assistant, who performs a desperate little tap dance to distract the audience while he tries in vain to get out of chains and a strait-jacket. Sid and Imogene vying for the same seat on the subway. Strangers seated next to each other at a symphony who are swept away, literally at times, by Tchaikovsky's *Romeo and Juliet* (Sid's expressions of rapture over the romantic music and Imogene's totally deadpan responses to them—and him—make it one of the funniest of their pantomimes).

It's almost impossible to choose "a best of" their pantomimes, but two would be in the running, one for its sheer hilarity and the other for its mimetic realism. "In a Shoe Store" (1/10/53) has Sid as a clerk trying to fit a picky customer, Imogene, who insists that her feet are smaller than they really are. At one point, Sid attempts to pry a too-small shoe from her foot by putting his own huge shoe against her shoulder to brace his tugging. In the course of his strenuous effort, one of her stockings is ripped and Imogene demands he repair it. As he tries to thread a needle to do so, she directs him with her hands like a parking attendant guiding someone into a tight space; his concentration is worthy of someone trying to defuse a bomb. And when he "sews" the rip, every movement of the needle, the tug on the thread and the slight lifting of her leg in response, and his final tying off of the thread is perfectly mimed. As he sits back in triumph, however, they discover that he has somehow managed to sew his hand to her leg.

In a pantomime of two drum majors in a parade (4/12/52), everything that could go wrong of course does, to the accompaniment of a stirring John Philip Sousa march. Anyone who has ever been in a marching band

Part III—Rendering Unto Caesar

The best pantomime duo on television, unsuccessfully trying to hail a cab in the rain (courtesy Barry Jacobsen).

will immediately recognize the officious, self-important drum major played by Sid, whose over-direction and insistence on proper spacing results in a traffic jam of marchers. When that has been sorted out, he manages, in a dramatic thrust of his long baton, to impale a bystander with it. Tugging to get it out, in perfect time to the music, he resorts to using his foot as leverage against his victim's body to finally extricate it. He and Imogene then engage in a twirling contest, he so enthusiastically that he begins to be lifted off his feet (helicopter sound-effects are supplied) and she has to pull him back to earth. She, however, is the far more skilled twirler and in a running exchange of tossed batons back and forth, which he keeps dropping, their contest degenerates into a fencing match with them. Eager to regain the upper hand, Sid indicates he will perform with a flaming baton. The result is a foregone conclusion: twirling it across his shoulders, he sets himself on fire and Imogene has to frantically smother the flames. The Parade of Disaster ends with their marching offstage as solemnly as they entered. You, on the other hand, will never be able to listen to Sousa's *The Thunderer* with a straight face again.

Besides Caesar and Coca, the rest of the major comedic cast did pantomime well, including Carl Reiner (no surprise there). Yet, even in paired pantomime and in sketches, Sid was capable of supplying nuances that took his miming a step above anyone else's on TV. He so immersed himself

8. Caesar as Physical Comedian   123

into the character and action that he provided little bits of business that on some level he must have known would be picked up by only a few viewers. But that wasn't the point: his *character* would have done them. In "The Sewing-Machine Girl" (5/16/53) where he, as a tailor plying needle and thread, helps his sweetheart Imogene to rethread her machine, he does so only after pinning his imaginary needle to the front of his shirt. And his sense of continuity never failed him even in the midst of sketches where at least three different things were going on simultaneously. In "Boy at First Dance" (4/22/50), after he has mimed a shy awkward guy seeking a partner, whose feet he continually steps on once he has found her, he portrays the same boy five years later. Now an assured, gum-cracking ladies' man, he reviews the girls available, chooses a partner, twirls her around and throws her in the air, waits for her to come down, executes one more throw—and never stops chewing his wad of gum. When he's playing a tambourine in a sketch with Coca where they are percussionists in an orchestra, he not only makes you see it, he continues to hold it after his solo and, before he sits down, shifts it to his other hand so that he can carefully place it on the floor next to him. Or in a later, brilliant sketch on *Caesar's Hour* where he and Nanette Fabray have an argument set to Beethoven's Fifth, he packs a suitcase to leave home. Once he picks it up, he never puts it down, even while continuing the gesticulations of the argument (in time to the music), until his exit.

Caesar's keen sense memory would serve him well in his comic acting, especially in his monologues, but particularly in mime. It ranged from where objects should be placed (Carl Reiner was always impressed by his perfect positioning when he put an imaginary cigarette in his mouth, so that lighting it and taking a first drag would look natural) to how they were placed (Sid's personal physician claimed that he could walk into an unfamiliar room, look around for a few minutes, and then later describe the objects in it, down to the number and location of lamps and the color of an ashtray). And both absolute concentration and sense memory were evident even in the preparation stage of sketches. Reiner recalled Caesar rehearsing a bit in which he was miming trying to get the lid off a jar. It was going nowhere and they decided to move on to something else. But not before Sid screwed the imaginary lid back onto the imaginary jar and placed it on an imaginary table (without being conscious of what he was doing).[11]

Caesar's miming was self-taught and a talent he had developed from a very early age: "I had always been able to see the props in my mind's eye and then they became real to me."[12] How real was recalled by Lucille Kallen in a list of her favorite experiences as a writer for *Your Show of Shows*: Caesar and Coca were rehearsing a pantomime under the direction of Max Liebman. In it, she was tossing a salad, apparently badly, and the script called for her to relinquish the bowl to him. Max stopped the action briefly, then said to Sid, "OK, start from where you're tossing the salad." Sid remained motionless, staring at Imogene. "Start!" Max repeated, and Sid, pointing to the empty air between Imogene's outstretched hands, said, "She didn't give me back the salad bowl."[13]

Liebman, who had ample opportunity to observe Caesar's miming, would once comment that when Sid picked up an imaginary object, you not only knew what it was but how much it weighed.[14] And his attention to detail when working with those imaginary objects could be extraordinary. Only Caesar, in the midst of a monologue about a nervous father-to-be in a maternity ward waiting room, could do the following: after smoking one unfiltered cigarette after the other, he begins to talk to another expectant father, then pauses to use the tip of his tongue to spit out a piece of imaginary tobacco on his lip before continuing.

The relative delicacy of mime was one aspect of Caesar's physical comedy; broad slapstick was another. And it could be very broad. A sketch of January 9, 1954, "I Object!" is reminiscent of the old vaudeville routine, "Here Comes the Judge," but in this case might be titled "There Goes the Judge." The scene: a courtroom where Imogene, the plaintiff, and her attorney Carl Reiner are trying to recover money from a deadbeat defendant who is late to the trial. Enter Sid as the judge, who seats himself at the bench. The court officer points out that a glass of water and a gavel are at his side, then asks if he requires anything else. Sid responds, "Yeah, a chair. Do you expect me to stand stooped over the whole day?" as he rises to reveal he has been semi-squatting behind the bench the whole time. When he hears the particulars of the case, he is initially sympathetic to Coca—that is, until the defendant shows up. It is of course a stunningly beautiful woman and Sid promptly falls off his chair. He reappears back up at the bench with a toothbrush to freshen up, takes a sip of water, gargles, and then—to gasps and laughter from the audience—spits the water over the heads of Coca in the witness box and Reiner beside her. As the attractive defendant takes the stand, she sits rather provocatively and Sid smoothly inquires, "May I offer you something? Have you had lunch?" When Imogene complains that she refuses to continue "with her sitting like this," Sid responds "For once I agree with you. The witness will not sit in such a manner. You'll turn your chair a little toward me," and when she complies, he falls off his chair again. When order is more or less restored, and he is leering at her, she crosses her shapely legs. Crying "Ahh, no!" he falls off his chair yet again and has to be helped up repeatedly by court officials, each time popping back up with a goofier expression than the one before. The action and humor are as broad as at least two barn doors, but you laugh anyway. And admire Caesar's aim in expectorating.

8. Caesar as Physical Comedian   125

In "Twenty Minutes for Lunch" (4/10/54), he shows off his skills at "reaction" slapstick as a mild-mannered soul who is trying to get lunch in a busy restaurant and takes every kind of abuse that can be dished out to a customer. Ignored by the wait staff, he finds an empty table on his own. After pleading for a menu (he finally has one slapped in his face by a waiter) and service, he soon discovers why the table is empty—it's by the swinging door to the kitchen. And, yes, he soon gets smacked by it, repeatedly. What makes the sketch is the perfect timing of door swings, the crescendo of mayhem (from a poked eye to a blow to the nose to the wedging of a water glass in his mouth), and Sid's reactions to each smack as the door swings back. The final indignity is inflicted when he is served at last, takes his first bite, and the door swings open again. When it swings back, he is briefly stunned, then discovers to his horror his fork is halfway down his throat. His muffled cry and pointing to the fork is laugh-out-loud funny. The sketch concludes with an endless line of waiters pouring through the door, hitting Sid as they go. The writers must have enjoyed playing against type: the burly, easily provoked Caesar as Mr. Milquetoast with a nervous little laugh? But, as usual, Sid sells it.

Perhaps the most impressive bit of physical comedy Caesar did on *Your Show of Shows* was a sketch in which he played a genuine *klutz*, a character type he didn't do that often. In "Big Business Conference" (12/27/52), he is the CEO of a financially-troubled business in a meeting with the other execs in an attempt to revive the company's fortunes. Wearing the intent scowl he always adopted for businessman characters, he listens as the board members proceed to outline their plans. Or try to, for in the ensuing minutes, the following take place: Sid hits his shin on the conference table, leans back too far in his chair and bonks his head on the wall (twice), then angrily answers an interrupting phone call and almost breaks his jaw with the receiver. Intent on a speaker's presentation, he sharpens his finger instead of a pencil, and when he slams his hand on the desk for emphasis, he impales it on a pen (which he has smoothly palmed). In frustration, he gets up from his chair, and immediately trips over a telephone cord, pulling down the phone, a lamp, and other items from a table. His associates pick him up and disentangle him, then guide him to a chair. Still continuing to expostulate, he thrusts his arm upward—through a standing lamp—and ends up with the shade, which is opaque by the way, over his head. While not once looking down through it (employing a special form of comedian radar?), he lurches forward and steps into a wastebasket. As the rest of the execs drag him offstage, with his foot still in the wastebasket and holding his body at an almost impossible 10 to 4 slant, he announces that the meeting will have to be postponed: "Gentlemen, it's just not my day." A marvelous example of a character careering out of control while the actor maintains perfect physical control, it's 5 minutes of pure non-stop slapstick timed perfectly. And performed live. It's the kind of sketch vaudevillians honed with years of performance; Caesar was doing things like it weekly.

Certainly, other comedians could do physical comedy well. What set Sid's apart was its totality.[15] Beyond just his size, strength, and agility, every physical characteristic and feature became tools to be used in his performances. In this respect, he was one of the most physical of the comedians of his or—you could convincingly argue—any era.

Caesar was not handsome in the conventional sense; rather his looks were striking, with strong features and one very distinguishable one, a mole on his left cheek that invariably appeared in every contemporary caricature of him. The harsh black and white of early TV made him look older and darker than he really was (it's almost a shock to see him in color home movies—he looks like he's his own younger brother). Yet, that same stark black and white accentuated the most striking of his features, his eyes. John Crosby, the TV critic for the *New York Herald Tribune*, noted that "he could wring laughter from an audience with the violence of his great eyes."[16]

Two sketches in particular illustrate well the "wringing laughter from the audience" part of Crosby's observation. The first is one of *Your Show of Shows*' best known, a wicked parody of the schmaltzy TV show *This Is Your Life*. Sid is Al Duncey, the hapless and reluctant victim hauled up, literally, on the stage to have his life reviewed by the relentlessly smarmy emcee, played brilliantly by Carl Reiner. As Al sits on a couch, he listens to offstage voices from his past, which he is expected to identify (a standard part of the real show). When he hears the first, we see a camera close-up of Sid's face. His eyes display an impressive series of reactions: intense concentration—who could it be?—pondering—maybe it could be?—no—more pondering—delighted recognition?—no. And then asks, to Carl's dismay and the audience's loud laughter, "Can I hear it again?"

The second is in a monologue, "A Man Coming Down with a Cold." (11/1/52). In his attempts to self-medicate, Sid opens the medicine chest to find first a bottle of pills. He reads from the label: "Upon taking this pill, do not stand near an open flame. If the pain persists, see your doctor immediately and don't tell him about this pill. Keep your mouth shut." Wisely moving on, he finds a bottle of mouthwash; its label informs him that his throat has billions of germs on every square inch. "They can't be without oxygen," he declares. "I'll suffocate them." He claps his hands over his mouth and nose, so that all you see are his eyes in close-up. A standard comic progression would be realization that this probably wasn't a good idea, ensuing panic, an eye-pop, and a final gasp for breath. Caesar didn't go in for standard. Using only his eyes, he manages to convey an initial smugness and satisfaction ("those germs are toast!"), followed by two rapid but distinct stages of dawning realization ("wait a minute" and "this isn't good") before panic sets in, and only then comes the explosive gasp for air, followed by "*I need oxygen!*" And he never does pop his eyes.

"The violence of his great eyes"? Crosby's description here is spot on. Caesar could use them to convey a variety of emotions, including a sadness and pain that can almost be felt. But when he expressed anger with them, no doubt drawing from his own considerable reserve, it's almost unnerving to watch. In some of the earliest Hickenlooper sketches, Sid's edginess and darker side come through clearly in Charlie's arguments with Doris. When his eyes flash and then become cold, you know an explosion is imminent and any hatches in the vicinity had better be battened down. And in one memorable monologue of April 11, 1953, he goes far beyond the realms of incredibly good acting with his eyes to the extraordinary. He's A Man in a Bar, getting progressively drunk. Whether the writers were just using a standard comedic trope or hinting to Caesar himself something of his own growing problems with alcohol (there were a *lot* of drunk sketches on *Your Show of Shows*), the fact remains that Sid was playing the sketch sober—he never drank before a show—and it's a masterpiece. It's very funny and he goes through the stages of inebriation brilliantly, but there is one point at which his eyes *are* the wild and angry eyes of a drunk. It's neither comedic nor overdrawn, and, for an instant, it's absolutely frightening.

Caesar was blessed with another physical gift: an incredibly mobile and expressive face. He is usually described as rubber-faced; you could add other adjectives like "plastic" and "quicksilver" to the description and be just as accurate. With Sid, the phrase "emotions playing over one's face" was not a cliché. He could not only mold his features into practically every expression possible, he could do them simultaneously.

The variety of "takes" he was capable of doing seemed endless and he could ring infinite changes and variations on them. Pain takes? They could be broad, as in his reaction when Howie Morris, as a German general displeased with his underling Sid's fraternization with Mata Hari (Coca), orders him to put out his palm and then puts out his cigarette in it. Or, continuing the military theme, when, as U–Boat commander Captain Unterwasser (an in-joke for those who knew German), he has a torpedo dropped on his foot. They could also be subtle. In a pantomime with Imogene where she is a pianist accompanying him in his violin debut, Sid graciously helps her by propping up the supporting rod on her baby grand only to have the top dropped on his head when she accidentally jars it. He displays an only slightly pained expression on his face, "slightly" considering that his head is now bent at a 90-degree angle. His reaction takes served him well in mime; a classic early sketch (3/11/50) features his looks of exasperation when teaching his wife to drive, and his looks of stark terror when she does—hair-raisingly. And one of his best in the reaction category (from 9/27/52) was the subtlest—as a man at the movies with a blind date from hell (Imogene of course) who bounces up and down in her seat, annoys the other patrons, and continually looks up at him, trying to get a reaction. Sid stoically ignores all of this, his attention focused on the screen—until you see his left eye twitch.

Caesar's double-takes were a thing of comedic beauty. He could do a deadpan stare toward the audience, a broad "What the *hell*?" of surprise, or the briefest and most subtle of takes. In "Business Lunch" a.k.a. "What's on the Agenda" (12/19/53), Sid is a hungry executive who has ordered a lunch for his board, but when it arrives, his order isn't among the others and he bellows to his secretary, "Where in the *wide* world is my bacon and raisin sandwich?" Forced to watch the others eating, he suddenly notices that Carl Reiner has left his ham hock sandwich unguarded. Without moving his head, he does the double-take in a second with only his eyes.

Outright mugging was generally reserved for the movie parodies, part of the poking fun at their melodramatic moments. However, Caesar (as well as Coca, who could twist her features with the best) could at times rely too much on facial expressions to bolster a weak sketch or extend a laugh. Yet, any excesses were more than balanced by all of the times they worked, to hilarious effect. None more so than in a sketch of April 19, 1952, called "The New Neighbor," in which Sid pulls off what is conceivably The Funniest Face Ever Made by a Human Being. He is sitting innocently on the couch in his apartment reading the paper when there's a series of knocks at the door. After a progression of his yelling—"Come in, the door's open. It's *open!* All you gotta do is turn the knob"—the door opens to reveal the beautiful new neighbor, played by guest-hostess Arlene Dahl, who comes in to introduce herself. Sid greets her with embarrassment, failed attempts at suavity, and more than a little nervousness in her presence. The nervousness increases as she gushes that new neighbors shouldn't be strangers and that they should get to know each other well. It finally dawns on him that she does indeed want to know him better: She pursues him to the couch where they both sit, he with one leg crossed over a knee, and she goes into full flirtation mode. Leaning in closer, she puts her hand on Sid's leg. As he winces with one eye as though he's just received a mild but pleasurable jolt, his look, with eyes slightly crossed, is one of surprise, embarrassment, and just a soupçon of sheepish delight—all sweeping over his face at the same instant. Simultaneous with *that*, he semi-levitates off the couch. It's almost as though he can't keep his face still, and Dahl can't keep hers straight, breaking into laughter along with the audience. In fact, the sequence elicited the loudest audience laughter at one of Sid's facial expressions that I've heard on any episode.

8. Caesar as Physical Comedian

Caesar used another physical characteristic, although not a visual one, to create comedy. He employed his voice as yet another comedic tool. One of its hallmarks—and it is immediately noticeable—was his New York accent. And it was pronounced.

Like that of most New Yorkers then and now, his speech was, if you want to use the linguistic term, non-rhotic; that is, he dropped his 'r's. Spectacularly so: don't bother listening for any sounded "r" in his introduction to the Airplane Movie parody (3/1/52) when he refers to it as "the first number I ever did in show business. In the Coast Guard. *Tars and Spars*"—there are none. His speech patterns also included one that has by now largely died out in New York. Long identified, incorrectly, as a "Brooklyn accent," it can be best characterized, to use another technical linguistic term, as "interesting things to do with vowels." It resulted in word sounds like "the pills are starting to *woik*, dear," or "just *toin* the knob." He could suppress his accent in his stiff, formal introductions at the beginning of each show, but it didn't last for long, usually reappearing in the first sketch. At least in this instance, appropriately, as the first sketch was almost always a Hickenlooper one, and Charlie was, after all, a New Yorker too. Although he could suppress it, he never tried to change or drop his accent and Caesar no doubt realized he could get laughs with it. Fifties audiences outside The Apple still found a New York accent funny, and even today, it's difficult not to smile when Sid orders Howie Morris, at full volume, to "Geddouttaheah!"

Caesar's volume could range from *piano* (his own natural speaking voice was rather soft) to *fortissimo*. In fact, *ff* could easily become *fff*: he could turn the dial up to 11 with ease, and his bellow could rival Gleason's. His vocal range extended to far more than just amplitude, however. In "Aggravation Boulevard," a sketch from *Caesar's Hour*, Sid pulled off a notable vocal feat. He's a John Gilbert–like silent film star whose high-pitched voice (which Caesar turned into a hilarious falsetto) dooms his career with the advent of the talkies. Thanks to the kindness of his old director (Carl Reiner) and the persistence of his wife (Nanette Fabray), he's given one more chance, in a Western talkie where he plays a sheriff. But when he enters a barroom set for the first take, his heroic lines are immediately made ludicrous by his falsetto and the stagehands laugh at him. Hurt and humiliated (and here Sid does the pathos very well), he walks off the set. When he returns, to tell Reiner and Fabray that he realizes his career is over, he does so, to their surprise, in a plummy near-bass voice. He's been walking in the rain, caught a cold, and it lowered his voice. Carl declares that he can be a star again, so long as he can keep that lower register. In 4 seconds, Sid slides his voice up an entire scale, as his cold wears off:

But I can't have a cold all the time, (near-bass)
I'm a healthy man. (natural baritone)

I get over these things easily. (falsetto)
[Thinking fast, Nanette dumps a pitcher of water over his head, drenching him.]
Thank you, dear! (back to near-bass).

It's an amazing display of vocal gymnastics. And all ends happily in the sketch as Carl says they'll wet him down before each scene, and Sid adds "And keep the windows open!"

If he had wanted, Caesar could probably have done an entire act based on sound-effects, at which he was a master. Common sounds (doors opening and closing, hammering a nail into a board) were easy; esoteric ones (seltzer water, herds of horses, a slot machine) were also a specialty.[17] He could not only make familiar sounds, he made some you've never heard before and probably never will again. And he could riff with sounds, improvising with his voice the way he improvised with his saxophone. One of the best examples, and one that generated loud and sustained laughter from the audience, was in a sketch about a music recital (4/11/53). The Recital sketches (there were three versions) featured Sid disrupting musical performances without really meaning to; this one has him doing so by trying to fight off a sneeze. Realizing he's going to lose the battle, he runs offstage. You then hear an aria of agonized attempts to stifle the sneeze; when he can no longer contain it, he erupts in vocal paroxysms that, frankly, are impossible to describe, only marvel as well as laugh at. And he does it for 30 seconds. When he reappears on stage, the reaction is immediate: it's probably the only time in the history of live TV that members of an audience begin to applaud a sneeze. As well they might—it was indeed something.

One last tool used by Caesar in physical comedy should be added to the list: his hands. They were basketball-palming huge with very long fingers; yet he could achieve a delicacy of movement with them and execute both broad and subtle gestures to dramatic as well as comedic effect. The drumming of his fingers on a table was always an ominous indication of an explosion to come, usually directed toward Doris Hickenlooper. He could also use those long fingers to create a more than reasonable facsimile of flippers in a pantomime of a trained seal (who can also shuffle cards with them). In "The Birthday Present," he uses his hands as comic punctuation in his argument with Doris over whether or not he forgot her birthday. In a silent movie parody, "Bartered Souls" (10/7/50), he plays an unhappy husband who, although married to a rich woman, still pines for his old sweetheart. As he sits at a desk, with chin in hand, he wrestles with the temptation to drown his sorrows. Gazing at a bottle of liquor, he moves his hands and fingers across his face, in a choreography of indecision, putting them in at least six different positions in roughly as many seconds. It's not only funny, he does it so quickly, it's almost as if the film has been speeded up.

8. Caesar as Physical Comedian

In his solo pantomime, "Boy at First Dance" (4/22/50), his hands almost achieve co-star status. Shyly waiting for the dance to start, Sid's character doesn't know what to do with them. He first uses them to check that his suit jacket, tie, and pocket handkerchief are perfect, then moves upward to make sure that his ears and nose are as well. He tries standing with them by his sides, then palms in, palms out, and finally just dangles them. After at least four arrangements of his hands—several different places on his sides, in his jacket pockets—he ends up in a Napoleonic pose with one tucked in his jacket. At this point, his constantly moving hands take on a life of their own and he looks at them in alarm as they continue to move, in front of his chest and behind his head, and, ominously, toward his throat. Finally regaining control, he flings them behind his back. The script simply directed [has trouble with hands].[18] Indeed.

In his monologues in particular, when Caesar put all of these physical tools together in combination with his usual gale-force energy and intensity, it was a take-no-prisoners approach to comedy—and in it, he had no equal on television in the '50s. He could not only wring laughter from an audience, he could almost overpower it. Of all the aspects and dimensions of his performances, it was this kind of onslaught that the *New York Times* was referring to in its obituary of Sid when it called him "a comedic force of nature."[19]

9

Caesar as Comic Actor

> *The first time I saw Caesar, it was like seeing Brando.... He was first and always an actor.*
> —Neil Simon[20]

Simon would not be the only one to make the comparison: Richard Corliss, in his *Time* essay, described Sid as the Brando of TV comedy. Caesar certainly matched Brando in brooding and intensity, and Corliss would go further in his comparison, calling Sid the first Method comedian. Your initial reaction might be that it's somewhat of a stretch. Sid would do a number of parodies of movies on *Your Show of Shows* with method actors *in* them (Montgomery Clift in *From Here to Eternity* and *A Place in the Sun* and of course Brando in *A Streetcar Named Desire*). And in one of the best "interview" sketches from the first season (4/18/50), he was an expert on Stanislavsky, using the technique to turn himself into a nail and, hilariously, a pinball. But his acquaintance with the Method never went beyond just knowing what it was. (For that matter he never had any kind of acting training, let alone in the Method.)

However, you can see him, almost intuitively, using some of its techniques in his comic acting. Above all, in his absolute immersion into a character (Steve Allen would note his "Brando-like" talent for throwing himself into a role),[21] particularly in straight segments of sketches. Other comics on '50s TV could play straight on occasion and do it well, but their personae tended to get in the way; you're almost always aware that it's *them* playing a role. You don't have that perceptual barrier when Caesar plays it straight. There's not that kind of distinction between him and his characters. And those characters could be very different from who he was. A mild-mannered Milquetoast or the brutish Stanley Kowalski—the real Caesar was like neither, but he was always convincing. In an interview from 1994, Imogene Coca put it another way: "he gets into characters so honestly."[22] And he could play those characters, if called for, with an intensity and degree of emotion at times almost unsettling to watch.

Moreover, at least once, Caesar explicitly describes using the affective memory technique of the Method, even if he doesn't call it that, in evoking a character's emotion. In a *Caesar's Hour* silent film sketch, he's a drunk who has reformed for the sake of his daughter; unfortunately, he's unable to live down his former reputation, and he asks his boss to adopt her so that she can have a better life without him. The sketch ends with him standing outside of the gate of a house, in the snow, looking through a lighted window at his daughter's marriage. Unable to join her, he watches her happiness as tears roll down his face. It's touching—and Sid played that emotional scene by recalling what he described in *Where Have I Been?* as "one of the most devastating experiences of my life."[23]

It occurred when he had just started *Your Show of Shows*. Emerging from the Waldorf-Astoria, where he had been playing a benefit, Caesar saw his mother standing in the snow across the street. He was stunned that she hadn't come to the benefit with his brother Dave (or apparently even told anyone she wanted to). Despite her insistence that she didn't want to be any trouble, Sid told her to wait and he would get a limo to take her home. However, when he returned with Dave, she was gone—she had left to go back to Yonkers on the train. Some thirty years later, Sid would characterize it as "like something out of *Stella Dallas*." It was an apt comparison not only in the parallels with the later sketch (the movie Stella gives up her daughter, then watches her marriage through a window), but, more importantly for Sid, in the image of the self-sacrificing mother who watches her successful child from a distance. Except that Stella's daughter never sees her mother; Ida Caesar's son saw his. It took him years to get over his self-imposed guilt, but he used the memory and recalled emotion of "the time my mother stood in the snow watching me come out of the Waldorf-Astoria" in typical Method style to summon those tears in the sketch. It's difficult to believe that he didn't use the same technique in other sketches and monologues: drawing on his own inner demons and unpleasant childhood, as well as adult, experiences to evoke his characters' pain, anger, humiliation, and, yes, guilt.

Whatever technique comic actors use, Method or otherwise, if they're good sketch actors, they're good actors, period. Caesar was demonstrably both, particularly in his effortless facility in turning from comedy acting to straight (and back again) in seconds, leaving an audience touched at one moment and laughing the next.

Where did his talents come from? You suspect that most comedians don't know, and Caesar was no exception. He said on more than one occasion he didn't know their source, only that in darker moments (and for Sid, those were frequent), he feared he would someday lose them. How he developed them is more clear. Unlike most of his contemporaries, Sid hadn't served a long apprenticeship in vaudeville, radio, or nightclubs. Generally, a few summers in the Catskills working as a *tummler* and playing roles in the dramas and musicals put on for resort goers, followed by a tour in a service revue, do not a superb comedian make (there were many with similar experiences who never made it any further). However, that revue experience in *Tars and Spars* and his appearance on Broadway in *Make Mine Manhattan* would be formative in developing and refining his innate gifts for comedy. He would always be at heart a theatrical actor. His skills in sketch and physical comedy and pantomime could be wasted in a smaller room with a smaller audience. Although he had briefly played nightclubs successfully before *Your Show of Shows* (and would occasionally do them during the show's run), he was never going to be the kind of club comedian with rapid-fire "but seriously folks" delivery. His act was always characterization comedy; jokes and one-liners weren't his style. And Caesar and stand-up were never going to be a good match: being himself was always difficult.

Live television would be the medium in which he thrived and one in which he could display his talents fully. He was the first genuine television comedian. He used the skills he had developed as a comic actor in theatre, but realized the potential for comedy on TV, adapting to it quickly and making it his own. Many comedians with far more experience were uncomfortable with or apprehensive about the demands of live TV. Bob Hope, in his first television appearance in 1950 on *Star Spangled Revue* (directed incidentally by Max Liebman), was visibly nervous and relied almost exclusively on cue cards.[24] Caesar was comfortable playing on camera from the beginning and never relied on them. Even more important, he adjusted to the smaller venue of television. He could play it broad (some TV comics with vaudeville experience like Berle or Jerry Lester never went beyond that), but also learned to scale it down: "You have to. The camera's right in front of you. That's who you play to—not the last row of the Pantages."[25] He also knew where the cameras were—and where he wanted them to be. Greg Garrison, one of *Your Show of Shows*' television directors, remembered that during his monologues, "Sid didn't want the cameras to be mobile. He felt—correctly—that if you move a camera while he is performing, the audience peripherally will watch the camera, not him."[26]

However, one element of theatrical acting that always remained with him was the discipline of staying in character. It meant that, in refreshing contrast to some major comedians on '50s TV, he never upstaged fellow actors or used (or abused) guest stars in sketches for laughs, as Milton Berle was prone to do. Nor would he ever halt the flow of a sketch by turning to the audience, waiting for a laugh, as Red Skelton frequently did. He refused to break character no matter how funny or absurd the situation in

9. Caesar as Comic Actor   135

a sketch, and he insisted that everyone else do the same. Caesar disliked "corpsing," unscripted laughing onstage particularly at one's own performance. The practice has its defenders. Sid was not among them: "It was like a 'No Smoking' rule—no laughing on stage.... I think it's phony to laugh at your own jokes."[27] You can count on one hand, with four digits left over, the number of times he violated the No Laughing Rule on *Your Show of Shows*. Even on the rare occasions when he began to smile (as he and Imogene were looking at each other after a particularly funny situation or as he looked down at a disheveled Howie Morris, whom he and Coca have just dismantled), he immediately suppressed it by turning his head or rubbing the side of his nose to disguise it, then it was back to the serious business of comedy.

At times it must have been difficult to exercise that kind of control. Never more so than in the beach scene from the parody of *From Here to Eternity* where he and Coca are drenched with buckets of water. Imogene inhaled just as the first water hit and thought, "Oh my God, I'm going to drown in front of all these people." It struck her as funny and she had to bite her lip to keep from breaking up. To make matters worse, after several more dousings, Sid then ad-libbed "Kinda rough tonight, ain't it?" She recalled, laughing, "I needed that like a hole in the head," and turned her head into his shoulder to keep control.[28] Obviously amused by Coca's reaction to his ad-lib, Caesar almost loses his own control. Because he was now in a close-up, he couldn't turn his head and had to struggle mightily, blinking and looking upward, to keep a straight face.

Only once on *Your Show of Shows* did he laugh spontaneously. Not surprisingly, it was prompted by Coca. In a parody of a French film (2/10/51), he is a Parisian thief who has made off with a bag of money. Back in his apartment with his lover Imogene, he's standing watch at a window in case the police are in pursuit. Meanwhile, she begins stuffing the money into the top of her dress, which begins to acquire not only a spectacular bust-line but '40s-style shoulder pads. Turning from the window, as Sid catches sight of Imogene, now looking like a combination of Jayne Mansfield and a pocket Joan Crawford, he bursts out laughing. It wouldn't happen again (at least in the 140 or so episodes that can be seen today). "Caesar laughs" in a sketch was almost the TV comedy equivalent of "Garbo laughs" in film and was just as unexpected (and probably surprising for the writers, who regarded him as the comedic equivalent of a Stoic).

Besides his staying in character, his ability to portray emotions convincingly made him a superb comic actor. They would also serve him well in a variety of sketches in which he did more than just comedy. The *Caesar's Hour* silent movie sketch was not a one-off; he would do a number of them on *Your Show of Shows* as well, "The Drunkard" and "The Sewing Machine

Girl" for example. These were first-rate recreated comic versions of the real silent films, with accompanying piano music and, usually, title cards. The cast excelled in their replication of the heightened emotions and exaggerated gestures and facial expressions of the silents. When you watch Caesar in particular, whose mobile face and expressive eyes were made for the pathos as well as the broad comedy of the genre, it occurs to you that, if he had been born several decades earlier, he would have made an excellent silent film actor.

However, it was in the regular sketches on *Your Show of Shows*, especially the parodies, that you see the full range of his acting skills. Unfortunately, some of the best examples can't be seen widely today. Unfortunately, because in them he could be both a subtle and sensitive actor. The straight bits were usually brief (they occurred, of course, within sketches that were comedic), but what he did in them using his facial expressions, body language, a look, or just his voice could be remarkable. Caesar had very quickly intuited that on television you can play an emotion naturally, and he became expert at it. He could not only convey emotion in his facial expressions, which you would expect, but also when just listening to or looking at other actors; he could convey it especially with his eyes, which reflected a character's anger, happiness, or pain (and no one did pain as convincingly as Sid—he made it palpable). And that ability to shift back to comedy from drama made his performances distinctive. It's one thing to play an entire sketch straight or to play it strictly for comedy. But to switch from one to the other in the same sketch a number of times—and do it convincingly—is something else again.

His instincts in playing straight were almost always dead-on. For example, in "Das Vorgessenor Symphony," a sketch performed twice on the show and done entirely in German double-talk, Sid is an impoverished composer, struggling to complete his masterwork. He's supported by his loyal and self-sacrificing wife Hilda, played by Imogene. Just how supportive she is, he realizes when he notices she isn't wearing her wedding ring. To his dismay, she tells him (in an inspired bit of faux German), "Ich habe es gehockt" so that they can afford bread. When he finally finishes his symphony in a burst of energy and emotion, he staggers offstage. Unbeknownst to him, his friend (Carl Reiner) discovers it and arranges for it to be played. Wandering outside the symphony hall, he hears its strains. Thinking that the music must be in his head, he then realizes "Das ist Meine Musik!" (and here he plays his bewildered and half-crazed character very well). He bursts into the box where Reiner and Coca sit listening to the performance. Carl halts the music and announces that the composer will conduct his own symphony. The script called for Sid to cry as he conducts.[29] And in the first version of the sketch, he does. When it was repeated (4/26/52), that's not the way he performed the sequence on air. After embracing Coca, he looks at her (and that look is absolutely piercing), kisses her hands, takes the stage and accepts the baton. Rather than crying, and far more effectively, he permits his voice to break only slightly as he declares, "Für Sie, Hilda [then with a slight beat to return to comedy]—und die gehockte wedding ring." The audience, after watching several minutes of absolutely straight acting in silence, now laughs. And from pathos to comedy, Sid never breaks character.

In "I'm in Love" (10/17/53), a mixture of *The Blue Angel* and *Of Human Bondage* (you can never say the sketches weren't eclectic), Caesar is a Heidelberg professor who has a "psychological brain theory" that immediately calls into question the validity of German scientific degrees: "The brain is the head of the whole shooting match. Don't listen to your heart—it's just a bum. The brain is the topkick of the whole outfit." On the basis of his "research," he's been invited by a fellow scholar (Carl Reiner) to address the British Academy of Sciences. In a bar at the railway station where they are to catch a train for London, he forgets his theory entirely as he immediately falls for Ivy, a waitress (Imogene Coca doing her best slattern). The train and Reiner leave without him, and abandonment of his career and his self-respect promptly ensue.

The sketch has, as usual, sharp and funny dialogue: The professor asks Ivy to go out with him, pulling out a wad of money. He suggests going to a movie. She wants to know what's playing. Maybe she'd like a new hat. She's not sure, but she could use some stockings. As it dawns on her that this is the mark of a lifetime, she notes that "Mother does need an operation." He asks somewhat plaintively, "We start with that so soon?" She finally announces that she already has a date. Giving it one last try, he suggests, "Maybe you got a kid brother who wants to go to camp?" However, good as he almost always was in sketches, Caesar could occasionally overplay a comic character. This was one of those occasions: there's too much of "The Professor" in his Heidelberg professor and his playing is at times uncomfortably broad. However, there's a segment where he plays it straight, very effectively, then follows with the usual comic coda, also very effectively. Of course, the better the performance of the dramatic part, the funnier the abrupt switch—and here, both parts are done perfectly.

The professor's infatuation with Ivy has led to his losing his position at Heidelberg and reduced him to a menial job in the bar where he met her, and he's squandered what money he has on Ivy's whims. After she cruelly rejects his marriage proposal, laughing at him, light finally dawns that she's only been interested in his money all along. His degradation is complete, and he throws himself into a chair at a table with a how-has-my-life-come-to-this expression. He laments, "Everything is gone. She laughed at me. No money, no friends, everything is gone. What is left?" He buries his head in his hands, then after a pause, slowly lifts it. The camera in a close-up shot follows his marvelously expressive eyes, which reflect his desperation, as he looks slowly upward to a chandelier on the ceiling. There's a brief full-shot, in which his look changes to one of sudden determination. He rises, gets a rope, and, standing on the chair, ties one end of it to the chandelier. You and the audience (you can actually hear murmurs from it) know what he's going to do. Surely he won't—but by this point, he's sold the character's hopelessness so completely, you wonder if you're about to see something truly different on live TV. He picks up the other end of the rope but, instead of making a noose with it, yanks on it, sending the whole thing crashing to the floor. At this point, you wonder what's going to occur. Comedy does. Climbing down from the chair, he picks up the chandelier, rope still attached, announces with perfect timing, "I could hock this and get a coupla bucks," and exits stage left.

The audience reaction to Caesar's segues from comic to serious was a measure of his success. There's no sense of a shift of mental gears, as in "is he being serious now?" And when he does move from one to the other, the audience follows him as they would any dramatic actor on stage. This is apparent in one of the best straight bits he ever did, in a sketch performed on January 10, 1953. It was a parody of the 1937 version of *A Star Is Born*, with Fredric March and Janet Gaynor, called (and here the writers weren't trying very hard) "Birth of a Star." Caesar is the Norman Maine character, Rod Rodney, Hollywood's brightest light, who gives an unknown, Mary Sweet (Coca), her big break in one of his films. They fall in love and marry, but rather than becoming movies' greatest team, her star rapidly eclipses his. She is now "America's Sweetheart," and his career has tanked. To make matters worse, she wins the "Oswald Award."

What follows is the big scene in all the versions of *A Star Is Born* where the actor crashes the awards ceremony, drunk. In the film, March inserts a bit of sarcastic humor, demanding an Oscar for bad acting, and slightly overplays the drunkenness (for that matter, so does James Mason in the 1954 remake, who enters as an initially genial drunk who then pathetically asks for a role). So, how do you play him in a straight bit, in a parody no less? Other comedians might have gone for the stereotypical drunk; interestingly, the script called for just that [Sid enters, plastered] and has him practically unable to get his name out.[30] That's not how he played it and, considering that he stuck to the script for much of the rest of the sketch, he demonstrably made the bit his own. Sid, if anything, underplays it. He reels slightly in his entrance, after shrugging off the security guards who are trying to restrain him, but from that point, there's no staggering or exaggerated slurring of words, just the halting and disconnected speech of a drunk.

And that brief speech is one delivered with anger and resentment, with no humor whatever, until there's a conscious break to insert it. Just to add a degree of difficulty, he plays most of that portion of the scene with his back to the camera, his face in only slight profile. Almost all of the emotion is conveyed with his voice:

"What's going on here? What is it? They're throwing you a party, honey? They made you a star, huh?" [Mary's producer, appalled, says, "You're drunk!" He responds quietly and devastatingly, "I know it"]. "They gave you the Oswald. Lemme see it. I got a dozen of these—they don't mean a thing [throws it on the floor]. The public—what do they know? One day they give you the Oswald, the next day they throw mud in your face. You forget. [voice rising] You *all* forget! [Then, as the camera shifts to a close-up, an almost startling break into comedy] *I* was once America's Sweetheart. With the curls and everything." [Then, just as quickly, back to playing straight.] Waving his arm wildly, he accidentally hits Mary. Mortified by what he has done, he says softly and abjectly, "I'm sorry, Mary. I'm really very sorry.... Forgive me, Mary, please."

Caesar's shifts from playing it straight to getting a laugh (and the audience gives it to him—the lines and his delivery of them *are* funny) and then back to straight are not only effective, but almost split-second. And in his slight underplaying and his affecting, rather than pathetic, portrayal of his character, it's acting within comedy at its best. In moments like these, there was no other comic actor on TV who could match him. Sid was once asked in an interview if he had any desire to play serious roles. His answer was simple and direct: "No. There are much better actors around than me."[31] Not in '50s comedy, there weren't.

A more familiar part of his acting range, and one entirely comedic, is better known today—his remarkable talent for doubletalk, a form of verbal comedy in which nonsense words are mixed with real ones. Audiences could hear it in English, for example from Al Kelly or Danny Kaye; and Chaplin would use a mixture of French and Italian gibberish in a song in the otherwise silent *Modern Times* (1936) and faux German in a speech in *The Great Dictator* (1940).[32] Sid's doubletalk was of a different sort and was really in a class by itself. He did it exclusively in foreign languages, none of which he knew or spoke. He mimicked their sounds and would also throw in real words of whatever language he was imitating (which might or might not make sense in the context). English was interjected for exposition or comic effect. For example, interviewing Coca for a job in a bakery in a rapid stream of faux French, then pausing with a Gallic head slap: "Mon Dieu! Your social security number?" This mélange was not only entertaining but convincing: there are people who view the sketch today and assume he knew French. He didn't. Nor was his use of doubletalk only an occasional part of his comedy; it was featured in over 50 foreign film sketches on *Your Show of Shows* as well as in a number of monologues and "roving reporter" bits in which Caesar was the foreign interviewee.

Carl Reiner did doubletalk very well, Howie Morris could do a bit of it, Imogene Coca not at all. She never picked up the knack and her forays into foreign languages were obviously memorized, although, as usual, she managed to make them funny. No matter the degree of talent among the rest of the cast, however, none had Caesar's skill and range, as Reiner would later acknowledge. On *The Admiral Broadway Revue* and *Your Show of Shows*, Sid did doubletalk in German, French, Russian, Italian, Spanish, and Arabic (or at least some convincingly Semitic-sounding version). And he would add Japanese to his repertoire on *Caesar's Hour* in spoofs of samurai films. Although his Russian and Italian were very good, German and French were arguably his best and what he could do with them was amazing; he could keep up French doubletalk for entire 10-minute sketches in which, as usual, he had the majority of the "dialogue." Or, really going above and beyond the usual, he would *mutter* to himself in faux German. He could also mimic the rhythm of German very well, at times even suggesting the typical placement of a verb at the end of a sentence. As a German composer in one sketch, Caesar tells an orchestra how to play his symphony. His instructions are heartfelt, detailed—and total gibberish. If you know a bit of German, you're left thinking that Sid's version of it *should* make sense, even if it doesn't.

Where did his skill come from? Caesar always maintained that he picked it up as a young boy listening to the various languages spoken by the immigrant workers who frequented his father's Yonkers diner. His imitations made them laugh and also got the approval and attention of his mother

The man in front of the curtain: Caesar in mid-monologue (Getty Images).

and father, something he was always seeking as a child. The latter would have been encouragement enough for him to continue and refine them. (He could also have conceivably picked up the rhythms and sounds of Russian from his Odessa-born mother.) There was also another contributing factor—he had a very good ear. He had begun to play the saxophone at an early age and would develop considerable skill at it, and his talents for both music and mimicry reinforced each other. It's no coincidence that Sid would later describe his learning of other language sounds in terms of music: "Every language has its own song and its own rhythm."[33] Whatever the origins of his skill at doubletalk, it's one of the aspects of his comedy that was unique and that people tend to remember, deservedly so.

Another aspect of his comic acting is less well known. Today, Sid is usually associated with double-talk, the Professor, or sketch comedy like the parodies or the Hickenloopers. However, as skilled as Caesar was in all of these, it would be in his monologues that he could display all of his considerable talents. Yet, in recent written accounts and retrospectives of *Your Show of Shows,* his solo performances are not mentioned a great deal—or sometimes at all. For a good reason: there aren't a lot of them that can be widely seen. Fortunately, you can see some very good ones: "Five Dollar Date" (although that was from the *Admiral Broadway Revue*), "Boy at First Dance" and a few other pantomimes, and the Airplane Number. But they aren't examples of the type of monologues he did most often nor do they begin to suggest their variety or Caesar's comic range in performing them. There *is* one major exception to the relative lack of description of Sid's solos: Ted Sennett's *Your Show of Shows* devotes half of one chapter to them, for the same reason I'm writing about them here—he saw a lot of Caesar's monologues on Max Liebman's kinescopes and I've seen close to 70 of them that are available at the Paley Center in New York. The writers referred to them as Sid's "Specialties," and they are indeed special. The more of them you see, the greater your appreciation of just how superb a comic actor he was.

It's almost easier to describe the monologues in terms of what they were not: they were not stand-up routines nor did they feature a lot of jokes or one-liners. The comedy, and its frequent brilliance, came from Caesar's characterizations and his skills in physical comedy, timing, and, above all, his intensity and immersion into those characters. Other TV comedians at the time did comic characters, Jackie Gleason and Red Skelton, for example. But as usual, Sid's characterizations were a bit different. They were not pegged to one distinct character like Gleason's Reginald Van Gleason III or Rudy the Repairman or Skelton's Clem Kadiddlehopper. (He already had one of that sort, the Professor). Nor did his characters interact with real people, as Gleason and Skelton's often did. His monologues were genuine solos—he appeared on a bare stage in front of the curtain, the only occasional physical prop a straight-backed chair, which served as a bed, bench, or, obviously, a chair. He supplied any others with mime. And he could "people" the bits if called for by using different voices and facial expressions or just by looking at and reacting to "them."

Caesar's ability to literally lose himself in his characters' interactions with those imaginary "others" was demonstrated—startlingly—in a monologue from April 19, 1952, "Dance Hall Stag." In it, he is a man looking for a partner at a dance. As usual, it's a funny solo, but partway through it, something surprising happens—and it hasn't lost its capacity to surprise, some 60 years later. He's rejected in his first attempt: "Hello! ... Goodbye! ... Where'd she go?" His bewilderment is humorous, but then the comedy disappears. Shooting the departing woman an icy look, he responds to the snub by indignantly saying to her, "You think you're so hot? You're not so hot!" His reaction is the first indication that this is someone who does not take an impolite turndown easily—and makes what follows, while certainly unexpected, plausible. Gathering himself and looking around, he finds another prospect. He inquires politely, "May I have this dance?" You don't hear the response of course, but it must be an extremely rude one because the look on Sid's face in reaction to it is one of surprise; then almost instantaneously, his eyes flash with alarmingly cold anger. As he tells her "and this is for YOU—double!" he thrusts his right hand sideways and upward, with, yes, his middle finger slightly extended beyond the rest. The gesture is quick but unmistakable and the audience reaction is immediate: surprised laughter, and an undertone of "ooohs" and murmurs of the "did I just see that!?" variety. The reaction is understandable (you just didn't *do* that on live TV in the '50s), but what is striking is Caesar's lack of reaction to that of the audience. He's so immersed in his furious character, he's oblivious to it. He's totally focused in the moment, never breaking eye contact with the woman who has rejected him. He even ups the ante by backing away, then making a fist and inquiring, "You wanna make something of it?" He does some boxing footwork that, after what has preceded it, comes as genuine comic relief, as you see his anger dissipate. He then goes on to more successful attempts to get a dance.

The gesture, the ultimate non-verbal expression of anger and contempt, couldn't have been scripted—obviously. For that matter, when sketches were developed in the Writers' Room, Sid insisted on excluding anything controversial.[34] So why in the world would Caesar do something that clearly was just that? It was totally out of character for him in his comedy performances. But that's the point: *he* didn't make that gesture, the enraged *character* he had become did. His absorption into his characters and their emotions could be so complete it's entirely possible to believe that it didn't even register with him that he had just flipped off someone, albeit an imaginary someone, on live TV. You can almost imagine a conversation backstage afterward: "Uh, Sid? Do you know that you...?" Such total immersion into a character was the norm for him. (As the reluctant guest on a spoof of *This Is Your Life*, he ran down the aisles of the theater to escape the ushers attempting to get him on stage. In the process, he actually threw a punch at one of them, something he later had to be told about—he didn't remember doing it.) Nonetheless, it would never again be illustrated quite as it was in that memorable monologue. But Furious Man—and his furious gesture—were (perhaps thankfully) atypical of Sid's characters.

So who—or sometimes more appropriately, what—was he in the monologues? He could be practically anybody. And sometimes everybody—in his solo movie parodies he could play all the characters, from two or three to double-digit. Or he could be practically any*thing*. From the inanimate—a penny chewing gum machine, a pinball, or a whitewall tire—to the nonhuman—the family dog or a housefly. Or in one memorable bit of March 11, 1950, a very small human—a six month-old baby observing life. The physical comedy of it is absolutely first-rate: imploring his inept father to "Hold my head! Hold my head!" as his unsupported neck rolls backward, being jounced back and forth between relatives, and forced to walk while his father holds his hands. Staggering, with legs splayed at various angles, and dragging his feet, he complains with exasperation, "I gotta walk because the neighbor's kid is walking.... And he's 10!"

However, in most of his monologues, he was a comedy Everyman, going through life stages or just coping with everyday situations and confronting daily challenges, all familiar to any audience, but played with, as Caesar put it, "just that little one step crossover from the everyday to the ridiculous."[35] He was a Man Coming Down with a Cold, a Man Who Can't Fall Asleep, or a Man Trying to Cope with His In-Laws. In his intro to a bit, he would describe the situation, then frequently conclude with "Here he is." And there, with a momentary pause to assume the character, he would be—usually put upon or frustrated, slightly cynical about what life threw at him, sometimes introspective, sometimes frantic, generally resigned to the absurdity of life—and always funny.

His monologue was usually the last comedy segment of the show, after the 45 minutes or so of sketches or pantomimes that came before, all of which he was in. Sometimes, the only prolonged break he would get would be Coca's preceding musical number, and at that point, would often be damp with sweat when he came out for his solo segment. Nonetheless, he would then throw himself into it with just as much of, if not more than, his usual intensity.

In the run of *Your Show of Shows*, Caesar would do 71 different monologues. Some were repeated, although rarely in exactly the same way; some were done only once, including some of his best. And, until the last season, he did one every week. You might pause to reread those last three sentences and consider what that meant in terms of writing and performance after minimal rehearsal time. Bert Lahr, the great revue comic and Cowardly Lion, once did—and said, "It's impossible."[36] Well, it was possible, and although not all the monologues were brilliant and a very few were pedestrian (at least for Sid), his comedy batting average was a remarkable one.

Some of the monologues contain the offbeat humor Caesar and the writers delighted in. "You're a Man Now" (4/29/50) has him taking his little boy to his first day of school and having the kind of conference with the school principal that all educators dread (in this case, with good reason): "Just a few things I want to tell you. You can't say no to a child all the time. Don't do this, don't do that—you'll give him a complex. So I gave in to him over a little thing—he carries a knife." Reassuringly, maybe, he goes on, "I took the point off and dulled it a little." In "Asking for a Raise" (3/25/50), his character tries out various scenarios that he hopes will be successful with his boss. One is the sympathetic approach: "I haven't eaten in three days. I have lots of expenses, my kid went crazy in a candy store and the whole house is full of jelly beans. On top of that, my wife did a very foolish thing—she paid the rent.... And I'm going to have a baby."

Domestic situations—and their woes—were always fertile subjects for monologues. One in particular—stewing after an argument with his wife—is also a good example of the usual comic twists and misdirection in the writing and performing of them. It starts with Caesar trying to get to sleep in the aftermath of such an argument (10/14/50). After flinging himself into 12 different positions in "bed" (this is more impressive if you know that he's doing it on a straight-backed chair) without success, he launches into an exasperated tirade: "What argument am I working on? Case #5,094: Her Mother! She says I'm making a slave out of her, making her scrub floors on her knees, making her lose her looks, I don't give her my whole paycheck, that I put it in my pocket and I go get drunk with a bunch of bums. [Beat. Then, with puzzlement] How did she find out?" Reviewing the course of the argument, he decides, "That's what I should have said: What man goes out and breaks his neck to make a living making money for food, shelter, and clothes? [Increasing the decibels] Yeah! What man goes out and breaks his neck to make a living making money for food, shelter, and clothes? [Consideration] Everybody."

Then there are the important moments in a man's life, like proposing to his girl (10/7/50). Deciding that the direct approach might not be the most effective, his character rehearses several alternatives, first a romantic

9. Caesar as Comic Actor

one: "I'll take her out, go to one of those foreign restaurants with the atmosphere and the low light. Sure. Order a big meal, a wonderful meal with wonderful wine. And just at the right moment—the music is playing and the hour is a little late and the candles have burned down quite low, and she's dead drunk.... I'll ask her." Dismissing that one—"No, I can't do that. What's wrong with you?"—he decides to convince her that she's the most important thing in the world and, if he can't have her, nothing else is worthwhile: "Doris, you are a queen and I am but a slave. You are the moon and I but a tiny star beside you. You are the soft breeze that blows over the vast oceans, and I am but a pebble on the beach. You are everything, life itself. [With a dramatic downward sweep of his arms] I am nothing.... So you better get another guy."

The monologues could also showcase Caesar's talents for mime and sound effects. In one of October 4, 1952, he is a man afraid of, and with phobias about, everything. On entering his apartment, after nervously looking around him, he steps in, and closes the door. Then slides three dead bolts across it to secure it, spins a wheel lock, hammers several boards across the door, turns on an electric eye, and greets his barking guard dog (so huge he has to reach up to pet it). Only then does he feel secure enough to take out the gun he's been carrying, open the chamber, check for bullets, spin it, and snap it shut—then does the same with four more. And he supplies first-rate sound effects for all the precautions he takes. After a sleepless night, he decides he has to conquer his phobias, starting with leaving his building: "Today, I'm going through the revolving door." Mustering up enough courage to finally pick a space and get into it, he can't muster up enough courage to get out. His miming of being stuck in it, going round and round, his hands pressed against the bar, is belly-laugh funny. The inevitable happens: "Hiya mister! Gee, you're in here with me? Listen, you want to get me out? Take me out the next time you go around." This proves successful, as he's finally freed from the door and flung out onto the sidewalk. And can go off to his job as a lion-tamer.

If you watch a number of Caesar's monologues, you can discern patterns in their content and also in Sid's performance techniques. The monologues were basically little playlets, with each self-contained segment building up to a comic conclusion. Although Caesar could, and did, tinker with elements of a monologue, he stuck to its structural outline and didn't meander—he couldn't. He had 6–10 minutes in which to set up the sketch, perform it, get laughs, and get off stage. His exits were usually quick, because what almost always followed his monologue was the big production number that closed the show. Running over meant running the risk of the finale being cut off before its conclusion, something unthinkable, at least to Max Liebman. This additional element of pressure makes his sense of timing even more impressive. It's difficult to imagine that there were not times when the show was behind schedule by the time he went on stage, and there are occasions where he indeed seems to be editing on his feet, leaving out scripted parts or condensing others.

The technique by which he got through the monologues' content might seem a trivial topic, until you consider the sheer amount of material and memorization involved. Vaudeville routines, once learned and practiced, could see a comic through months, if not years, of performance for different audiences on the circuit. Sid did different monologues on a weekly basis, with limited rehearsal time, for a TV audience of millions. Besides having an obviously good memory, he used a method—and aid—for getting through their structure. It's one of the oldest in a monologists' toolbox, going back to ancient oral story-telling—the repetition of phrases or brief interjections to move from one part of a story to the next or within a particular segment. In this case, the interjections were distinctly 20th-century American: "Sure…. That's all…. What are you gonna do? … That's the way…." They could be used not only as segues but provide spaces in which to gather himself mentally. Their repetition could be made funny by Caesar's delivery and their addition in performance made his speech sound more naturalistic than just sticking to a written script.

Another form of repetition was distinctive of his solo comedy in general. The writers referred to it as Sid's "drilling down." You can also think of it in terms of an oxymoron, creative repetition: repeating the same phrases or actions, with slight variations or emphasis. It was a risky approach—at what point do you lose an audience?—but it generally worked and was funny because the repetition had a pay-off. You can see it in his solo pantomimes: in one he first did on *The Admiral Broadway Revue*, a woman puts on a dress, pulls up a zipper on one side, then the other, then progresses to zippers on the front, back, diagonal, and, improbably, a circular one in the middle. Then completes the process, after endless zipping, by fastening a few buttons at the top. Or a man tying a tie, which involves a good sixty seconds of endless adjustment of the ends for evenness, flinging them over his shoulder, looping them, and adjusting the knot so it's just perfect. Finally ripping off his creation because he can't get it quite right, he starts all over—and does it perfectly in about four seconds. And you can hear it in his monologues: in "The Jealous Husband" (9/9/50), he arrives home to find that, for the first time in seven years, his wife isn't there to greet him. In several wonderfully modulated minutes, Caesar ascends from mildly suspicious to crazed—she must be having an affair with his best friend Jim. On the verge of total mania, he exclaims, "*Now* I see! Now I *see*! I see *now*!" And gets laughs with each variant of the phrase.

Among his best monologues, and perhaps not coincidentally the longest (he could fully develop the character), are "Man at the Bar" and "A New Leaf." Although very different in situation and performance (another indication of his comic range), both are classic Caesar solos. In them, you can also see elements of his characteristic repetition.

Sid would do "Man at the Bar" twice on *Your Show of Shows* and in each version, he departed somewhat from the script, leaving out bits or extending others.[37] The first version was funny, but the second, performed on April 11, 1953, after he had fine-tuned his performance of the monologue, was a *tour de force*. He's in that titular bar, getting progressively, hilariously, and at times frighteningly, drunk. In the course of the sketch, he has not just one too many, but six too many. As he downs seven shots, the reaction takes, as expected, are first-rate (the best is simply a poleaxed look as the alcohol hits), as is the physical comedy as he gets progressively sloshed. At one point, he throws one shot back—onto the side of his face instead of into his mouth ("Oh, I'm all right, George," he assures the bartender)—and later has to manually adjust his booze-paralyzed tongue so he can speak more or less coherently.

Above all, he captures the stages of drunkenness superbly, as he moves from one to the next with each drink. At first, he's the Genial Drunk, telling everyone about taking his wife and kids to the park. Another shot, and he becomes Surly Drunk: "You're all a bunch of bums. You won't take your kids on a picnic. Get away from me. The little woman is home cooking supper. She can't even reach the top of the stove. Why don't you marry someone your own size?" Another shot, and he's Maudlin Drunk: "Life has passed me by. Time just went tick, tock. I'm all tocked out. Know what I could've been? I could've been an airplane pilot." (Or, as he struggles to get the words out, "An air-hair-hair-plane pilot") He then spreads his arms and begins to fly around the room—"Flaps down on Runway Number 4!"—and lands, of course, at the bar: "I'll have another, George."

And in the best, he becomes the Drunk You Least Want to be Cornered By: "Artie, I like you. You're a swell fella. How long have I known you? I want to ask you a personal question. And if you don't want to answer, don't give it another thought. Just wipe it off your mind. I don't want to butt into your personal affairs. I won't get offended. I'm not trying to be a busybody. You don't have to answer me if you don't want to.... So, ask me anything, and if I don't want to answer it, I won't. I won't be offended. What's the question? [He pauses for a beat, during which you and the audience catch on to what he's just done] You haven't got a question, Artie? You're wasting my time then, aren't you?" [Sits back with a beatific, drunken smile].

In the next stage, he's Pugnacious Drunk. Noticing a commotion in one corner of the bar, he asks "What's the diff ... disc ... (searching for a more than two-syllable word he can get out and giving up). ... What's going on over there?" Someone has taken a regular's seat and won't relinquish it. Lurching over, he announces "That's his stool—off!" Encountering resistance, he says, "Oh, so that's the way you want it." In preparation for the fight to come, he goes to spit on his hands—and is so stewed by this point that he spits before he can get them together. Nothing daunted, he throws the intruder out and declares triumphantly, "She won't bother you any more, Harry." Dimly realizing it's late, he asks George for a cup of black coffee, downs it, and, instantaneously cold sober, wishes everyone a good night—"See you gentlemen tomorrow—Taxi!"

In its range of comic acting, perfect timing, and great physical comedy, "Man in a Bar" is among the most impressive monologues Caesar ever did. As is "A New Leaf" (10/8/1950), one of the best examples of Sid absolutely losing himself in his Everyman character, as he confronts his mortality and realizes he may have wasted his life. As he gets into each segment of the monologue, particularly at the end, the script becomes only a point of departure, as he adds lines and adlibs and repeats phrases, drilling down into the situation, before the payoff:

> I'm going to turn over a new leaf. You never know what's going to happen. Like the earth smashing into another planet. Boom! Like that. A little thing like that and it's all over....
> Sure! I know what's I'm going to do—I'll buy a farm. That's the life. Get up at 4 o'clock in the morning, go down, clean out the whole barn, get the horses out in the field, till the soil, plow that field, rebuild your fences. That's the life. When it gets dark, you take those fences in, you carry the horses back, you pull in the tractor. When it's 8 o'clock, after dinner, you feel that honest tired feeling, that wonderful pain in your back, those beautiful blisters on your hands. You're a wreck—you can't breathe, you can't move—you're dead! Who needs it?!
> I'm a city guy. I'm a guy from the city. I gotta do mad, crazy, impulsive things—things I always wanted to do, things I would never dream of doing before. I'll send money to my mother. What am I talking about? My mother lives with us. That's it! You hear that word "us?" I never said that before. *Us.* It was always me, me, me, me. I never brought anything home for the family. Nothing. From now on, I'm not coming home empty-handed. I'll bring them something—a box of cigars, a rifle, a bottle of whiskey. Something for the house.... [As he reaches the end, his delivery gets faster and faster, and you're watching someone work himself into something very close to a comedy stream of consciousness.]
> After that, I'll go out, get in my car, shoot down that highway. Just me alone. Get that relaxed feeling. Who cares where, what, when? Feel a little hungry, stop off at a little diner, get something, back in the car, shoot down that highway. Drive—that's the way. Love thy neighbor. Say hello to your fellow man. Hiya, Farmer Grey. Hiya, Farmer Brown. Look, there's a boy, wants a hitchhike. Love thy neighbor. Sure, pull over the car, stop—"You bum, why don't you get a job? I worked for this car!" Shoot down the highway, that's the way to be—unchain yourself from that desk. Twenty years at a desk. Why? *Why*? For what? *For what*? What do I have to show for it? Where's all the money? *Where's all the money*? ... In the bank! And that's where it's going to stay. Sure. And I'm 5 minutes late for work now. I gotta get going!

Of course, any description or recapitulation of his monologues can only suggest the amazing energy and intensity he puts into them. Sennett summed it up well: "Alone on stage, with his entire physical being involved in a specific situation, he was at his most riveting, his most memorable."[38]

When you review the body of Caesar's work on *Your Show of Shows*— the sketches, the monologues, the pantomime—and his incredible comic skills, you can understand why Carol Burnett, then just starting her career in New York, gave up tickets to a hot Broadway show to stay home and watch Caesar live—"if you missed one of Sid's shows, it was gone forever."[39]

Of course, they weren't just "Sid's shows." He had superb material supplied by extraordinarily gifted writers and superb players to work with in Imogene Coca, Carl Reiner, and Howie Morris. It was a marvelous instance in television history when a number of giant talents meshed at one time on one show produced and directed by one of early TV's best impresarios, Max Liebman. However, having given credit where it is certainly due, after viewing most of its episodes, you reach an inescapable conclusion: Caesar was the indispensable straw that stirred the drink. Without him, *Your Show of Shows* wouldn't, and couldn't, have been the success it was. What he did, live, for over 30 weeks a season, over 5 seasons, was extraordinary. Not just in its quantity, although that too was staggering—when people see individual sketches today, and with only a few exceptions that's all that can be seen, they might not realize he was in *every* comedy sketch in every episode. Above all, it was extraordinary in its quality—there was simply no comedian in '50s television as multi-talented as Sid.

Howie Morris, in an interview given eighteen years after *Your Show of Shows* ended, reflected: "Somewhere in that marvelous and troubled man was a drive and an instinct, a kind of satiric creativity I can't quite explain."[40] Anyone who has seen Caesar in his prime *can* explain it—he was a comic genius.

PART IV
The End of *Your Show of Shows*

10

"Well, this was it"

Of course, it wasn't going to last forever. Ratings had declined; by 1953, the show was no longer in the top ten. There were also rumors of dissension in the Triumvirate, contemporary newspapers' shorthand term for Liebman, Caesar, and Coca (no one then, or later, could resist Caesarean references). By early 1954, speculation was widespread among TV columnists that the show was ending. And on February 25, 1954, appropriately the month and day on which the program had debuted four years before, the speculation became fact. Pat Weaver, NBC president, announced that the Triumvirate would come to an end. *Your Show of Shows* would not be back for the 1954-55 season. It was not cancelled; rather, continuing with a Caesarian theme, it, like Gaul, was divided into three parts—Liebman would do "spectaculars," as specials were then called, and Caesar and Coca would have their own separate shows, all to be aired on NBC. According to Weaver, "the new plans arose from mutual understanding and the desire of each of them to go forward to still greater attainments in their own shows."[1]

However, the mood at the news conference with Max, Sid, and Imogene that followed, held in Liebman's offices in City Center, was hardly celebratory. One report described Coca as "bawling like a baby" and Caesar as "looking pale, glum, and a little sick to his stomach." Liebman tried to put the best face on it, insisting, despite all visual evidence to the contrary, "this is a happy occasion." He commented that "these things are natural developments in show business. It seems sometimes the best way to carry on in a creative manner," and urged his stars to put on happier faces for the camera (which they eventually did).[2]

That was how the announcement was made, but Weaver's statement, particularly the "mutual understanding" and "desire of each of them for their own shows" parts, would be later contradicted by one member of the former Triumvirate. Imogene Coca always maintained that she had been blindsided when she was summoned to the room full of reporters and photographers for a conference and announcement she hadn't expected. Her agent had told her of rumors that the show was ending, but when she asked

Preparations for the opener of the show's last season of 1953-54 in a much heralded revised format—which lasted for only one month (1953). Left to right: Judy Johnson, Carl Reiner, Imogene Coca, Lily Pons, Sid Caesar, Max Liebman (Sam Falk/The NewYorkTimes/Redux).

Liebman and Caesar about its fate, they (and here her accounts vary) were either noncommittal or told her they would get together to talk about it. When she was asked by a reporter how she felt about the show ending, "That's the first I knew about it. Like an idiot, I broke into tears." A photograph accompanying the *Daily News*' coverage shows her dabbing her nose with a handkerchief, visibly upset. She later admitted, however, that "there were people pushing me to have my own show," but "I needed a show like I needed a hole in the head."[3]

Pat Weaver, in his memoir of his career in radio and television, identified her agent, Deborah Coleman, as the one doing the pushing: "She was determined to have Imogene split with Sid Caesar and launch a show of her own."[4] Caesar, decades later, repeated the story about Coca's agent, then added, "Max wanted his own show, Imogene wanted her own show."

That might, if you're a cynic, be regarded as retrospective cover for his own desire for one. Except that, in an interview from 1953, Liebman said that Imogene had "once asked about doing a half-hour situation comedy, but nothing developed."[5]

Caesar himself, in his later accounts, could be both maddeningly vague ("It was a rumor. And then the reporters showed up, and it was true.") but also quite specific, describing himself as stunned when Hal Janis, the NBC exec who was the liaison to the show, came to see him in his dressing room to tell him that the rumors were indeed true—"There's a big shake-up coming."[6] Howie Morris, on the other hand, in an interview from the late 1990s, said "Sid wanted his own show. He staged that news conference unbeknownst to us."[7] The first part of the comment is conceivable; the second isn't. The notion of Caesar somehow dragooning Liebman into a conference Max had no prior knowledge of is almost laughable. There's no way Caesar would have done something like that on his own without consultation with Liebman, particularly as the conference was held in Max's offices and he, judging from the newspaper accounts, presided over it. Caesar never mentions the news conference, and for what it's worth, Imogene, other than lamenting a lack of communication about it, doesn't mention any machinations by Sid, simply saying that she never knew why *Max* hadn't told her about it before-hand.

The one person who, years later, might have shed at least a little light on the whole affair was Pat Weaver. However, other than blaming, accurately or not, Coca's agent for the break-up, he was oddly silent about his role in all of it. In his memoir, he absents himself from any scenario, which is inconceivable. As president of NBC, he would have known about, if not been deeply involved in, the discussions and negotiations with the principals—in particular for Liebman's contract for twenty-odd "spectaculars" and Caesar's 10-year contract with NBC, signed the day of the announcement. As for Liebman's take on the conference and what role he played in setting it up, there's a similar silence. If he ever discussed it with Ted Sennett in the interviews conducted and reminiscences shared for Sennett's *Your Show of Shows*, it's not mentioned in the book.

Nonetheless, it's difficult to believe that Liebman and Caesar formed a cabal of two to purposely sandbag Coca, given the demonstrated regard the three had for each other, not to mention their long and to all appearances amicable professional relationship. Did Max and Sid, realizing the inevitable, make the best deals they could, assuming Imogene, or at least her agent, was doing the same? You can't help feeling that she had to have had some inkling of what was going to happen, even if not exactly when. It's equally difficult to believe that Weaver would have made the statement about "mutual agreement" without some basis for it. In fact, his announcement included the statement that Coca was working with NBC on development of a new program.[8] Any speculation is, of course, moot. Over 60 years later, we're likely to never know exactly who did what or who knew what, not to mention when they knew it.

That's *how* it ended. *Why* it ended is a different issue entirely. There was a great deal of speculation then and there still is in accounts or retrospectives today. Mike Dann, at the time an NBC exec, said, "Everybody had a point of view on why it went off, and they were probably right. It's like backing into a buzz-saw and asking which tooth cut your ass."[9] However, sorting out and analyzing the different reasons from the many given can be helpful in understanding why a successful and innovative program ended. They can be divided into speculation about internal factors having to do with the show itself and its cast—inflated egos, particularly Caesar's; personality clashes; or a precipitous decline in the quality of the show. Although rumored or talked about at the time, the first two can be largely discounted; the third is inaccurate, at least for the comedy segments. More important were external factors—the changing nature of programming and the TV audience and, above all, how commercial television had evolved by 1954. And here, the biggest tooth in Dann's buzz-saw would ultimately be NBC's.

As for those internal factors, it was suggested, or at least rumored, at the time that Sid didn't want to share the spotlight. Except that he did. On *Your Show of Shows* the spotlight he shared would have been with, of course, Coca, but there's little if any evidence of his reluctance to do so. It's easy to assume on the basis of watching video collections of sketches that it was all Caesar, all of the time. It's only when you watch complete episodes that you realize that was not the case. Yes, he was in all of the ensemble sketches and had his solo, either a monologue or pantomime. However, and this is what you don't see in those collections, Coca had a weekly number of her own: a ballet parody, a song-and-dance routine, or a full-scale production number with the singers and dancers. She also participated in almost all of the ensemble sketches, and it's striking that in them both Caesar and Coca have their big moments; in fact, Sid in some sketches is almost a straight man for Imogene. In the Hickenlooper sketches and pantomimes, they are very much equal in terms of dialogue or action. Offstage, he supported her ideas for sketches, sometimes when Liebman didn't think they were worth pursuing, and after the first full season of the show when Max approached him about changing the billing on the show's opening titles from "Sid Caesar *with* Imogene Coca" to "Sid Caesar *and* Imogene Coca," he agreed with no indication of an egotistical fuss about it. Coca once remarked, decades later, of their relationship on *Your Show of Shows*, "I can tell you that Sid and I, I know it sounds impossible, never really had an argument."[10]

Max Liebman was always quick to quash any rumors of clashes among the three of them, whether it was Sid and Imogene arguing with Max or each other, or Liebman yelling at anyone, let alone his two stars: "There is absolutely no truth to this. No one has ever raised his voice to anyone else on the show." In 1953, he was repeating what he had maintained since the beginning of the show: "The harmony between Sid, Imogene, and myself is sometimes frightening."[11] That supposed lack of discord extended to the rest of the cast as well. Coca insisted that "Nobody was out there saying, 'I don't have as much to do as so-and-so,' or 'I didn't get enough laughs'— there was none of that."[12] According to Carl Reiner, that included Caesar as well. When asked if Sid was the kind of performer who wanted all the good lines for himself, he responded, "No, no ... as a matter of fact, he was very good about the piece being right. And if you got a laugh, and if you did something funny, he would never say, ooh, let me do that. He just let you do it."[13] That attitude apparently extended to the later *Caesar's Hour* as well, Nanette Fabray remembering that "He was never impervious to the people around him ... with his cast, he was always generous and gracious. One of the warmest men I've ever worked with."[14]

All of this may sound too good to be true, and certainly Sid argued with Max over cutting time from comedy sketches for production numbers, but he always gave in (at least over that) and moved on. Caesar, by all accounts, reserved his temper for the Writers' Room; when it came time for rehearsals and performance, he was all business. Mel Tolkin later said, "Tensions there were, but very little temperament. For that we didn't have the time. We couldn't be competitive—the important thing was to get the show *on*."[15]

All of this may also sound as if Caesar didn't have an ego. Of course he did—no comedian or actor lacks one. He said that he could be at times arrogant. And egotism certainly became apparent by the early 60s, when, as he would admit later, his drinking and pill-popping, rapidly approaching the out-of-control stage, made him paranoid when he thought others were getting more applause. But there's little indication of an over-inflated ego or swelled head on *Your Show of Shows*. Pat Weaver found him remarkably "gracious and even quite modest" about his success (which is not to say that he didn't enjoy it).[16]

Did he want a show of his own? Probably. Even if not in 1954, at least eventually. When he did get one, *Caesar's Hour*, he recalled that "I was cocky; I looked forward to being the complete and total boss," but was also honest enough to admit, "I was scared."[17] It would be the first time since 1949 that he had not worked with Max Liebman on TV. Perhaps a better way of framing an answer might be that he wanted to be in a different *kind* of show—one with fewer production numbers and more comedy and one that wasn't 90 minutes long. In an interview he gave in September of 1954, right before the debut of *Caesar's Hour*, he repeated much the same thing he had said seven months earlier about the split, that it had become time for each to grow and develop by themselves, but then went on to criticize the length of the show: "I guess it was psychological or something. We'd have a fast-moving show for an hour and then come up against the fact that we still had 30 minutes to go." However, he also mentioned a more significant factor in his possible restiveness with *Your Show of Shows*. Commenting on what his new show would be like, he said, "One thing I'm certain of ... is that we won't fall into the format trap. It's a slow form of strangulation to get into this rut...."[18]

The format was indeed an issue remarked on at the time, at least by television columnists and critics: they thought the show had become predictable and was getting static. There were some complaints about Caesar and Coca exhausting their material and repetitious routines, but there was little complaint about any diminution of their talents. Jack Gould, reviewing the first show of the 1952-53 season in the *New York Times* of September 8, 1952, commented that the show needed freshness and greater variety, but thanks to Caesar and Coca, it "remains an island of engaging literacy in TV's sea of vaudeville mediocrity." Two years later, his critique was even more pointed: "Mr. Caesar and Miss Coca have not lost their technique or artistry. Their performances individually may be just as good as they were four years ago." The main issue seemed to be indeed the format: the "production as a whole does not vary materially ... it is lavish rather than imaginative."[19] Ironically enough, the comments about predictability began to emerge during the 1952-53 season when, arguably, the show was at its peak. Not just in the dance routines or vocal numbers (the Billy Williams Quartet continued to be popular and Jack Russell's songs were generally excellent); some of the best parodies, Caesar monologues, pantomimes, and Hickenlooper and Professor sketches came from that season. Certainly, if you watch enough episodes from the second season onward, you can predict the running order—if it's 9:30, it's probably time for a parody. However, if you watch the seasons in sequence, your reaction might be who cares, so long as the sketches in that running order are first-rate comedy and they generally were. Another reaction, over 60 years on, to contemporary criticism might be that it was a classic case of "you don't know what you've got till it's gone."

Your Show of Shows was not the only comedy-variety show in revue format to be the target of similar criticism about predictability and repetition. The big comedy-variety show had dominated programming in the earliest days of TV and NBC had four of the biggest: *Texaco Star Theatre*, *All Star Revue*, *Your Show of Shows*, and the *Colgate Comedy Hour*. By 1953,

10. "Well, this was it" 159

Texaco Star Theatre was gone, *All Star Revue* went off the next year, and the *Colgate Comedy Hour* would follow in 1955. The entire genre was demonstrably in difficulty, one of the earliest victims of the cyclical nature of programming. From a peak in 1952 with 25 on the air, by the 1954-55 season, there were 20 and they were now outnumbered by half-hour, cheaper to produce, sitcoms. By 1957, there were only 10.[20] The comedy-variety show would never go away entirely, but of those that remained or were put on air later, they tended to be hosted not by comedians but singers, for example, Perry Como, Dinah Shore, and later Andy Williams and Dean Martin. One of the longest lasting from the early era of TV was *The Toast of the Town*, which eventually did in its competition, the *Colgate Comedy Hour*. It was hosted by Ed Sullivan, demonstrably not a singer, but who also could hardly be called a comedian either, at least intentionally. With only a few exceptions, it would not be until the late '60s and early '70s that you would see a return to traditional comedy-variety with the shows of Flip Wilson and, especially, Carol Burnett, who consciously modeled hers after *Your Show of Shows*.

There were attempts by Max Liebman to shake things up on the program. Much was made of a new format for the 1953-1954 season.[21] It would be on for three weeks a month instead of four, more in line with the usual NBC comedy-variety show schedule. (For that matter, most of those shows featured three or four comics who rotated their hosting and performance duties; they tended to regard Caesar's four weeks a month for 90 minutes with a mixture of admiration and wonder, and a tinge of horror at his workload). The show would also move from the International Theatre on Columbus Circle that had a seating capacity of 1500 to the Center Theatre in Rockefeller Center, with 3700 seats and more space for production numbers. There were to be fewer guest-hosts, more guest stars. To make room for them (and their salaries—top stars could command up to $5,000 for an appearance), some of the regulars were let go and would appear only occasionally. This was unfortunate, in that two of them, Marguerite Piazza and Jack Russell, had contributed much on a weekly basis. Piazza, a soprano at the Met, not only sang operatic excerpts but could be an excellent comedian. Russell had sung with the New York City Opera; his solo numbers were usually excellent, and he was an effective straight man in comedy bits. Caesar and Coca were also to appear more often, particularly at the beginning of the show, as themselves rather than characters. You have to wonder whose idea that was. Let's take two shy comic actors, one of whom was very uncomfortable at being himself, and give them scripted banter? Anyone who knew them offstage could have predicted what looked like their occasional discomfort with the whole thing. Ironically, their unscripted interaction was far more appealing, and sometimes charming, in terms of showing glimpses of their "real" personalities. Finally, the running order of sketches was sometimes juggled and more dance routines and longer parodies sometimes eliminated Caesar's monologue.

However, some of these changes had already been in evidence the season before, and the entire experiment was a brief one. The first episode opened with a belabored and not very funny "welcome back" introduction sketch, followed by, thankfully, an impressive Caesar pantomime. There was a longer-than-usual parody (of *From Here to Eternity*), numbers by new dance teams, and songs by guest-stars Nat King Cole and Lily Pons. More traditionally, there were also Hickenloopers and Professor sketches. However, by the fourth episode, things had reverted pretty much to what they had always been, guest-hosts, for example, made a return. About the only lasting change was in the running order of sketches. The short-lived tinkering had not been enough to satisfy the critics; but just enough, one suspects, to irritate viewers who expected the traditional running order or didn't care what it was, so long as they got their Hickenlooper or parody fix. It was difficult to break a mold, particularly when, in the case of *Your Show of Shows*, it had been very successful.

However, issues with the show or its cast aside (some of them were either not valid or perhaps not all that important in the long run), external factors would play a far larger role in NBC's decision to end it. Whether or not Caesar or Coca were unhappy with the restrictive nature of *Your Show of Shows* in terms of format or its 30-plus-week schedule that permitted little to no time for them to pursue films or Broadway productions, didn't really matter.[22] They were under contract to NBC and as Coca's agent, the much-maligned Ms. Coleman, would emphasize at the time of the split, as would Caesar later, the network made the call to end the show.

Was it because of the decline in ratings? (Although it should be noted that the show was not exactly in free fall.) One of the factors behind it was increased competition, not necessarily from better shows but from different kinds—boxing and sitcoms, for example. There was simply more to watch and more people to do the watching. It's one thing to say that TV viewership expanded in the '50s. You really have to look at the figures to see how quickly and exponentially: the percentage of TV households was 9 percent in 1950; by 1951, it was 23.5 percent; by 1956, 71.8 percent. And *where* people watched TV was rapidly changing. In 1949, 41.6 percent of TV sets were in New York; most of the rest were in urban areas like Philadelphia, Chicago, and Los Angeles. Then the two coasts were linked in 1951 via coaxial cable and an FCC freeze on new television stations in 1948 was lifted in early 1952. The resulting increase in stations, 104 in 1950 to 380 in 1954, and in the percentage of TV households, 23.5 percent in 1951 to 59.4 percent in 1954, was dramatic. And much of that increase in viewership was

10. "Well, this was it"   161

in small towns and rural areas. A "national audience" in TV's early days was by definition an urban one. By the mid-50s, it was becoming a truly national one.[23]

As television began to expand into non-urban areas, the South and Midwest in particular, viewing preferences by region began to emerge. Increasingly, what might be a ratings success in the Northeast was not what was popular in, say, the South. For example, by May of 1954, the rating of Milton Berle's *The Buick-Berle Show* (the two-season successor to *Texaco Star Theatre*) in Charlotte, North Carolina, was 1.9; that of its competition, *Death Valley Days*, was 56.3. The trend would continue: ten years later, Red Skelton's and Andy Griffith's shows were in the top 10 in ratings in the South; neither appeared on the top 10 in the Northeast, where Jackie Gleason and the Smothers Brothers topped the list.[24]

Urban humor, at least as far as can be judged by these few examples, might not have always appealed to that expanded audience outside of large cities. And *Your Show of Shows* was a very urban, specifically New York-centered, program—from its theme song "Stars Over Broadway" to the settings and concepts of many of its sketches. A notable number are set in the subway; in one pantomime, Caesar and Coca literally fight other passengers to get on a train (conditions at the 42nd Street stop haven't changed all that much) and then vie for a seat once they're inside. And, of course, Charlie and Doris Hickenlooper are New Yorkers. In most of the Hickenlooper sketches, they are apartment dwellers who contend with the usual problems (noisy neighbors, for example) and sometimes the not so usual (a neighbor who insists on throwing garbage into the hall instead of down the incinerator chute). When Doris, in a sketch about taking phone messages for Charlie, reels off a series of telephone exchanges—Plaza, Trafalgar, Chickering—they are ones that were familiar to any New Yorker at the time. One entire Hickenloopers sketch of May 31, 1952, is built on how guests are going to get home after a party at an apartment on 12th St. The couple are set to drive back to their apartment in Chelsea and everyone else agrees to walk to the nearest subway station or take a bus. However, Doris helpfully volunteers Charlie as a chauffeur. Hoping to divide the task with another potential driver, he asks for a show of hands—Uptown or Downtown? (all hands are raised for Uptown)—then East Side or West Side? (all hands for West)—as the New York audience laughs at his resulting frustration. And everyone keeps forgetting Mary, who lives "across the river." Throwing up his hands, Charlie finally just gives her cab fare.

Was the show, as in the famous initial assessment of *Seinfeld* by NBC execs, "too New York"? Today, with a more sophisticated national audience, the answer would be no. But by 1954? The sketches are funny on their own, but you can't help feeling that some of the nodding-your-head-in-recognition laughter at aspects of New York life (or Manhattan geography) might not have been shared by a viewer in Atlanta or Dubuque.

Besides being firmly planted in New York, both physically and conceptually, the show's humor was urban—smart, sophisticated for its time, and satirical. Was it becoming too hip for the expanding 1950s TV room? Carl Reiner and Larry Gelbart, who wrote for the later *Caesar's Hour*, thought so. Reiner regarded the coast-to-coast linkup, which Caesar announced on the episode of September 29, 1951, as the beginning of the dumbing-down of television. To reach a broader audience, networks wanted programming that would appeal to the greatest number; whether it was smart or sophisticated became depressingly beside the point. Gelbart put it another way: in the early days of TV, with fewer sets owned by people who tended to be more well-educated and could also afford the expense (and adults in control of what would be seen on them), viewers tended to be more demanding and expected higher standards—"You could write much smarter material."[25] Even if this wasn't always the case—there were plenty of non-urban, non–East Coast folk who enjoyed *Your Show of Shows*—the assumption among some network executives was that it was. After *Caesar's Hour* ended, Sid and Imogene reunited in 1958 and signed for a half-hour show on ABC. One of the network VPs remarked that it would probably work, given their talents, but only "just so long as they don't get egghead and do stuff that gets esoteric—I mean take-offs on Japanese movies nobody has ever been to an art theatre in New York to see. They've got to give it that old common denominator—empathy."[26] Caesar and the writers for the show *Sid Caesar Invites You*, who included Larry Gelbart and Danny and Neil Simon, continued with a sketch-comedy and satire format and did spoofs of not just bullfighter movies but one of *Omnibus*, a high-toned series on the arts and sciences financed by the Ford Foundation. This was apparently not the kind of empathy ABC was looking for. The show had a half-season run.[27]

The VP's comment could have been a line from *Network*. However, it was also a portent for the comedy shows that followed in the early '60s, which certainly targeted not just a common denominator, but frequently the lowest. *The Flintstones, Dennis the Menace, Mr. Ed, The Beverly Hillbillies*—all had their appeals in some fashion (who doesn't like horses?) but could hardly be accused of wit or sophistication. Among the few exceptions were *The Bob Newhart Show* and *The Dick Van Dyke Show*, a sitcom created by Carl Reiner.

All of these factors may have played a role in the ratings decline, but it's possible to over-emphasize that decline in determining the chief reason NBC decided to end *Your Show of Shows* in 1954. It was still in the top twenty at the end of 1953, still NBC's prestige comedy-variety show, and critics' carping about predictability aside, still delivering the smartest humor and most sophisticated satire on television. More important than any other factors were, simply, money (there's a reason why they call it commercial television) and, ironically, the show's success.

Comedy-variety shows were very expensive to mount, especially one that was 90 minutes long, had a more or less permanent cast of singers and dancers to perform those elaborate production numbers, its own choreographer, and a live orchestra. And of course it had a superb writing staff and a superb cast of comedians, all of whom were paid very well, particularly its stars: by 1954, Caesar was making $25,000 an episode, Coca $10,000. Sponsors, not surprisingly, were growing increasingly restive about the price tag for comedy-variety in general. Texaco was paying program costs of $90,000 plus the bill for 60 minutes of network time for its eponymous Milton Berle show, a total of $150,000 per episode. It would indeed pull out of its sponsorship at the end of the 1953 season. Colgate was paying $6 million a year in time-and-talent costs for its *Comedy Hour*; that would end in 1955. And *All Star Revue* would go under because of insufficient sponsor support.[28]

Your Show of Shows was more expensive than most, with its talent cost of $85,000 a week and total production costs of $220,000 a show. Camel, one of its major sponsors, was paying $2,250,000 yearly for the ads for one half-hour of the program by the 1953-54 season. And NBC, or at least David Sarnoff, the chairman of RCA which owned NBC, wasn't happy with that talent budget. Sarnoff was notoriously more invested in the returns from NBC's shows than their quality (Pat Weaver was usually the guiding force behind that), and in a barely veiled reference to Sid, grumbled that, "It's a sad state of affairs when a couple of talent deals can represent the difference in profit in network leadership."[29] Yet, Camel, despite its qualms about cost, continued its sponsorship (after the first season, although sponsors might change, the show never lacked in numbers of them), and it wasn't as if NBC wasn't getting its money's worth from Caesar or the program—the network was reaping profits of $8,000,000 a year from *Your Show of Shows*.

It had become a double-edged programming sword. The show was successful, so its popular stars got step-up clauses in their contracts (and resultant salary increases) and production costs continued to mount. It was expensive, but because it was successful, NBC was reluctant to abandon the format despite its costs. The dilemma was illustrated beautifully in a letter of October 12, 1953, from *TV Guide*'s Hollywood bureau chief Dan Jenkins in California to Max Liebman in New York.[30] It was after the jettisoning of the revised format for the 1953-54 season, and Jenkins offered advice on what to do with the show. He predicted, on the basis of ample evidence, that the days of the big comedy-variety show were numbered, in part because of the cost to sponsors, and also because its rapid consumption of acts and material would inevitably result in a lack of freshness and vitality. His suggestion? Drop *Your Show of Shows* at the end of the season while it was still popular and return with a half-hour show with Caesar, Coca, Carl Reiner, and Howie Morris, "perhaps the four most talented damn people working together anywhere in the world." It could have Hickenlooper sitcom sketches for a half-hour, but also other segments that would feature movie satires as well as completely different comedy situations to fit the skills of both writers and cast. Liebman's letter in reply was both charming and witty—and let Jenkins down gently. Max thought Jenkins' analysis of the problem with TV comedy-variety was spot on, saying that he hadn't expected the show to last more than two seasons before it gave way to the trend toward half-hour programs. While agreeing that what he proposed could "very well be the greatest thing on the networks," he pointed out the hitch. The cost. With the salaries of all four, it would be economically unfeasible. They were currently doing the equivalent of three half-hour shows for the same money they would probably ask for one half-hour. NBC's solution to the conundrum was to split the comedy and variety segments of the show. They didn't reduce *Your Show of Shows*' 90 minutes to a comedy half-hour, but by splitting Caesar and Coca, got two comedy shows, Sid's hour and Imogene's half hour, that added up to 90 minutes. Max got the variety end with his 90-minute spectaculars.

In the end, it wasn't an issue of not getting enough money from the show, NBC just wanted more of it. They had a goose that had laid a demonstrably golden egg; the hope was that it contained three more inside. And the timing was right in terms of going out on top—the show was still successful, hardly on its last legs creatively, and its stars still popular. And it escaped no one's notice that Caesar's expensive contract was up for renewal. It must have seemed perfect from a corporate standpoint: launch Imogene in a solo half-hour; give Sid an hour he could primarily devote to comedy; and let Max concentrate on what he felt he did best, staging big revues. Three successful shows could conceivably increase profits beyond *Your Show of Shows*' 8 million and the network was willing, for the sake of profit, to take the gamble. As it would turn out, not all of the eggs were equally golden, and in killing the goose, NBC broke up the most creative team in TV comedy. Although each had subsequent success after *Your Show of Shows*, they would arguably never match individually what they had achieved together.

After the announcement of the split, there were still 10 more shows to do before the final episode of June 5. Whatever their feelings about the show's upcoming end, there's no indication of a let-down by either writers or cast. There was some repetition of sketches, although with the usual variation and tinkering, but there were also brand new ones, among them two excellent Hickenloopers sketches; the classic "The German General," performed by Caesar and Morris; "Twenty Minutes for Lunch," one of Caesar's best physical comedy bits; "How's Production," a zany look at a creative session of the Acme Novelty Company; and of course, one of *Your Show of Shows'* best, if not *the* best, the parody of *This Is Your Life*. The last three episodes featured audience-requested sketches and, even here, they were not just carbon copies of the originals.

And then it was time for the last show. *Life* magazine sent a reporter and photographer to the last day of rehearsals on Saturday, which was an emotional one. The pictures featured Imogene in tears and Sid looking off into space, morosely chewing his cigar. Max Liebman attempted a farewell speech, but finally gave up and said, "to Hell with it."[31] That night, Faye Emerson was the final guest-host, appropriately, as she had been not only a frequent one, but one of the best. She and Sid and Imogene appeared together at the beginning, the two stars struggling to maintain their composure, Coca trying to smile and Caesar looking exceptionally glum. After a few remarks by Emerson, Sid, brightening with a noticeable effort, said, in a line you have to suspect was scripted, "C'mon, Imogene, let's have some fun."

What followed, interspersed with the usual songs and dance, were a Hickenloopers sketch, a French World War I film parody, the 1812 Overture pantomime, a silent, "The Sewing Machine Girl," Imogene in her tramp persona singing "Wrap Your Troubles in Dreams," and a final comedy sketch with The Four Englishmen. The dancers and singers performed at the end of the show, for one last time, "Stars Over Broadway," and then it was time for the final curtain call. The regulars came out on stage, in groups or one-by-one, all smiling, and then Sid and Imogene, who were not. After thanking the audience, Sid, somewhat awkwardly as usual, and with his voice slightly breaking, said "Well, this was it. It's been a wonderful five years," and turning to Imogene, "I just want to say, I love you," and kissed her. Fighting back tears, she thanked the audience as well. She was now openly crying, and he, with his arm around her, looked like he was going to, biting his lip to keep control. Pat Weaver came on stage to announce the "great plans for all next year," and that's the way it ended, with everyone on stage and the audience slowly filing out. After four years, *Your Show of Shows* was over.

During its run, it had reached a peak audience of more than 25 million. It had received every award possible: two Emmys as best variety show, one each for Caesar and Coca as best actor and actress, as well as nominations every year; Sylvania awards (in the early days of television, equivalent to the Emmys) for Liebman as best director and for Caesar and Coca as best actor and actress; a Peabody for Coca; and every magazine award you can think of. It had created stars of Sid and Imogene and, in their pairing with its miraculous chemistry, arguably the best male-female comedy duo ever. Its writing staff was one of the best, if not the best, in television history, and its troupe of performers, Caesar, Coca, Carl Reiner, and Howie Morris, was unmatched. It was the first genuine television comedy and provided the template for every comedy program that followed it, and, in Caesar, featured the first genuine, and brilliant, television comedian.

Perhaps the best epitaph for the show was one given by critic Gilbert Seldes: "In the four years of the Caesar-Coca combination, [there was] not a single program of its quality, or anything near it...."[32] Several decades later, anyone who has seen all of its episodes would agree—and perhaps add that there never has been anything quite like it since.

Afterword

After the end of *Your Show of Shows*, what were the results of NBC's gamble in splitting up Liebman, Caesar, and Coca? For both the network and the former Triumvirate, they were mixed. Max Liebman had success in putting on the big shows and revues he felt he did best. From 1954 through 1956, he produced and directed over twenty-five Spectaculars (sometimes titled *Max Liebman Presents*). Active into the early '60s, he then refused to follow TV production to the West Coast, preferring to stay in New York in semi-retirement. His last major production was in 1972, a compilation of sketches, *Ten from Your Show of Shows*, for theatrical release.

Imogene Coca unfortunately did not have success in her solo venture. The half-hour *Imogene Coca Show* lasted only one season. Lucille Kallen, along with Max Wilk and, briefly, Mel Brooks, wrote for it, but it seems never to have been decided what exactly it was to be—it started out as a sitcom, changed to a comedy-variety format after the first three episodes, then returned to a sitcom. Kallen would later say that it was "not a happy experience. I think Imogene was—I know she was—very unhappy to be alone without Sid...." Max Wilk would echo Kallen in his recollection of writing for the show—"that was not a happy experience"—and stated rather bluntly that Coca was "lost without Sid." Kallen perhaps summed it up best: "the other thing [*Your Show of Shows*] was so perfect for her—she was a star without the burden."[1]

The star who had always borne the burden on *Your Show of Shows* would arguably fare the best of the three on his solo show. On *Caesar's Hour*, you can see Sid's attempts to break out of the comedy-variety format he had come to dislike: it obviously wasn't ninety minutes, there were guest-stars but no guest-hosts, and the emphasis was firmly on comedy. And he had the writers to create it—besides Mel Tolkin, the Simons, and Mel Brooks, he added Larry Gelbart, Sheldon Keller, Michael Stewart, and Selma Diamond to the staff. He also brought on board, along with Carl Reiner and Howie Morris, Nanette Fabray. You might say he was fortunate in finding her as a new female partner, except that he already knew how good she was from her appearances on *Your Show of Shows*. She was not

Imogene, but she was a gifted comedian in her own right and she and Sid developed a chemistry of their own. The show, as you might expect, had superb parodies, for example, "Aggravation Boulevard," in which Caesar played a John Gilbert–type silent film actor whose career seems doomed by the talkies when his speaking voice turns out to be a hilarious falsetto, and "On the Docks," a spoof of *On the Waterfront*, featuring conceivably the best-ever Brando impression by Sid. There was the occasional pantomime (including the brilliant argument between Sid and Nanette set to Beethoven's Fifth) and Professor sketch, but also new additions, for example, a domestic sitcom, "The Commuters," with Caesar and Fabray as a couple living in suburbia. Sketches in general were far longer than they were on *Your Show of Shows*. Some of the parodies could take up close to a half-hour of the show, as did the Commuter segments (some of which took up almost all of it), and "Abandon Ship for Love," an ambitious parody of *On the Town*, with singing, dancing, and a big final production number, *did* take up the entire hour. *Caesar's Hour* would run for three years and garner a number of Emmys, one for Nanette Fabray, two for Carl Reiner, and one for Sid to join the one he had received for *Your Show of Shows*.

The complete cast of *Your Show of Shows* would reunite for one last time in 1967 with the *Sid Caesar, Imogene Coca, Carl Reiner, and Howard Morris Special*. A new generation got a glimpse of *Your Show of Shows'* comedy style, in a Strangers sketch with Sid and Imogene and a sketch with Sid, Carl, and Howie as submariners attempting a new record for length of immersion (Of course, after starting out as best buds, they end up unable to stand each other; when informed they're to stay down even longer, they open the hatches). Above all, they saw it in a hilarious spoof of *Who's Afraid of Virginia Woolf?* with Caesar and Coca as the battling couple and Carl Reiner as one-half of the hapless couple who gets caught up in the combat. After almost ten years of being apart, they hadn't lost much. Caesar said the interval was "just like a long weekend," and Howie Morris, when asked why the old chemistry was still there, responded simply, "because we missed each other."[2] The program would win Emmys for Outstanding Variety Special and Outstanding Writing Achievement in a Variety Special. But after that, they would not work as an ensemble again.

Its cast may have gone their separate ways; however, *Your Show of Shows* would never really be over and never be completely forgotten. How could it be? In the earliest days of television it had shown what TV comedy could be like, smart and sophisticated, and, in Caesar, that TV comics could go beyond vaudeville and radio routines to develop comedy specifically for the new medium. Its DNA can be traced in almost all the successful comedy shows that followed. Its writers would go on to create such programs as *Get Smart* (Mel Brooks) and *The Dick Van Dyke Show* (Carl Reiner). Later comedy-variety shows bore its imprint; Carol Burnett modeled her show after it (particularly in its own brilliant movie parodies). When CBS tried to dissuade her from doing a comedy-variety show in favor of a half-hour sitcom, they condescendingly explained to her that the genre was for comedians like Gleason or Caesar. She replied, "I don't want to be [the same character] every week, I want to be different people. I want to have music. I want to have guest stars. I want to be like Sid Caesar."[3] And, of course, *Saturday Night Live* was a direct descendant; in appropriate acknowledgment, Sid was made an honorary member of the cast on his appearance on the show in 1983. More strikingly, after you have seen a number of episodes or sketches of *Your Show of Shows*, you can recognize and *hear* it in subsequent successful TV comedy—in sharp parodies of movies or TV shows, in sitcoms with married couples who don't always get along, but argue hilariously about it. And Caesar's brand of characterization comedy can be heard in Jonathan Winters and Lily Tomlin's performances, among others. Jon Stewart would go further than that as he closed his *Daily Show* for February 12, 2014. Announcing Sid's death, he said, "The news was, today, for everybody that is in comedy … we all lost our grandfather."[4]

When choosing the title for this book, *Sid Caesar and Your Show of Shows*, I did so because the two literally can't be separated. *Your Show of Shows*, with its stellar cast, writers, and producer/director, made the program the standard for sketch comedy and made a star of Caesar. In turn, the comic actor whom Larry Gelbart referred to as "the single most gifted man ever to grace the small screen"[5] would make the show the success that it was; it simply would not have been the same without him. The two, in a sense, created each other and, in the process, television comedy to come.

Occasionally, in retrospective articles on the show, you will see comments that suggest it's perhaps better *not* to see all of *Your Show of Shows*, rather than be disappointed if it doesn't live up to people's memories of it. After all, a lot of programs popular in the early '50s don't and leave you wondering what people ever saw in them. That's not the case with this one. When you see a pitch-perfect movie parody or a flawless Caesar-Coca pantomime or hear some hilarious Caesar snark in a monologue, you almost have to remind yourself you're watching American television of over sixty years ago. And, if you're lucky enough to see most of those full episodes, you realize why, over sixty years ago, people stayed home on Saturday nights from 9:00 to 10:30 glued to their TV sets. The show they watched on that small screen was that good. And Caesar was that good on that small screen, except as Gelbart would go on to comment, when Sid was on it, it grew in size. There's a reason why he gets top billing in the book's title. Comic geniuses deserve it.

Appendix: Comedy Sketch Guide

This guide was constructed by viewing as many episodes of *Your Show of Shows* as possible, with my primary source being the 141 digitized episodes held by the Paley Center for Media in New York. I also made use of several sketches and episodes digitized from kinescopes at the Moving Image Section in the Library of Congress, as well as individual sketches contained in various home video releases on VHS and DVD. The UCLA Film and Television Archive also has a substantial collection of kinescopes of complete episodes, a handful of which are not in the digitized Paley collection, but which I was unable to view.

Note that no archive has a complete collection of episodes, with some episodes missing entirely and others existing in only partial form. Every sketch I could view has a brief description added. I was also able in a few cases to fill in descriptions for sketches unavailable for viewing, using scripts from the Sid Caesar and Max Liebman papers at the Library of Congress and the papers of Lucille Kallen at the New York Library for the Performing Arts.

In order to reconstruct as far as possible the contents of episodes I was unable to view first hand, I have relied on a sketch list compiled by Max Liebman (my thanks to Barry Jacobsen for providing a copy). Liebman's list noted only the air dates, titles, and types of sketches, not their running order, nor any further descriptions of the sketch contents. In these instances, I've used the information from Liebman's notes to just list the sketches and their titles and, if possible, the cast members in them.

The sketches in this guide are all categorized by genre, with a cast list, and a list of locations where sketches can be viewed, in the following format:

CATEGORY: Sketch Title [Cast List] (Available Viewing Locations, if any)

The cast list uses the following abbreviations:

- **S:** Sid Caesar
- **I:** Imogene Coca
- **C:** Carl Reiner
- **H:** Howard Morris
- **GH:** Guest Host

The viewing locations list uses the following abbreviations:

- **YT:** The Sid Caesar Channel on YouTube (Channel name: "Sid Caesar: *Your Show of Shows*/Caesar's Hour/Admiral Broadway Revue")
- **SF:** Shout! Factory's 2018 5-disc DVD collection, "Sid Caesar: The Works"
- **SC:** Sid Caesar's 9-disc DVD collection (long out of production, but sometimes still available for purchase from resellers)

To assist readers interested in seeking out any of the complete episodes held by various archives (as opposed to individual sketches released on home video and posted to YouTube), I've also provided a list, in brackets, of where they can be found, using the following abbreviations:

- **Paley:** Paley Center for Media (in NYC and Los Angeles), 141 episodes
- **UCLA:** UCLA Film and Television Archive, 152 episodes
- **LOC:** Library of Congress, 121 episodes

An asterisk (*) following "Paley" indicates an incomplete episode; a plus (+) following indicates that the only available portion of the episode is Sid's monologue. Listings of episodes on kinescope at UCLA or the LOC do not provide information as to whether episodes are complete or partial.

Season 1 (1950)

Technically a half-season, the show debuted in February and ran through May. Along with Caesar and Coca, Tom Avera appeared in many of the sketches primarily as a straight man; Howard Morris only occasionally (he would not become a regular until 1952). The Strangers/Clichés sketches first appear in this season, as do the proto–Hickenloopers (only in pantomime, not yet in sketch form) and the Professor (in the earliest interview format). Some sketches were reworked from The Admiral Broadway Revue; Caesar-Coca pantomimes were, save for only two, brand-new and excellent from the very beginning.

Appendix: Comedy Sketch Guide

Ep #1 • Air Date: 2/25/50 • Host: Burgess Meredith • [Paley+, UCLA]
PROFESSOR: Interview with Professor Wolfgang [S, GH]
GUEST SKETCH: Live Versus Theatre [S]
 Life in a Noel Coward play versus real life (with Gertrude Lawrence)
OTHER: Christopher Columbus [S]
 Chris (Sid) encounters the usual perils, but continues despite them when his crew reminds him of what will never be discovered—"What about Columbus Circle?"
PANTOMIME: Courtship [S, I]
OTHER: Smorgasbord [I]
MONOLOGUE: It'll Be Nice [S]
 Thoughts of a nervous groom—all apprehensive—before the ceremony

Ep #2 • Air Date: 3/4/50 • Host: Burgess Meredith • [Paley, UCLA]
PANTOMIME: Author at Work [S, I]
 Author types a play as a young married couple, Sid and Imogene, mime the action
SONG/DANCE: Venetian Gondolier [I]
 A gondolier who bears a striking resemblance to a New York cabbie
PROFESSOR: Interview with Professor Habeas Corpus [S, GH]
 The professor as an expert on law; done in English and Russian doubletalk
SONG/DANCE: Story of Cinderella [I]
 The put-upon Cinderella gets her prince, sort of
OTHER: History as She Ain't: Samson and Delilah [S, I]
 Sid's Samson is shorn by Coca's Delilah, but likes the new look
PANTOMIME: Woman Getting Up in the Morning [S]
 A woman's morning routine, including getting into a dress with endless zippers in odd places

Ep #3 • Air Date: 3/11/50 • Host: Rex Harrison • [Paley, LOC, UCLA]
OTHER: Italian Painter [S, H]
 An artist attempts to instruct a numbskull student
SONG/DANCE: Mr. Rockefeller [I]
 Coca as tour guide at Radio City Music Hall
PANTOMIME: Driving Lesson [S, I]
 A husband teaches his wife how to drive; the results are hair-raising; the first new Caesar-Coca pantomime on *Your Show of Shows* and still one of the best
PROFESSOR: Interview with Kurt von Rhinestone [S]
 The professor as an expert in realism
GUEST SKETCH: Haberdashery [S, GH]
 A fast-talking salesman (Harrison) overwhelms a meek customer (Caesar)
SONG/DANCE: Madame Galli [I]
 Spoof of various types of opera divas
MONOLOGUE: What the Baby Thinks [S]
 Life through the eyes of a six-month-old baby with an inept father—"Hold My Head! Hold My Head"

SONG/DANCE: Hobo Ballet [S, I]
> Closing number featuring Caesar and Coca in a hobo pas de deux, their first dance together on *Your Show of Shows*. A parody, with low culture imitating high, but one that showcases their individual physical skills ().

Ep #4 • Air Date: 3/18/50 • Host: Melvyn Douglas • [Paley, LOC, UCLA]
PANTOMIME: Movie [S, I]
> Couple on first date, featuring mirror reactions to scenes

OTHER: The Wedding Picture [S]
> A bumbling photographer ruins a photo shoot

PROFESSOR: Interview with A Russian Ski Instructor [S]
> The professor provides unorthodox takes on ski techniques

OTHER: Slowly I Turn [S, I]
> Adaptation of the old vaudeville routine; a man is assaulted by a crazed woman every time he says "Niagara Falls"

GUEST SKETCH: The Importance of Being Earnest [S, I, GH]
> Spoof of the Wilde play, with Douglas in multiple roles

SONG/DANCE: Too Many Parties, Too Many Pals [I]
> A turn-of-the-century party girl

MONOLOGUE: Punching Bag [S]
> Spoof of boxing movies with Sid as the kid from the neighborhood who makes it big in the ring

Ep #5 • Air Date: 3/25/50 • Host: MacDonald Carey • [Paley, LOC, UCLA]
OTHER: Doctor [S]
> A hypochondriac doctor attempts to treat an increasingly nervous patient

PANTOMIME: Coney Island [S, I]
> On a date at Coney Island, which ends disastrously after a roller-coaster ride

OTHER: Interview with Giuseppe Macaroni [S]
> An expert on pasta who shares his expertise—and his spaghetti—with the audience

SONG/DANCE: Mon Amour Americaine [I]
> Apache/torch song in which Coca laments her lost GI lover

GUEST SKETCH: Movie Set [S, GH]
> Trouble on the set when a director insists on the perfect shot

MONOLOGUE: Asking for a Raise [S] (YT)
> Man tries out various approaches, including a plea for sympathy ("I'm going to have a baby")

SONG/DANCE: Pocahontas [I]
> Final production number featuring Coca as the Indian princess

Ep #6 • Air Date: 4/1/50 • Host: Jose Ferrer • [Paley*, UCLA]
OTHER: Butcher Shop [S, I]
> A demanding customer makes life miserable for a butcher, when he's forced to go into the freezer multiple times

PANTOMIME: Picnic [S, I]
> Couple on a picnic, beset by usual al fresco mishaps

STRANGERS/CLICHES: I Wonder Who That Was [S, I]
    A couple meet and exchange clichés as if they know each other; they don't (first Strangers sketch)
OTHER: Interview with Jungle Boy [S]
SONG/DANCE: Overcoat Striptease [I]
    A striptease under a huge overcoat—with a surprise ending
MONOLOGUE: Technicolor Western [S]
    Spoof of Westerns in which Sid plays at least 12 characters, including a horse

Ep #7 • Air Date: 4/8/50 • Host: Basil Rathbone • [Paley, UCLA]
PANTOMIME: Getting Dressed for Dinner [S, I]
    Getting dressed for dinner, with the usual stuck zippers, missing buttons, etc.
OTHER: Passion for Fashion [I]
    A preview of the latest, i.e., 1950, fashions
OTHER: Radio City Music Hall [S, H]
    Preparing for a big premiere, with Caesar as chief usher and Morris as nervous rookie
GUEST SKETCH: Slave Market [S, I, GH]
    A seller (Rathbone) tries to convince the shah (Caesar) to buy the girl no one wants (Coca)
PROFESSOR: Interview with a Stanislavsky Expert [S]
    One of the best of the early interview sketches, as Sid demonstrates the method by turning himself into a nail and a pinball
SONG/DANCE: Swan Lake [I]
    Ballet parody by Coca and dancers; her swan molts
OTHER: History as She Ain't: Henry VIII [S, I]
    Henry's queen tries to make him clean up his act; gluttony ensues
MONOLOGUE: Life Through the Eyes of a Dog [S]
    Between cats and a demanding owner, life's not easy for a canine

Ep #8 • Air Date: 4/15/50 • Host: Rudy Vallee • [Paley, LOC, UCLA]
OTHER: Drycleaners [S, I]
    A drycleaner ruins clothes in a variety of inventive ways, but not without reminding the disgruntled customers, "Be sure to recommend us to your friends!"
SONG/DANCE: Modern Music [I]
    Spoof of modern versus classical music
OTHER: Interview with Lemuel Cornball [S]
    A country folk singer performs one of his songs, "Cry of Crazy Crow," a ditty supposedly written by Mel Brooks
PANTOMIME: Bringing Baby Home [S, I]
    Couple taking extreme care with their first baby; contrasted with their laissez-faire attitudes toward the second
GUEST SKETCH: Saxes and a Trombone [S, I, GH]
    Vallee and Caesar attempt a sax duet, interrupted by Coca on trombone
MONOLOGUE: Man After Fight with His Wife [S]
    Man can no longer deal with his wife's quirks, keeping a shark in the bathtub among them

176   Appendix: Comedy Sketch Guide

Ep #9 • Air Date: 4/22/50 • Host: Melvyn Douglas • [Paley*, LOC, UCLA]
OTHER: Perfume [S, I]
   Parisian perfumier tries to make an expensive sale to an American tourist
SONG/DANCE: Jim [I]
   Torch song about a less than desireable lover
STRANGERS/CLICHES: Wedding Reception [S, I]
   A couple enjoy gossiping about the happy couple and their new house
OTHER: Russian Milton Berle [S]
GUEST SKETCH: Sagebrush Serenade [S, I, GH]
MONOLOGUE: Boy at First Dance [S] (YT, SF, SC)
   Shy, awkward boy at first dance; five years later, he's an assured ladies' man.
   A classic, notable for Caesar's comic acting of the transition and excellent physical comedy

Ep #10 • Air Date: 4/29/50 • Host: Jose Ferrer • [Paley, UCLA]
OTHER: Cavemen [S, I]
   Life Among the Neanderthals
OTHER: Pizzicato [S, H]
   The frustrations of a virtuoso in teaching an inept student to play the violin
MONOLOGUE: You're a Big Man Now [S]
   A man takes his son to his first day at school, including a talk with the principal, alerting him to his son's quirks—"he carries a knife"
STRANGERS/CLICHES: The Movie Line [S, I]
   Waiting to see a show, a couple exchanges trite observations on the movie and its cast
SONG/DANCE: Afternoon of a Faun [I]
   Parody of the ballet, with Coca as a nymph on the prowl
MONOLOGUE: Coming Attractions [S]
   Spoof of formulaic gangster movies, in which Sid meets a predictable bad end

Ep #11 • Air Date: 5/6/50 • Host: Al Capp • [Paley, LOC, UCLA]
OTHER: Chickenhearted [S]
   The world's worst waiter, in a restaurant that seems to serve nothing but chicken
PANTOMIME: Dance Hall Pick-up [S, I]
   Man in search of a dance encounters inept, aggressive dancer; all ends well with a jitterbug
OTHER: Interview with Three Directors [S]
   Three foreign film directors discuss their masterpieces (French, Italian, and Russian doubletalk)
OTHER: Fur Fashions of 1950 [I]
   Modeling by Coca, with a demonstration of how to make a muskrat stole fashionable
OTHER: Hillbillies [S, I]
   A shout-out to the *L'il Abner* comic strip of the host, Al Capp, which just doesn't work as a sketch; there's no time to develop the satire of the strip, leaving just the cornpone

SONG/DANCE: Babs [I]
    Popular flapper with suitors abounding
PANTOMIME: Man Getting Up in Morning [S]
    The morning routine of the other sex, featuring the world's most complicated tying of a necktie

Ep #12 • Air Date: 5/13/50 • Host: Jack Carson • [Paley, LOC, UCLA]
OTHER: Efficiency Expert at Breakfast [S, I]
    Wife serves her husband breakfast while he times her with a stopwatch, leading to rebellion
STRANGERS/CLICHES: Grand Central [S, I]
    Couple leaving New York trade clichés about the city and its inhabitants
PANTOMIME: Baby Carriages [S, I]
    A man and woman play one-upmanship with their offspring
GUEST SKETCH: Honeymoon [S, I, GH]
    An overbearing friend almost wrecks a couple's honeymoon before it starts
SONG/DANCE: Maywalk [I]
    A young girl with her Maypole laments missing the dance
MONOLOGUE: Zero Hour [S]
    Spoof of World War I movies contrasting English and French (French double-talk)

Ep #13 • Air Date: 5/20/50 • Host: Cedric Hardwicke • [Paley, LOC, UCLA]
OTHER: Nervous Suitor [S, I]
    Ill-at-ease man meets sweetheart's parents, destroying their afternoon tea, but somehow winning their approval (earliest version of a classic sketch)
STRANGERS/CLICHES: Restaurant [S, I]
    Couple have to share a table in a crowded restaurant where they exchange clichés about home-cooking and discuss items they have taken for souvenirs (including enough matchbooks to make a bedspread)
PANTOMIME: Quiet Evening at Home [S, I]
    Which turns out to be anything but, as the man wrestles with a recalcitrant TV and windows, among other objects
GUEST SKETCH: Caesar and Caesar [S, GH]
    Caesar (Hardwicke) and the other Caesar (Sid) compete for Cleopatra
OTHER: International Parade of Models [I]
    Coca versus a line-up of beautiful models, featuring many ludicrous hats
MONOLOGUE: Boy Growing Up [S]
    Man in waiting room of a maternity ward imagines various stages of his son's life, all exasperating

Season 2 (1950-51)

The first full season, in which Carl Reiner becomes a regular cast member, replacing Tom Avera. The earlier interview sketches with Caesar in

Appendix: Comedy Sketch Guide

"Nonentities in the News" are now regular Professor sketches with Reiner as the "roving reporter" interviewing Sid. Morris appears occasionally. From the sixth episode onward, the Hickenloopers as identified characters appear in sketches, usually first in the running order. Silent movie parodies as well as foreign film spoofs in doubletalk make their first appearance. Starting in 1951, Sid and Imogene finally get breaks, taking two-week vacations in early Spring and around Christmas. Because the emphasis in this guide is on the comedy of Caesar and Coca, I have provided only the air-date and guest hosts for these episodes and noted "Sid and Imogene on vacation."

Ep #14 • Air Date: 9/9/50 • Host: Bob Cummings • [Paley+, UCLA]
OTHER: Perfect Host [S, I]
PANTOMIME: New Car [S, I]
STRANGERS/CLICHES: First Day at School [S, I]
GUEST SKETCH: Producers [S, C, GH]
MONOLOGUE: Jealous Husband [S] (YT)
    Man returns home from work to find his wife isn't there for the first time in 7 years; in a few wonderfully modulated minutes, Sid escalates from mildly suspicious to totally crazed—she must be having an affair!

Ep #15 • Air Date: 9/16/50 • Host: Arlene Francis • [Paley, UCLA]
First female host
OTHER: Sleeping Baby [S, I]
    Couple with baby cope with noisy neighbors, not helped by the husband's acceptance of a drink every time he goes to quiet them down
PROFESSOR: Animal Authority [S, C]
    How to deal with, tame, and otherwise cope with animals
STRANGERS/CLICHES: Superstitions [S, I]
    Couple meet in gypsy tearoom, comparing superstitions and their own methods of warding off bad luck
SILENT FILMS: Intrigue [S, I, C]
    Spoof of Valentino films (first silent film sketch)
SONG/DANCE: One Gay Night in Boston [I]
    Turn-of-the-century frolics
PANTOMIME: Woman Dressing [S]
    A woman's morning routine, including getting into a dress with endless zippers in odd places

Ep #16 • Air Date: 9/23/50 • Host: Lee Bowman • [Paley, LOC, UCLA]
OTHER: Caveman Restaurant [S, I, C]
    Paleolithic diners with paleolithic manners
PROFESSOR: Authority on Psychology [S, C]
    The Professor discusses the nature of reality and demonstrates, badly, the

power of mind over matter. Few comedy sketches of the early '50s took
excursions to the boundaries of logic and back again ()
SONG/DANCE: Die Fleidermaus [I]
   Spoof of the operetta
PANTOMIME: Cocktail Party [S, I]
   A couple argue on the way to a party; the argument escalates once they're there
   over his flirting and her jealousy
GUEST SKETCH: Infernal Triangle [S, I, GH]
   Woman with two suitors, a gentleman and a slob; getting nowhere, the former
   turns into the latter with success
MONOLOGUE: She's a Nice Girl [S]
   Man complains to friends about wife's quirks

Ep #17 • Air Date: 9/30/50 • Host: Ralph Bellamy • [Paley, LOC, UCLA]
OTHER: French Restaurant [S, I, H]
   A French chef is offended by the crude tastes of an American tourist; she'd just
   like a meal that doesn't take hours to prepare
PANTOMIME: Carnegie Hall [S, I]
   Two symphony-goers mirror the emotions aroused by Tchaikovsky's Romeo
   and Juliet; the first, but not the last, example of Caesar and Coca's incredi-
   ble skills at combining mime and music
GUEST SKETCH: It's Certainly Been [S, I, GH]
   A party guest just won't leave despite all efforts by his hosts
STRANGERS/CLICHES: Dogs [S, I]
   Couple compare their dogs and their tricks; his begs, hers plays dead (all too
   convincingly, as the man observes "she's dead again")
SONG/DANCE: The Sensitive Matador [I]
   Coca confronts El Toro and can't dispatch him
MONOLOGUE: Airplane Movies [S]
   Spoof of World War II aviation movies, with a lone pilot taking on the Luft-
   waffe (Sid's first number in show business, from the film *Tars and Spars*)

Ep #18 • Air Date: 10/7/50 • Host: Nanette Fabray • [Paley, LOC, UCLA]
STRANGERS/CLICHES: Courtroom [S, I]
   Couple meet in a courtroom and discuss juicy trials they have attended and
   evaluate judges
OTHER: Slowly I Turn [S, I]
   A man's innocent mentions of "Niagara Falls" set off a woman he encounters;
   they would do this old vaudeville routine a number of times, but Coca's
   crazed monologues and Caesar's bemused, then wary, reactions to them
   make it one of the best
PROFESSOR: The Brain [S, C]
   Gangsters preparing for a heist, with the Professor as the brains of the outfit;
   disaster is the result
SILENT FILMS: Bartered Souls [S, I, C, GH]
   Sid is the unhappy husband of a rich woman (Nanette); reunited with his old

sweetheart (Coca), tragedy results, abetted by a devious butler (Carl). One of the best of the silents, with superb miming and physical comedy, particularly by Caesar
SONG/DANCE: Les Sylphides [I]
Two ballet dancers intersperse moves with conversation ranging from gossip about other dancers to their romantic lives
MONOLOGUE: Man Proposing to Wife-to-be [S]
Man tries out various scenarios in which he will ask his girl to marry him

Ep #19 • Air Date: 10/14/50 • Host: Jose Ferrer • [Paley, LOC, UCLA]
HICKENLOOPERS: Life Begins at 7:45 [S, I] (YT, SC)
Charlie is driven to exasperation, and a striptease, when he can't get Doris to decide on an outfit and get to a show on time
PANTOMIME: School Kids [S, I]
Goody-two-shoes girl and misbehaving boy unite to face a bully and find they like each other
PROFESSOR: Marriage (a.k.a. Authority on Marriage) [S, C] (YT)
Advice on married life, taken from the Professor's book "Happy Tho' Married"
STRANGERS/CLICHES: The Readers [S, I]
Strangers discuss Great Literature of the World, including "The Bobbsey Twins in Africa"
OTHER: Surgery Strikes Back [I, C]
Coca as a doctor who performs unorthodox surgery on a hapless patient
MONOLOGUE: Trying to Sleep After an Argument [S]
A man's attempt to sleep is undermined by his rehashing of an argument (Case #5,094) with his wife

Ep #20 • Air Date: 10/21/50 • Host: Madeleine Carroll • [Paley, LOC, UCLA]
HICKENLOOPERS: The Sneeze Sketch (a.k.a. An Evening at Home) [S, I] (YT)
A quiet evening is interrupted by Charlie's attempt to conceal a cold; featuring an epic sneeze when he fails
FOREIGN FILM/DOUBLETALK: Jean-Pierre Fleurette [S, I, C]
A jewel thief has to deal with his lover who has betrayed him to the police (French doubletalk)
GUEST SKETCH: Unluckiest Man in the World [S, GH]
A man and woman are alone on a desert isle, hardly a romantic situation because they don't like each other
MONOLOGUE: The Schmoe (Boxing Movies) (a.k.a. Punching Bag) [S] (YT)
Spoof of boxing movies with Sid as the kid from the neighborhood who makes it big in the ring
OTHER: Football [S, I]
Coca as the unlikely hero of the big game

Ep #21 • Air Date: 10/28/50 • Host: John Conte • [Paley, LOC, UCLA]
HICKENLOOPERS: First Homecooked Meal [S, I]
Charlie's attempts to deal with Doris' inedible food without hurting her feelings include tossing it out the window, with collateral damage to passersby

Appendix: Comedy Sketch Guide   181

STRANGERS/CLICHES: Cocktail Party [S, I]
    Out-of-towners at a New York cocktail party marvel at the native customs
SILENT FILMS: The Foundling [S, I, C]
    A father's attempt to reclaim his daughter, whom he had given up to a wealthy couple after his wife died; superb miming with an element of pathos and a first-rate take on Chaplin in *City Lights* by Sid ()
SONG/DANCE: The Sleighride [I]
    Coca and the male singers on that titular sleigh
MONOLOGUE: A New Leaf [S]
    A man is worried that he might have wasted his life and decides to change—briefly; one of the best examples of Caesar's absolute immersion into his Everyman characters ()

Ep #22 • Air Date: 11/4/50 • Host: Wendy Barrie • [Paley, UCLA]
HICKENLOOPERS: Putting Romance Back into Marriage [S, I]
    Doris follows a friend's advice, with the usual negative results
PANTOMIME: Sleep [S, I]
    A good night's sleep proves difficult for a man when his partner reads aloud, hogs the covers, and eats crackers in bed
SONG/DANCE: Madame Galli [I]
    Spoof of opera divas
MONOLOGUE: Annoying Next-door Neighbor [S]
    A man attempts to deal with his neighbor, who has a horde of annoying kids and a dog that jumps the fence and buries things in his backyard, among them his own dog

Ep #23 • Air Date: 11/11/50 • Host: Douglas Fairbanks, Jr. • [Paley, LOC, UCLA]
HICKENLOOPERS: Divorce [S, I]
    The first, and edgiest, version of a classic Hickenlooper quarrel over, among other things, her cooking ()
OTHER: Kids on Scooters (a.k.a. Kids on the Block) [S, I] (YT)
    Neighborhood kids who talk about kid things and discover they have mutual crushes
PROFESSOR: Sleep (a.k.a. Sleep Expert) [S, C] (YT, SC)
    Sigmund von Sedative describes his treatment of insomniacs and how to get a good night's sleep
FOREIGN FILM/DOUBLETALK: Poison [S, I, C]
    The eternal triangle; all points end up dead (Italian doubletalk)
SONG/DANCE: Beauty and the Beast [I]
    A beauty is more than apprehensive about the beast—at first
PANTOMIME: Boy at First Dance [S]
    Shy, awkward boy at first dance; five years later, he's an assured ladies' man

Ep #24 • Air Date: 11/18/50 • Host: Veronica Lake • [Paley, LOC, UCLA]
HICKENLOOPERS: Potluck Dinner [S, I, C]
    The couple's dinner of left-overs is interrupted by an early-arriving friend

182   Appendix: Comedy Sketch Guide

GUEST SKETCH: Bad for Good [S, C, GH]
   A femme fatale at a bar, who earns the title by eliminating most of its patrons
STRANGERS/CLICHES: In a Bank [S, I]
   Couple meeting at a bank discuss long lines, tellers, and other clichés about financial institutions
PANTOMIME: Sunday Driver [S, I]
   Dealing with traffic, engine trouble, and a flat tire (made worse when the woman throws away the lug nuts)
SONG/DANCE: Mon Amour Americaine [I]
   Apache/torch song in which Coca laments her lost GI lover
MONOLOGUE: Zero Hour [S]
   Comparison of English and French war movies (French doubletalk)

Ep #25 • Air Date: 11/25/50 • Host: Henry Morgan • [LOC, UCLA]
HICKENLOOPERS: Party List [S, I]
SILENT FILMS: Happy Days [S, I]
PROFESSOR: Eating Authority [S, C]
GUEST SKETCH: Two Friends [GH]
MONOLOGUE: Zero Hour [S]

Ep #26 • Air Date: 12/2/50 • Host: Glenda Farrell • [Paley, LOC, UCLA]
HICKENLOOPERS: Dining Out [S, I, C]
   The couple eat at an expensive restaurant and are intimidated by the waiter who has great expectations for a tip; all of Charlie's money, his watch, and his car payment eventually meet it. Reiner did a number of snooty waiter bits; this is one of his best
STRANGERS/CLICHES: On the Weather [S, I]
   A couple meet under an awning seeking shelter from the rain; clichés about the obvious topic, the weather, ensue
PANTOMIME: Sunday at Home [S, I]
   Every presumably peaceful Sunday activity, from watching TV to a game of checkers, goes wrong for a husband
GUEST SKETCH: Midsummer's Day Tempest [S, I, C, GH]
   A community theatre production of *The Tempest* goes awry when Professor von Intermission is brought in to direct it
OTHER: Models in Furs [I]
   Coca up against stiff competition in a modeling contest
MONOLOGUE: Thoughts of a 6-month-old Baby [S]
   The thoughts include, directed at his inept father, "You know if you drop me, your life isn't worth a nickel"

Ep #27 • Air Date: 12/9/50 • Host: Melvyn Douglas • [Paley, LOC, UCLA]
HICKENLOOPERS: The New Suit [S, I, C]
   Doris accompanies Charlie to a haberdashery; the result is several unsuitable outfits, including cuffed pants that don't break at the shoe heel but extend three feet beyond his shoes

Appendix: Comedy Sketch Guide 183

PANTOMIME: At the Movies (a.k.a. Movie Pest) [S, I] (YT)
   A woman movie-goer is plagued by a man whose fidgeting, eating and drinking, and snoring drive her out of the theatre—his plan all along
STRANGERS/CLICHES: Housewarming (a.k.a. Wedding Reception) [S, I] (YT)
   A couple enjoy gossiping about the happy couple and their new house
FOREIGN FILM/DOUBLETALK: Hate [S, I, C]
   A jewel thief has to deal with his lover who has betrayed him to the police (French doubletalk)
SONG/DANCE: American Beauty Rose [I]
   Coca in big production number
MONOLOGUE: Husband Walks Out (a.k.a. A Husband Returns) [S] (YT)
   After fleeing his home because of his wife's quirks, he returns to reconcile things

Ep #28 • Air Date: 12/16/50 • Host: Marsha Hunt • [Paley, LOC, UCLA]
HICKENLOOPERS: The Phone Messages (a.k.a. Did Anyone Call?) [S, I] (YT)
   Charlie is frustrated when Doris can't get messages straight, or forgets to give them to him
PROFESSOR: Expert on Flying [S, C]
   Rudolf von Rudder explains the mechanics of flight and ace pilots he has known, whose major achievements seem to have been getting airborne
PANTOMIME: Photographing Baby [S, I]
   A couple take turns photographing the baby and each other, including Sid's molding of Imogene's face into the expressions he wants
GUEST SKETCH: Hamburger Joint [S, I, GH]
   A man refuses to give up his seat so that two women can sit together; they make his meal miserable
SONG/DANCE: You Can't Get a Man with a Gun [I]
MONOLOGUE: Asking for a Raise [S]
   A man tries out various scenarios he hopes will be successful

Ep #29 • Air Date: 12/23/50 • Host: Paul Winchell • [Paley, UCLA]
   Winchell, the scheduled host, was replaced by Marguerite Piazza when he objected to his routines being shortened by time constraints
HICKENLOOPERS: The Budget [S, I]
   The couple argue about how much money is being spent and who spends it
PANTOMIME: Winter Visit [S, I]
   A man visits his girlfriend for a romantic afternoon, continually interrupted by her dog
FOREIGN FILM/DOUBLETALK: La Bicycletta (a.k.a. Who Stole My Bicycle?) [S, I, C] (YT, SC)
   A semi-spoof of *The Bicycle Thief*, in which Imogene has her eye on Carl's bicycle as Sid tries to stop her thievery (Italian doubletalk)
MONOLOGUE: Gangster Films [S]
   The clichés of gangster films are demolished

SONG/DANCE: Giselle [I]
　　Spoof of the ballet
MONOLOGUE: It's Better This Way [S] (YT)
　　A man muses on, and rationalizes, his breakup with his girl

Ep #30 • Air Date: 12/30/50 • Host: Arlene Francis • [Paley, LOC, UCLA]
HICKENLOOPERS: Midnight Snack [S, I]
　　Charlie on the hunt for something to eat in the wee hours, but there's no food in the house
PROFESSOR: Expert on Love (a.k.a. Expert on Love and Courtship) [S, C]
　　The Professor's usual skewed advice on how to win a woman and keep her
SILENT FILMS: Belle of the South [S, I, C]
　　A wounded Union soldier takes refuge with a Southern belle, then her Confederate sweetheart arrives on the scene; aka The Hand of Fate, which is in this case Sid's—once he takes someone's hand, he won't let go. Hilarious physical comedy from a very simple premise
GUEST SKETCH: At the Opera [S, I, GH]
　　Two opera snobs have to share a box with a slob, who has acquired a ticket
SONG/DANCE: I'm Yours [S, I, C]
　　Sung to a number of men, who assume she's exclusively theirs
MONOLOGUE: A Plague of Brother-in-law [S]
　　A man complains to his wife about his freeloading brother-in-law who has taken over the house

Ep #31 • Air Date: 1/6/51 • Host: Bill Goodwin • [Paley+, LOC, UCLA]
HICKENLOOPERS: The Quarrel [S, I]
PANTOMIME: Life of the Party [S, I]
OTHER: The Doctor [S, I]
SONG/DANCE: I've Got a Passion for Fashion [I]
MONOLOGUE: Boy Growing Up [S]
　　Father-to-be imagines various stages of his child's life

Ep #32 • Air Date: 1/13/51 • Host: Martha Scott • [Paley, LOC, UCLA]
HICKENLOOPERS: Home Late [S, I]
　　Charlie offers the standard excuses, as well as some inventive ones, for why he's returning home at 3 a.m.
GUEST SKETCH: The Bus Riders [S, I, GH]
　　A long bus trip, with Caesar as the man in the uncomfortable middle
STRANGERS/CLICHES: At the Pediatricians [S, I]
　　A couple in the waiting room exchange experiences and give each other advice on child-rearing
SONG/DANCE: Red Silk Stockings [I]
　　Coca in a production number with Jack Russell
PANTOMIME: Woman Getting Up in the Morning [S]
　　Depiction of woman's routine from awakening to dressing and going out for the day

MONOLOGUE: Breaking the News [S]
    A man prepares his parents for the announcement of his marriage

Ep #33 • Air Date: 1/20/51 • Host: Lena Horne • [Paley, LOC, UCLA]
HICKENLOOPERS: Railroad Station [S, I]
    Charlie sees Doris off at the station—if she ever stops questioning him and reminding him of things and actually goes
PANTOMIME: Child's Play [S, I]
    A doting mother wants her husband to play with the child—constantly
PROFESSOR: The Doctor [S, C]
    The Professor on anatomy: "The Human Body and How to Avoid It"
FOREIGN FILM/DOUBLETALK: A Fella Needs a Girl [S, I, C] (YT, SC)
    A man meets a prospective wife, who seems ideal (he tests her strength), but then sees a more attractive woman (Italian doubletalk)
SONG/DANCE: It's a Natural Thing to Do [I]
MONOLOGUE: It'll Be Nice [S]
    Thoughts of a nervous groom before the ceremony

Ep #34 • Air Date: 1/27/51 • Host: Nanette Fabray • [Paley*, LOC, UCLA]
OTHER: Nervous Suitor [S, I, C]
    A man visits his girlfriend's parents and, despite wrecking their tea and much of their house, wins their approval
PROFESSOR: Animal Psychiatrist [S, C]
    Advice on how to plumb the psyches of animals, from cowardly lions to snakes that don't think they're snakes
GUEST SKETCH: Telephone Sketch [S, I, GH]
    A man consults a directory and then tries to make a call from a phone booth; two women who also want to make a call complicate things
SILENT FILMS: Fool's Destiny [S, I, C, GH]
    A king (Caesar) copes with plots against his life by two women (Coca and Fabray), helped by an evil counselor (Reiner)
MONOLOGUE: Man Getting Up in Morning [S]
    A man's wake-up routine before leaving his apartment—without an important piece of clothing

Ep #35 • Air Date: 2/3/51 • Host: Dane Clark • [Paley, LOC, UCLA]
HICKENLOOPERS: Where's Dinner [S, I]
    Doris is in the mood for culture; Charlie is in the mood for food
PANTOMIME: Taking Out Baby [S, I]
    Rivalry between doting parents in the park over whose child is more precocious
STRANGERS/CLICHES: Golden Wedding Anniversary Reunion [S, I]
    Distant relations discuss their kin, including the black sheep of the family, who is literally that
GUEST SKETCH: A Movie is Born [S, C, GH]
    A producer deals with an actor's temperament by calling in the Professor, Roland von Close-up

SONG/DANCE: Grand Opera [I]
  Parody of Romeo and Juliet
MONOLOGUE: Husband's Third Complaint [S]
  A man's argument with his wife leads to his purchase of a bullet-proof vest—if she'd only give him time to put it on

Ep #36 • Air Date: 2/10/51 • Host: Sarah Churchill • [Paley, LOC, UCLA]
OTHER: Baby is Ill [S, I]
  Doting parents are beside themselves when their baby becomes mildly sick
PROFESSOR: Fitness (a.k.a. Sports Expert) [S, C]
  Advice based on the Professor's book "Watch Your Body, Buddy"
GUEST SKETCH: School Days [S, I, GH]
  Disruptive kids make a principal's life miserable
FOREIGN FILM/DOUBLETALK: The Killer [S, I, C]
  A criminal on the run after a bank job; his lover makes a terrible accomplice (French doubletalk)
SONG/DANCE: All You Want to Do is Dance [I]
  Coca as a woman who wants to do just that
MONOLOGUE: How About Breakfast? [S]
  A man's wife won't make breakfast, among many other things she won't do

Ep #37 • Air Date: 2/17/51 • Host: Bob Cummings • [Paley, LOC, UCLA]
Sid and Imogene on vacation

Ep #38 • Air Date: 2/24/51 • Host: Fred Allen • [Paley, UCLA]
Sid and Imogene on vacation

Ep #39 • Air Date: 3/3/51 • Host: Joan Bennett • [Paley, LOC, UCLA]
HICKENLOOPERS: Sunday Morning at Home [S, I]
  The couple consider buying a house, but it's very expensive: $9500
STRANGERS/CLICHES: Tourists in Mexico [S, I]
  A couple observes that foreign places are so quaint, so exotic ... so expensive
GUEST SKETCH: The Wild Blue Yonder [S, I, GH]
  A man so nervous about an airplane trip, he gives new meaning to the term Fear of Flying
SILENT FILMS: Father Come Home [S, I, C]
  The earliest silent melodrama about the Perils of Demon Rum
SONG/DANCE: Gypsy Dance [I]
MONOLOGUE: Life Through the Eyes of a Dog [S]
  The family pet reveals what he really thinks about life with humans, and the occasional cat

Ep #40 • Air Date: 3/10/51 • Host: Tom Ewell • [Paley, LOC, UCLA]
HICKENLOOPERS: Anniversary Dinner [S, I, C]
  Doris and Charlie are about to break up at their anniversary dinner over their recollections of their marriage; a waiter, who thinks they're the perfect couple, reconciles them

PANTOMIME: New Camera [S, I]
  A couple go to the zoo to try out their new acquisition by taking pictures of animals; an accommodating monkey takes shots of them
PROFESSOR: Archeology I (a.k.a. Archeology Expert) [S, C] (YT, SC)
  The Professor's best advice on how to succeed in a career in archeology: "Don't Lift Heavy Rocks"
GUEST SKETCH: In the Movies [S, I, GH]
  Two movie-goers drive the man sitting behind them crazy with talking, eating, and blocking the screen; when an usher is summoned, the victim has to leave
SONG/DANCE: Get Outta Town [I]
MONOLOGUE: Rejected Suitor [S]
  A man trying to figure out why his girl left him for his best friend Jim

Ep #41 • Air Date: 3/17/51 • Host: Signe Hasso • [Paley, LOC, UCLA]
HICKENLOOPERS: Where Shall We Eat? [S, I, C]
  An endless debate between the Hickenloopers and another couple over where to spend their night out
STRANGERS/CLICHES: Old Friends [S, I]
  A couple assures each other "you haven't changed a bit," even while they can't quite place who the other is
FOREIGN FILM/DOUBLETALK: Il Nuovo Telephono [S, I, C]
  The installation of a telephone leads to jealousy and murder (Italian doubletalk)
GUEST SKETCH: At the Fights [S, I, GH]
  Two women at ring-side who don't quite understand The Sweet Science frustrate a man who does
SONG/DANCE: Those Were the Good Old Days [I]
MONOLOGUE: You're a Big Man Now [S]
  A man takes his son to his first day at school, offering useful advice on how to get along with teachers and his fellow classmates

Ep #42 • Air Date: 3/24/51 • Host: Richard Carlson • [Paley*, UCLA]
HICKENLOOPERS: After the Party [S, I]
  An argument after a social engagement in which Charlie conducts to Doris's off-stage bickering
SILENT FILMS: A Fool's Fate [S, I, C]
  A husband falls for a femme fatale, abandoning his wife and children for her; featuring one of the longest falls down a staircase on a TV show by Sid
SONG/DANCE: Rigoletto [I]
  Coca as a sub in a touring company of Rigoletto; her infatuation with the tenor almost derails the performance
GUEST SKETCH: You Done It [S, GH]
STRANGERS/CLICHES: Superstitions [S, I]
MONOLOGUE: Sunday Ride with Big Family [S]
  A man takes his extremely large family out for a drive, complicated by Jimmy, one of the brood, constantly taking the keys

Appendix: Comedy Sketch Guide

Ep #43 • Air Date: 3/31/51 • Host: Virginia Field • [Paley, LOC, UCLA]
HICKENLOOPERS: Spring Cleaning [S, I]
  Doris decides to clean out the closet; most of what she wants to get rid of is, of course, Charlie's
PANTOMIME: Let's Have a Party [S, I]
  A couple copes with a large party, then its aftermath
PROFESSOR: Engineering 2 (a.k.a. Engineering Expert) [S, C]
  Hans von Bulldozer on principles of architecture and how not to build a skyscraper
GUEST SKETCH: Natives are Restless [S, C, GH]
  The Eternal Triangle in the tropics
MONOLOGUE: I Can't Sleep [S]
  Man tries various methods to get some shut-eye, some ludicrous, none of which work
SONG/DANCE: Tom Sawyer [I]
  Routine based on the Twain classic

Ep #44 • Air Date: 4/7/51 • Host: John Conte • [Paley, LOC, UCLA]
OTHER: Let's Be Neat [S, I]
  A very fussy husband makes serving breakfast a nightmare for his wife (he measures wheatcakes with a compass)
FOREIGN FILM/DOUBLETALK: It's a Lovely Day [S, I]
  A man prevents a woman from jumping into the Seine, and is rewarded by a succession of her lovers beating him up (French doubletalk)
GUEST SKETCH: Country Club Reunion [S, I, C, GH]
  A man becomes increasingly jealous as all his wife's male classmates greet her a little too warmly
STRANGERS/CLICHES: Public School [S, I]
  A couple watches their offspring graduate from 6th grade while trading trite observations on education and praising their kids
MONOLOGUE: Wedding Invitation [S]
  A man can't figure out why he wasn't invited to a wedding—after all, it's his daughter's
SONG/DANCE: Tickle-toe [I]

Ep #45 • Air Date: 4/14/51 • Host: Marsha Hunt • [Paley, LOC, UCLA]
HICKENLOOPERS: Reconciliation [S, I, C]
  A friend tries to get Charlie and Doris to make up after an argument; they reconcile only after turning on him
PROFESSOR: Movies (a.k.a. Film Expert) [S, C] (YT)
  Kurt von Close-up describes movies he has made and how to deal with stars
GUEST SKETCH: The Cruise [S, I, GH]
  A seasick man is badgered by two woman on a cruise
SILENT FILMS: Doctors' Wives [S, I, C]
  The neglected wife of a doctor is attracted to a friend; the doctor finds out about it and then has to perform brain surgery on his rival

SONG/DANCE: I Haven't Got Time to be a Millionaire [I]
   Coca in her tramp persona
MONOLOGUE: Trust [S]
   After declaring the importance of trust in a marriage, a man undermines his with his jealousy

Ep #46 • Air Date: 4/21/51 • Host: Richard Greene • [Paley, UCLA]
HICKENLOOPERS: Auto Smash Up [S, I]
   Doris wrecks the car and has to find a way to tell Charlie
STRANGERS/CLICHES: At a Housewarming [S, I]
   Touring a home, a couple dish about the owners and the house
PANTOMIME: Dance Hall Pick-up [S, I]
   A man seeking a dance is stuck with an awkward, pushy partner
GUEST SKETCH: Adventure in Bangadoor [S, I, C, GH]
   Betrayal and intrigue in the Colonies
MONOLOGUE: Diet [S]
   A man decides he has to lose weight, as he observes that his suit jacket used to be a topcoat
SONG/DANCE: Gypsy Dance [I]

Ep #47 • Air Date: 4/28/51 • Host: Wendy Barrie • [Paley, LOC, UCLA]
HICKENLOOPERS: Trying to Get a Table in a Restaurant [S, I, C]
   Charlie gives a head waiter exorbitant bribes to get a table; after the meal, he takes it with him, having paid for it
PROFESSOR: Marriage Consultant [S, C]
   Advice on courtship and romance from the Professor's work "Love: its cure and prevention"
GUEST SKETCH: The Gay Party [S, I, C, GH]
   A man flirts with various women at a party, neglecting his wife; when a man flirts with her, trouble ensues
SILENT FILMS: Dancing Mothers [S, I, C]
   Flapper neglects her husband and child; then the child falls ill
SONG/DANCE: Queen of the Maywalk [I]
   A young girl with her Maypole laments missing the dance
MONOLOGUE: Man Proposing to Wife-to-be [S]
   A man acts out various methods to propose

Ep #48 • Air Date: 5/5/51 • Host: Skitch Henderson • [Paley, LOC, UCLA]
HICKENLOOPERS: Doris Gets a Maid [S, I]
   After his initial disapproval, Charlie finds that he enjoys having a maid
STRANGERS/CLICHES: The Separation [S, I]
   A couple enjoy watching the cases in a divorce court and gossiping about the people involved

190   Appendix: Comedy Sketch Guide

FOREIGN FILM/DOUBLETALK: Café Paradise [S, I, C, H]
    A parody of *The Blue Angel*, with Imogene singing "Falling in Love Again" and Sid as the professor doing just that (German doubletalk)
GUEST SKETCH: Music Salon [S, I, C, H, GH]
    Sid's coughing and sneezing not only disrupts Henderson's piano playing, it spreads to the audience
SONG/DANCE: Ev'ry Little Movement Has a Meaning All Its Own [I]
    Coca in a 1910 musical
MONOLOGUE: Big Family at the Beach [S]
    An excursion to Coney Island with a family so large they play four games of volleyball simultaneously and at least one kid is temporarily lost when a sibling buries him in sand

Ep #49 • Air Date: 5/12/51 • Host: Faye Emerson • [Paley, LOC, UCLA]
HICKENLOOPERS: Front Seat Driver [S, I]
    The usual misadventures on a drive, including road rage, misleading directions, and an inventive scheme to avoid a speeding ticket
PROFESSOR: Self-Help Expert [S, C]
    Ludwig von Backslapper explains techniques to build self-esteem
GUEST SKETCH: Next-Door Neighbor [S, I, GH]
    A man is flummoxed by the attentions of an attractive new neighbor; his wife is not amused
FOREIGN FILM/DOUBLETALK: Escape [S, I, C]
    A convict on the lam who takes over the house of a father and daughter (French doubletalk)
SONG/DANCE: San Antone [I]
MONOLOGUE: Second-Hand Car Buyer [S]
    A man thinks he's being shrewd in trying to negotiate the price of a used car

Ep #50 • Air Date: 5/19/51 • Host: Signe Hasso • [Paley]
HICKENLOOPERS: The Maid Leaves [S, I]
    After becoming disappointed in their new maid's performance, the couple finds, to their shock, that she's leaving
PANTOMIME: Country Hotel [S, I]
    A stay in a room so small they can't turn around, the windows don't open—and there are bats
FOREIGN FILM/DOUBLETALK: The Happy Event [S, I, C]
    A man is ecstatic to find that his wife is going to have a baby, but is insistent on its sex: "A boy—or forget about it" (Italian doubletalk)
GUEST SKETCH: Quartet [S, I, C, GH]
    Adventures of two couples on a double date at the movies
SONG/DANCE: Crazy Rhythm [I]
MONOLOGUE: Anti-Marriage Advice [S]
    A man tries to dissuade his best friend from marrying, supplying reasons from his own unhappy marriage

Appendix: Comedy Sketch Guide   191

Ep #51 • Air Date: 5/26/51 • Host: Larraine Day • [Paley, UCLA]
HICKENLOOPERS: Dishwashing [S, I, C]
    Charlie and Doris's argument over household chores spills over to affect a happy couple who are visiting
PROFESSOR: Child Psychology [S, C]
    Ludwig von Pablum explains, among other things, misbehaving children— sometimes, they're just rotten kids
SILENT FILMS: Great-Grandson of the Sheik [S, I, C]
    Desert intrigue, in a spoof of Valentino movies
GUEST SKETCH: Let's Eat [S, I, GH]
    A man and two women try to co-exist after they're forced to share a table
SONG/DANCE: Les Sylphidea [I]
    Parody in which two dancers exchange gossip between plies and arabesques
PANTOMIME: Boy at First Dance [S]
    Shy, awkward boy at first dance; five years later, he's an assured ladies' man

Ep #52 • Air Date: 6/2/51 • Host: Constance Bennett • [Paley, UCLA]
HICKENLOOPERS: Vacation [S, I]
    The couple argue over where to go: he wants the deep-woods, she wants the tropics
PANTOMIME: Magicians [S, I]
    An inept magician whose tricks fail, usually to the detriment of his assistant, and who just can't escape from a strait-jacket and chains
FOREIGN FILM/DOUBLETALK: Forgotten Symphony [S, I, C]
    A composer finally sees his masterpiece performed, thanks to his wife and friend (German doubletalk)
GUEST SKETCH: Picnic [S, I, C, GH]
    A double-date at a turn-of-the-century picnic, in which the men vie for the attention of a glamorous visitor from New York
MONOLOGUE: Soft-hearted Harry [S]
    A man's friend threatens their relationship when he asks for a loan

Season 3 (1951-52)

Howard Morris becomes a regular. Parodies of specific films (rather than genres) first appear with spoofs of *A Streetcar Named Desire* and *A Place in the Sun* and will become a standard feature of *Your Show of Shows*. With the episode of September 29, 1951, the show goes live coast-to-coast via coaxial cable. From this season forward, on weeks when there were no guest hosts, regular cast members (Carl Reiner, Howard Morris, and the occasional singer or dancer) filled in and provided introductions to guest stars and sketches.

Ep #53 • Air Date: 9/8/51 • Host: Wendell Corey • [Paley, LOC, UCLA]
One of only two full episodes released on DVD
HICKENLOOPERS: It's Only a Movie [S, I]
    She thinks the movie was tragic; he thought it was hilarious
PANTOMIME: Day at the Beach [S, I]
    Building sand sculptures, finding "buried treasure," and getting sunburnt
GUEST SKETCH: French Without Food [S, I, GH]
    An American couple want to experience real French cuisine; the woman, much to the dismay of the waiter (Sid), wants ketchup
SONG/DANCE: Over a Bottle of Wine [S, I, C]
    Sid and Imogene drink wine, flirt, sing a scat song, and dance to Latin rhythms "under a tropical sky"; the first of only two full-scale song and dance numbers on *Your Show of Shows*
MONOLOGUE: You Never Looked Better [S]
    A man cheers up his hospitalized friend by telling him that he's lost his job and probably his wife—"but you never looked better"

Ep #54 • Air Date: 9/15/51 • Host: Marguerite Chapman • [Paley, LOC, UCLA]
HICKENLOOPERS: Handling the Servant Problem [S, I]
    Charlie and Doris part ways with Annabelle, the maid
PROFESSOR: The Legal Expert [S, C]
    Ludwig von Loophole shares his expertise of legal systems
GUEST SKETCH: City Gal [S, I, C, GH]
    Two country boys are enamored of a glamorous city girl, leaving her plain cousin in the lurch
SILENT FILMS: Fools in Love [S, I, C]
    Love among the royals when a prince falls for a commoner, much to the disapproval of his father the king
SONG/DANCE: Glowworm [I]
    A number in which Imogene does indeed glow—intermittently
MONOLOGUE: Just Relax [S]
    A businessman can't relax, thinking about his partner whom he suspects is leading the company to ruin

Ep #55 • Air Date: 9/22/51 • Host: Tom Ewell • [Paley, UCLA]
HICKENLOOPERS: Parking [S, I]
    The couple, on their way to the theater, search endlessly for a parking space; to Doris' dismay, Charlie resorts to driving on the sidewalk ("I can make better time")
STRANGERS/CLICHES: Hollywood [S, I]
    A couple meet on a studio tour and discuss picture-making and Hollywood stars
FOREIGN FILM/DOUBLETALK: Bambino [S, I, C]
    A man rescues a baby, which may or may not be abandoned (Italian doubletalk)
GUEST SKETCH: The Cafeteria [S, I, GH]
    A man and a woman taking a leisurely lunch in a cafeteria drive a man who only wants a piece of apple pie to hysterics

SONG/DANCE: Life on the Rails [I, C]
   Coca in her tramp persona
MONOLOGUE: Note from Principal [S]
   A man sees a principal about his misbehaving son and must attempt to straighten things out

Ep #56 • Air Date: 9/29/51 • Host: Eva Gabor • [Paley, UCLA]
First coast-to-coast live broadcast
HICKENLOOPERS: The Train [S, I, C]
   Charlie is extremely nervous about missing his stop, driving Doris and the conductor to distraction
PROFESSOR: Magic I (a.k.a. Magic Expert) [S, C] (YT, SF, SC)
   Professor Hocus von Pocus demonstrates his legerdemain with the bottle-glass trick and hypnosis, all of which don't go as planned
PANTOMIME: Coney Island [S, I] (YT, SC)
   A couple visit the attractions, try out various venues, and get sick after an epic roller-coaster ride
GUEST SKETCH: Monte Carlo [S, I, C, GH]
   A French duc has his plan to recoup his losses at the gambling table thwarted by two women and the croupier
SONG/DANCE: When the Bell in the Lighthouse Rings [I]
   Coca as an unlikely Lorelei
MONOLOGUE: The In-Law Problem [S]
   A man defends his wife to his mother, who disapproves of her

Ep #57 • Air Date: 10/6/51 • Host: Kim Hunter • [Paley*, UCLA]
HICKENLOOPERS: The Wife Works [S, I]
   Doris announces one morning that she's off to a job; Charlie is horrified—doesn't he support the house? Also, who's going to make his breakfast? Some surprising proto-feminist twists for a comedy sketch of 1951 ()
GUEST SKETCH: Baseball [S, I, C, H, GH]
   Sid as a pinch-hitter for the Yankees in the World Series; all looks grim when two women heckle him from the stands and the count goes to 3 and 2
FOREIGN FILM/DOUBLETALK: Grand Disillusion [S, I, C, H]
   A German officer is lured into divulging secrets by an attractive woman who just happens to be Mata Hari
OTHER: Suicide Sketch
MONOLOGUE: Penny Chewing Gum Machine [S]
   The saga of a polite chewing gum machine in a subway station who comes to a bad end as a downtown slot machine

Ep #58 • Air Date: 10/13/51 • Host: Charlton Heston • [Paley, LOC, UCLA]
HICKENLOOPERS: Theatre Tickets [S, I, C]
   Charlie gets tickets to a sold-out show, but the couple's tickets are far too close to the stage

HICKENLOOPERS: First Homecooked Meal [S, I]
   Charlie can't eat Doris's inedible cooking; to avoid hurting her feelings, he throws each course out the window, resulting in collateral damage to passers-by
PROFESSOR: Distaff Expert [S, C]
   Advice is offered from the Professor's book "Women and Their Behavior—Look out, Men!"
SILENT FILMS: A Rich Man's Joke (a.k.a. The Huge Jest) [S, I, C, GH] (YT, SC)
   To get back at an obnoxious friend, a man transforms a poor woman into a beauty the friend will fall for; the joke's on him as he falls for her himself
MONOLOGUE: Chance of a Lifetime [S]
   A man who can't decide on anything including his career choices
SONG/DANCE: Wildflower [I]

Ep #59 • Air Date: 10/20/51 • Host: Geraldine Fitzgerald • [Paley, LOC, UCLA]

The video for this date at the Paley Center is actually a compilation of 8 Caesar monologues from various episodes

PANTOMIME: Old-fashioned Courtship [S, I]
FOREIGN FILM/DOUBLETALK: Frere Jacques [S, I, C]
STRANGERS/CLICHES: Doctor's Office [S, I]
GUEST SKETCH: Out of Your Mind [S, GH]
OTHER: For the Defense [I]
MONOLOGUE: Phobias [S]

Ep #60 • Air Date: 10/27/51 • Host: Ilona Massey • [Paley, LOC, UCLA]

HICKENLOOPERS: Dinner at Twelve [S, I, C]
   The couple are invited to a friend's for dinner, which is interminably delayed as Charlie becomes more and more ravenous
FOREIGN FILM/DOUBLETALK: The Tree [S, I, C, H]
   A man's beloved tree has to give way to a railroad—maybe (Italian doubletalk) One of the best of the doubletalk sketches, with a touch of pathos as well as humor—you actually find yourself rooting for Sid and his tree
GUEST SKETCH: Gypsy Countess [S, I, C, GH]
   Sid and Imogene are Sasha and Tasha, gypsy musicians who are summoned to entertain at a party thrown by a Hungarian countess
PROFESSOR: Airplane Expert [S, C]
   Rudolph von Rudder explains the mechanics of flying
SONG/DANCE: Place Pigalle [I]
   Imogene gets a French lesson as well as a dance
MONOLOGUE: Punching Bag [S]
   Spoof of boxing movies with Sid as the kid from the neighborhood who makes it big in the ring

Ep #61 • Air Date: 11/3/51 • Host: Richard Arlen • [Paley, LOC, UCLA]

HICKENLOOPERS: Fear of Flying [S, I, C]
   Charlie is an extremely nervous not-so-frequent flyer

Appendix: Comedy Sketch Guide   195

PANTOMIME: Taking Baby Home [S, I]
    A couple take extreme care with their newborn; to feed him, the man dons surgical mask and gloves
SONG/DANCE: Striptease [I]
    Coca does a striptease under a huge overcoat
SONG/DANCE: Basin Street [S, C, H]
    Sid as a Parisian entertainer at a jazz club, playing sax, singing a patter song, and dancing a jitterbug (French doubletalk)
GUEST SKETCH: The Eyewitness [S, I, GH]
    The Hickenloopers attempt to aid a policeman in reconstructing an accident they have witnessed; their accounts of course vary
MONOLOGUE: Absentminded Man [S]
    A man whose wife told him to do something important, if he could only remember what

Ep #62 • Air Date: 11/10/51 • Host: Marguerite Piazza • [Paley, LOC, UCLA]

HICKENLOOPERS: Overnight Guest [S, I, C]
    Carl as a guest who just won't leave, and Sid and Imogene have to accommodate him for the night
STRANGERS/CLICHES: Aboard Ship [S, I]
    Couple meet and exchange observations about life on a cruise ship (there really are crows in the crow's nest)
GUEST SKETCH: Football Hero [S, I, C, GH]
    A soda jerk has a crush on a coed; unfortunately, she only has eyes for a football star
SILENT FILMS: They Always Get Their Man [S, I, C]
    Adventures in the Great White North, as Mounties search for an escaped convict
SONG/DANCE: Scots Number [I]
MONOLOGUE: She's a Nice Girl [S]
    A man complains to his neighbors about his wife's less-than-desirable qualities

Ep #63 • Air Date: 11/17/51 • Host: Nina Foch • [Paley, LOC, UCLA]

HICKENLOOPERS: Insomnia [S, I]
    Charlie can't get to sleep; after all of Doris's advice fails, she suggests something sure-fire: exhausting himself with a polka
PANTOMIME: Carnegie Hall [S, I]
    Couple seated next to each other at a symphony mirror the emotions of Tchaikovsky's "Romeo and Juliet"
OTHER: Readin', Writin', and Weltschmerz [S, I, C, H]
    A Heidelburg professor has difficulty controlling his students (German doubletalk)
GUEST SKETCH: Le Grand Prix [S, I, GH]
    An experienced bettor on horse races is confounded when two novices keep laying winning bets

196　　　　Appendix: Comedy Sketch Guide

SONG/DANCE: Me and My Imagination [I]
　　Coca in her tramp persona
MONOLOGUE: Any Messages? [S]
　　A man worries over a mysterious caller who didn't leave a message

Ep #64 • Air Date: 11/24/51 • Host: Robert Preston • [Paley, LOC, UCLA]
HICKENLOOPERS: Poker Game [S, I, C, H]
　　Charlie goes to a poker game—and forgets he was supposed to meet Doris
STRANGERS/CLICHES: Dogs in the Park [S, I]
　　Trading clichés about canines; his begs so well, it's sending his son through college
FOREIGN FILM/DOUBLETALK: L'Arsenique [S, I, C]
　　A love triangle, in which all points are dead by the end (French double-talk)
GUEST SKETCH: Producer's Dilemma [S, C, GH]
　　A producer asks the help of the Professor in turning a nice-guy actor into a movie killer
OTHER: Fur Model [I]
　　Coca models the latest fashions in fur
MONOLOGUE: Wedding Ceremony [S]
　　Thoughts of a man whose daughter is about to be married

Ep #65 • Air Date: 12/1/51 • Host: Patrice Munsel • [Paley, LOC, UCLA]
OTHER: Lost Kids [S, I, C]
　　Two lost kids end up in a police station, complicating things for all officers concerned
PANTOMIME: Day at the Park [S, I]
　　A couple enjoys a day at the park, with an emphasis on avian relations: feeding songbirds almost results in a scene from Hitchcock; Sid grants a request from a duck for a cigarette
GUEST SKETCH: The Country Relations [S, I, C, GH]
　　Country cousins almost ruin an engagement party for their wealthy kinswoman
HICKENLOOPERS: Making Up Again [S, I, C]
　　A neighbor tries to reconcile the battling couple; no good deed goes unpunished
MONOLOGUE: English/French War Pictures [S]
　　Different versions of World War I movies, English and French (French double-talk)
SONG/DANCE: Scheherazade [I]
　　Final production number with Coca as the story-teller

Ep #66 • Air Date: 12/8/51 • Host: Herb Shriner • [Paley, LOC, UCLA]
Sid and Imogene on vacation

Ep #67 • Air Date: 12/15/51 • Host: Herb Shriner • [Paley, LOC, UCLA]
Sid and Imogene on vacation

Ep #68 • Air Date: 12/22/51 • Host: Charlton Heston • [UCLA]
HICKENLOOPERS: Hangover [S, I]
STRANGERS/CLICHES: Christmas Shopping [S, I]
GUEST SKETCH: Unter den Test Tube [S, GH]
OTHER: Lobster Sketch [S, I]
MONOLOGUE: Woman Preparing for Sleep [S]

Ep #69 • Air Date: 12/29/51 • Host: Madge Evans • [UCLA]
HICKENLOOPERS: Modern Furniture [S, I]
PROFESSOR: Culinary Expert [S, C]
GUEST SKETCH: Subway [GH]
MONOLOGUE: My Son, a Doctor [S]

Ep #70 • Air Date: 1/5/52 • Host: Marguerite Piazza • [Paley, LOC, UCLA]
HICKENLOOPERS: Justice of the Peace [S, I]
   In a bit of back history, Charlie and Doris plan to be married before a justice of the peace
PANTOMIME: Shoe Salesman [S, I]
   A clerk attempts to fit a fussy customer
HICKENLOOPERS: It's My Treat [S, I, C]
   Couples who go to the movies argue about who's going to pay for everything from tickets to popcorn
FOREIGN FILM/DOUBLETALK: Roses are Blooming in Picardy [S, I, C]
   An escaped convict holds two people hostage (French double-talk)
SONG/DANCE: Madame Galli [I]
   Spoof of opera divas
MONOLOGUE: But I Love Her [S]
   A man asking advice about his girlfriend

Ep #71 • Air Date: 1/12/52 • Host: John Hodiak • [Paley, LOC, UCLA]
HICKENLOOPERS: Toothache [S, I]
   When Charlie develops a toothache after eating candy, Doris's advice ranges from "Suffer!" to anesthetizing the pain with whiskey, a remedy he readily embraces
STRANGERS/CLICHES: In a Pet Store (a.k.a. In the Pet Shop) [S, I] (YT)
   A couple compare possible pets, some highly inappropriate, and admire those on display
GUEST SKETCH: Sagebrush Serenade (*Double Indemnity*) [S, I, C, GH]
   Actors filming a quickie movie (an excellent mini-parody of *Double Indemnity*) have to speed up the action—hilariously—so that they can relinquish the set to a western
SILENT FILMS: Ticker Mad [S, I, C]
   A man who thinks of nothing but money, neglecting his wife and daughter in the process, realizes that money isn't everything

MONOLOGUE: Boy Growing Up [S]
  Man waiting in maternity room at hospital imagines various stages of his son's life, all exasperating
SONG/DANCE: Dangerous Dan McGrew [I]
  Final production number with Coca as the shady lady who's responsible for Dan's demise

Ep #72 • Air Date: 1/19/52 • Host: Signe Hasso • [Paley, LOC, UCLA]
HICKENLOOPERS: Baby in the Park [S, I, C, H] (YT)
  The couple take their baby, over whom they fuss, to a park where they encounter extremely laissez-faire parents
PANTOMIME: Life of the Party [S, I] (YT)
  A man makes himself thoroughly obnoxious at a party with pranks and practical jokes
FOREIGN FILM/DOUBLETALK: U-Boat-749 (a.k.a. Submarine) [S, I, C, H] (YT, SC)
  Submarine warfare, highly ineffectual, in World War I with Sid as the captain who discovers a spy is on his boat
GUEST SKETCH: Quartet [S, I, C, GH]
  Double-dating at the movies
SONG/DANCE: The Dixie Belle [I]
  Coca as a Southern charmer with a coterie of admirers
MONOLOGUE: Vacation Time [S]
  A businessman on vacation can't relax, as he worries about his business and his partner

Ep #73 • Air Date: 1/26/52 • Host: Binnie Barnes • [Paley, LOC, UCLA]
HICKENLOOPERS: Taking Messages [S, I]
  Doris can't take down, or remember, Charlie's important messages
STRANGERS/CLICHES: Community Bazaar [S, I]
  At a bazaar, with much satirizing of small town events and sampling largely inedible baked goods
PROFESSOR: Money Expert [S, C]
  Financial tips from Professor Filthy von Lucre
SPOOFS/PARODIES: A Place in the Streetcar [S, I, GH]
  Parody of *A Streetcar Named Desire* with Sid as Stanley and Imogene as Blanche (the first spoof of a specific film rather than genres)
SONG/DANCE: Jim [I]
  A torch singer laments a highly unsuitable lover
MONOLOGUE: Early to Bed, Early to Rise [S]
  A man takes extraordinary measures to ensure he gets up in time to catch a train

Ep #74 • Air Date: 2/2/52 • Host: Teresa Wright • [Paley, LOC]
HICKENLOOPERS: Lost Dog [S, I]
  The couple has lost their pampered dog Brownie; all is well when he's discovered in a bar—he'll return when he's finished with his drink
PANTOMIME: Driving Lesson [S, I]
  A man attempts to teach his wife how to drive

Appendix: Comedy Sketch Guide 199

FOREIGN FILM/DOUBLETALK: The Cobbler's Daughter [S, I, C]
    A cobbler tries to find a suitable suitor for his daughter (Italian double-talk)
PANTOMIME: Two Musicians [S, I]
    Sid and Imogene as percussionists in an orchestra mime their parts in the 1812 Overture
SONG/DANCE: Fish and Chips [I]
MONOLOGUE: It's Better This Way [S]
    A man has been jilted by his girl and tries to get over it

Ep #75 • Air Date: 2/9/52 • Host: June Lockhart • [Paley*, LOC, UCLA]
HICKENLOOPERS: Smorgasbord [S, I]
    Doris introduces a reluctant Charlie to a new cuisine; the prospect of all-you-can-eat is too much for him
GUEST SKETCH: The Couple Upstairs [S, I, H, GH]
    When the woman upstairs complains of her treatment by her fearsome husband, Doris enlists Charlie to deal with him
SONG/DANCE: Swan Lake [I]
    Parody of the ballet, with Coca as the swan with molting feathers
SILENT FILMS: The Love Bandit [S, I, C, H]
SONG/DANCE: Lily of Laguna [S, I] (YT)
    A loving couple perform a vaudeville/music hall act which turns into an anything-you-can-do-I-can-do-better contest; the second of only two full-scale song and dance numbers Caesar and Coca would perform
MONOLOGUE: Man Without a Dime [S]
    A man leaves his wallet in the office and tries a variety of methods to get a dime for the subway

Ep #76 • Air Date: 2/16/52 • Host: Arlene Francis • [Paley, LOC, UCLA]
HICKENLOOPERS: Standing Room Only [S, I, C, H]
    In a crowded movie theatre, after trying various ways of getting seats, Charlie leads the rest of the patrons in a revolt
PANTOMIME: What's on TV Tonight? [S, I]
    Watching TV in the '50s: endless adjustment of horizontal and vertical controls and the antenna; then you fall asleep in front of it
FOREIGN FILM/DOUBLETALK: Avoir, Ma Cherie [S, I, C, H]
    Spoof of a World War I movie; a woman bids goodbye to her lover as he leaves for the front (French doubletalk)
GUEST SKETCH: The Gay Party [S, I, C, GH]
    A man flirts with various women at a party, neglecting his wife; when a man flirts with her, trouble ensues
MONOLOGUE: What Does the Baby Think? [S]
    Musings of a 6-month-old baby
SONG/DANCE: Ratchey-Coo [I]
    Final production number with Coca as a dancing dove, accompanied by lots of real ones

Ep #77 • Air Date: 2/23/52 • Host: Margaret Lindsay • [Paley, UCLA]
One of only two full episodes released on DVD
HICKENLOOPERS: A Big Surprise [S, I]
 Charlie is excited about going to his reunion—until Doris reveals a new hairdo
PANTOMIME: On the Subway [S, I]
 Two people fight other passengers, and each other, to get a seat
GUEST SKETCH: Drugstore Counter [S, I, C, GH]
 A truck driver who needs both his lunch and a seat is frustrated by two women taking their time
FOREIGN FILM/DOUBLETALK: Ich Liebe die Halls of Ivy [S, I, C, H]
 A student (Carl) introduces his father the Baron (Sid) to his fiancée (Imogene); the Baron was once in love with her mother (German doubletalk)
SONG/DANCE: Rigoletto [I]
 Spoof of the opera
MONOLOGUE: Just Once of Those Days [S]
 A man's bad day begins as soon as he wakes up—while stretching, he dislocates his shoulder—and goes downhill from there

Ep #78 • Air Date: 3/1/52 • Host: Leo Genn • [Paley, LOC, UCLA]
HICKENLOOPERS: The Quarrel [S, I]
 The couple argue over his cigar smoking and her cooking
PROFESSOR: Self Defense (a.k.a. Self-Defense Expert) [S, C] (YT, SF, SC)
 Demonstration of various techniques, all of which backfire
GUEST SKETCH: King Solomon's African Queen [S, I, GH]
 Years after a boy goes missing in the jungle, an explorer and a woman search for him; Sid as jungle boy in a Tarzan spoof
FOREIGN FILM/DOUBLETALK: Bambino [S, I, C]
 A couple await the birth of their child (Italian doubletalk)
SONG/DANCE: It's Raining Sunbeams [I]
 Coca in her tramp persona
MONOLOGUE: Airplane Movies [S] (YT, SF, SC)
 In a satire of World War II movies, a lone pilot takes on an entire Luftwaffe squadron

Ep #79 • Air Date: 3/8/52 • Host: Larry Storch • [Paley, LOC, UCLA]
Sid and Imogene on vacation

Ep #80 • Air Date: 3/15/52 • Host: Dave Garroway • [Paley, LOC, UCLA]
Sid and Imogene on vacation

Ep #81 • Air Date: 3/22/52 • Host: Virginia Grey • [Paley, LOC, UCLA]
PANTOMIME: Music Recital [S, I]
 A violinist's debut is ruined by his own ineptitude and his piano accompanist's antics
GUEST SKETCH: The Wayward Bus [S, I, C, H, GH]
 A crowd of passengers make a bus driver's run impossible

Appendix: Comedy Sketch Guide 201

HICKENLOOPERS: The Scented Letter [S, I] (YT)
 Charlie receives a scented letter in the mail; Doris's suspicions are immediately aroused
FOREIGN FILM/DOUBLETALK: Das Vild Vild West (a.k.a. Hopalong Dingle-Dangle) [S, I, C, H]
 Spoof of a Western in which the good guy defeats the bad and helps the heroine, but one performed entirely in German doubletalk
SONG/DANCE: Galli Curci Rag [I]
MONOLOGUE: Putting Baby to Sleep [S]
 A man tries every known tactic to get his four-year-old daughter to go to bed

Ep #82 • Air Date: 3/29/52 • Host: No guest host • [Paley, LOC, UCLA]
HICKENLOOPERS: Restaurant [S, I, C]
 Doris has too much to drink while waiting to meet an important client of Charlie's
OTHER: Punch and Judy [S, I, C]
 A Punch and Judy show with real people instead of puppets; a rare total misfire—Punch and Judy just aren't funny, even with this cast
STRANGERS/CLICHES: Dentist's Office [S, I]
 Trading trite observations about dentists, teeth, and pain
SILENT FILMS: Siren's Spell [S, I, C]
 Imogene as a siren with a magnetic attraction (a real one) that Sid and Carl can't escape
SONG/DANCE: Water sprite [I]
 Ballet spoof
MONOLOGUE: The Mumbler [S]
 A very unusual monologue. A man who mumbles to himself is regarded by onlookers with some alarm; Sid turns himself into a proto-Travis Bickle when he notices their stares ("Are you lookin' at me? Are you lookin' at me")

Ep #83 • Air Date: 4/5/52 • Host: Betty Furness • [Paley, LOC, UCLA]
HICKENLOOPERS: Don't Mind Me [S, I, C]
 An obnoxious guest ruins the couple's dinner
PANTOMIME: Sleep [S, I]
 Trying to get some shut-eye amid various distractions
PROFESSOR: Business Expert [S, C]
 Filthy von Lucre gives financial advice; unfortunately, it's more along the lines of How to Fail in Business Without Really Trying
SPOOFS/PARODIES: A Streetcar Named ??? (a.k.a. A Place in the Streetcar Named Desire) [S, I, GH] (YT, SF, SC)
 Parody of *A Streetcar Named Desire*, with Sid as a very slobbish Stanley and Imogene as Blanche ()
SONG/DANCE: I'm Yours [S, I, C]
 A woman assures several men she's exclusively theirs
MONOLOGUE: Marriage Consultant [S]
 A man tries to convince his bachelor friend to get married

Ep #84 • Air Date: 4/12/52 • Host: Patrice Munsel • [Paley, LOC, UCLA]
HICKENLOOPERS: Easter Parade [S, I, C, H]
　Charlie and Doris crash it, in an attempt to get close to the celebs who are there
PANTOMIME: The Paraders [S, I]
　Two drum majors lead a marching band to disaster; featuring twirling and flaming batons, one of which ignites Sid. Mime at its funniest ()
FOREIGN FILM/DOUBLETALK: I Love You Strongly [S, I, C, H]
　In the casbah, a gangster (Sid) copes with his spitfire lover (Imogene) and fights with a rival (Carl)
OTHER: Music Recital [S, I, C, H]
　A man disrupts a musical performance without meaning to
SONG/DANCE: Life is Just a Bowl of Cherries [I]
　Coca in her tramp persona
MONOLOGUE: Second-Hand Car Buyer [S]
　A man thinks he's being shrewd in trying to negotiate the price of a used car

Ep #85 • Air Date: 4/19/52 • Host: Arlene Dahl • [Paley, LOC, UCLA]
HICKENLOOPERS: Priceless Antique [S, I]
　Doris buys a Louis XV table; when he finds out the cost, Charlie wants her to return it to him
PANTOMIME: Trained Seal [S, I] (YT, SF, SC)
　A seal who really doesn't want to balance a ball on his nose and his insistent trainer
GUEST SKETCH: The Girl Next Door [S, I, GH]
　A man discovers that his new, and glamorous, next-door neighbor really wants to get to know him better; his wife is not amused. Featuring, arguably, the Funniest Face Ever Made by a Human Being ()
SPOOFS/PARODIES: A Place at the Bottom of the Lake [S, I, C, H]
　Parody of A Place in the Sun, in which the unhappy man just can't kill his obnoxious wife-to-be, despite his best efforts; one of the first—and among the best—spoofs of a specific film ()
MONOLOGUE: Dance Hall Stag [S]
　A man is turned down repeatedly in his quest for a dance, to his increasing frustration. A rather startling illustration of Caesar's ability to not only immerse himself in his characters but react to imaginary "others" ()
SONG/DANCE: The Tickle-Toe [I]

Ep #86 • Air Date: 4/26/52 • Host: Kukla, Fran, and Ollie • [Paley, LOC, UCLA]
HICKENLOOPERS: Four in a Car [S, I, C]
　Sid and Imogene's drive in the country is disrupted by Carl as an annoying passenger
HICKENLOOPERS: Hypochondriac [S, I]
　Charlie is coming down with a cold; featuring a whole-body sneeze
GUEST SKETCH: Watching the Wedding [S, I, GH]
　The Strangers join Kukla, Fran, and Ollie to trade clichés about weddings

Appendix: Comedy Sketch Guide

FOREIGN FILM/DOUBLETALK: Das Forgessenor Symphony (a.k.a. Forgotten Symphony) [S, I, C]
: A composer finally sees his masterpiece performed, thanks to his wife and friend (German doubletalk). An excellent example of Caesar's ability and instincts in playing it straight within a comedy sketch ()

SONG/DANCE: Ever So Slightly Late [I]

MONOLOGUE: Rejected Suitor [S]
: A man tries to figure out why his girl has dumped him, perhaps for the best— "No good can come from a girl who steals hubcaps"

Ep #87 • Air Date: 5/3/52 • Host: Marguerite Piazza • [Paley, LOC, UCLA]

PANTOMIME: The Magicians [S, I]
: An inept magician (chains and a strait-jacket are hard to get out of) and his assistant

GUEST SKETCH: The Secretary (a.k.a. The New Secretary) [S, I, H, GH]
: Doris assists Charlie in interviews for a new secretary; unfortunately, one of them (Piazza) is a real knockout

PROFESSOR: Memory Expert [S, C]
: The Professor shares tips from his book, "I Remember Mama, but I Forget Papa"

FOREIGN FILM/DOUBLETALK: Say You'll Be Mine [S, I, C]
: The search for a wife (Italian doubletalk)

SONG/DANCE: Siamese Dance [I]

MONOLOGUE: Man at the Bar [S]
: A man enters a bar, has seven shots, and his mood changes with each

Ep #88 • Air Date: 5/10/52 • Host: Colleen Gray • [Paley, LOC, UCLA]

HICKENLOOPERS: The Diet [S, I]
: Doris decides on a weight-loss regimen and drags Charlie into it

PANTOMIME: Photographing Baby [S, I]
: Getting the right poses for both baby and parents is difficult; at one point Sid molds Imogene's face into exactly the right expression

GUEST SKETCH: Greyhound Bus [S, I, GH]
: Three people take a bus to Los Angeles, with the man uncomfortably in the middle

OTHER: Slowly I Turned (a.k.a. Suicide Sketch) [S, I, GH] (YT)
: Or don't attempt to help someone who wants to jump off the Empire State Building

SONG/DANCE: Maywalk [I]
: A young girl with her Maypole laments missing the dance

MONOLOGUE: Breaking the News [S]
: A man tells his parents that he's going to be married: "Ma, get your head out of the stove"

Ep #89 • Air Date: 5/17/52 • Host: No guest host • [Paley, UCLA]

HICKENLOOPERS: The Point Killer [S, I, C]
: Doris can't resist correcting a story Charlie is trying to tell, to his increasing consternation; among the best of the Hickenlooper sketches, illustrating

the moments in every marriage that elicit stray thoughts of spousal homicide ()
PANTOMIME: School Children [S, I]
    Kids dealing with teachers, lunch, and schoolyard bullies
PROFESSOR: Pain Expert [S, I, C]
    Tips on avoiding pain by tricking your brain (the only appearance of Imogene in a Professor sketch)
SPOOFS/PARODIES: Buzz and Bubbles [S, I, C, H]
    Spoof of the vaudeville trope in which a couple breaks up when Ziegfeld wants her, not him
SONG/DANCE: Sleeping Beauty [I]
    This beauty only wants to go back to bed
MONOLOGUE: Killing Time [S]
    A man misses a train and creates havoc in the station

Ep #90 • Air Date: 5/24/52 • Host: No guest host • [Paley, UCLA]
OTHER: Butler and Maid [S, I, C]
    An argument between the couple escalates dramatically as they serve dinner to their employer and his guests
STRANGERS/CLICHES: Kids at Summer Camp [S, I]
    A couple meet while sending their respective kids off to camp
HICKENLOOPERS: Auto Smash-up [S, I] (YT, SF, SC)
    Second version of the classic "wife wrecks car" sketch
SILENT FILMS: Sewing Machine Girl [S, I, C, H]
    Sweethearts in a sweat-shop, whose relationship is doomed by the lascivious boss and her ominous cough
SONG/DANCE: Fatback, LA, USA [I]
MONOLOGUE: I Can't Sleep [S]
    Man tries a variety of methods to get some shut-eye, all ludicrous and none work

Ep #91 • Air Date: 5/31/52 • Host: Dennis King • [Paley, LOC, UCLA]
HICKENLOOPERS: Drive You Back Home? [S, I, C, H]
    Trying to get guests home after a party in Manhattan isn't easy for Charlie
GUEST SKETCH: Garbage Sketch [S, I, C, H, GH] (YT)
    A super takes a tenant to court when she insists on throwing garbage out her window
HICKENLOOPERS: Midnight Snack [S, I] (YT)
    Charlie's search for food goes unrewarded until Doris comes up with singularly unpalatable "Limhoffer" cheese
FOREIGN FILM/DOUBLETALK: Mata Hari (a.k.a. Grand Disillusion) [S, I, C, H] (YT, SF, SC)
    A World War I German officer is attracted to a woman; unfortunately, she's Mata Hari
SONG/DANCE: Die Fleidermaus [I]
    Excerpts from the operetta

MONOLOGUE: Civic Pride [S] (YT)
    A man takes a little too much pride in his civic duties, becoming a nuisance to all

Season 4 (1952-53)

There was some tinkering with the running order (Hickenlooper sketches didn't always appear first). The number of comedy sketches was frequently reduced as parodies became longer. Coca was out for almost a month with an appendectomy; female guest-hosts appeared in her traditional roles and Caesar doubled up on pantomimes and monologues until her return. The Four Englishmen sketches make their first appearance.

Ep #92 • Air Date: 9/6/52 • Host: No guest host • [Paley, LOC, UCLA]
HICKENLOOPERS: The Joke (a.k.a. A Difference of Opinion) [S, I]
    Charlie tells Doris a joke he finds hilarious; to his increasing frustration, she doesn't get it
PANTOMIME: Hailing a Taxi in the Rain [S, I]
    None of their stratagems work, including Sid standing in the path of a cab and Imogene showing a bit of leg
FOREIGN FILM/DOUBLETALK: Das Schwinging Cirküs (a.k.a. The Circus) [S, I, C]
    The Eternal Triangle at the circus; a strongman's wife and her lover attempt to get rid of him (German doubletalk)
SPOOFS/PARODIES: The Doorknob [S, I, C, H]
    A community theatre's production goes awry, starting with a door that just won't open; farce and physical comedy worthy of Feydeau ()
SONG/DANCE: Doll Song from Tales of Hoffman [I]
MONOLOGUE: It's the Heat [S]
    A man copes with an extraordinary heat wave

Ep #93 • Air Date: 9/13/52 • Host: Marilyn Maxwell • [Paley, LOC, UCLA]
HICKENLOOPERS: How to Entertain at Home [S, I, C, H]
    Charlie gets a tape-recorder to entertain friends; unfortunately, it has a monumental case of feed-back
OTHER: Last Night in Camp [S, I, C]
    A man tries to convince a summer romance he'll see her back in the city
OTHER: School Days [S, I]
    Sid and Imogene as elementary school kids; she's a good student, he's anything but
SPOOFS/PARODIES: Young Man with a Lip [S, I, C, H, GH]
    Semi-parody of *Body and Soul*; Sid is a saxophone player who's given it up to go into the ring; Imogene is his girlfriend who reminds him continually of his lost career
SONG/DANCE: Gypsy Number [I]
MONOLOGUE: Man in Restaurant [S]
    A man suspicious of other patrons, including accusing them of coat-theft

206 Appendix: Comedy Sketch Guide

Ep #94 • Air Date: 9/20/52 • Host: Jack Palance • [Paley, LOC, UCLA]
HICKENLOOPERS: The Lost Diamond Ring [S, I]
   Doris loses her ring; Charlie tries to help her find it. However, she manages to lose other things along the way
SILENT FILMS: Enchanted Ballerina [S, I, C, GH]
   A Svengali-like villain (Sid) hypnotizes a dancer (Imogene); she's saved by another dancer (Carl) and a mysterious stranger (Palance)
OTHER: Fitting Room [I]
   A woman is bullied into trying on outrageous outfits; desperate to escape, she tries on one last totally unsuitable one—and loves it
PROFESSOR: Mountain Climbing I (a.k.a. Mountain Climbing) [S, C] (YT, SC)
   Kurt von FraidyCat explains and demonstrates techniques of mountain climbing, even if he doesn't follow them
GUEST SKETCH: Goldmine [S, C, H, GH]
   A *Treasure of the Sierra Madre* spoof, in which, not surprisingly, few of the prospectors make it out alive
MONOLOGUE: My Son, a Doctor [S]
   A proud parent at his son's med school graduation

Ep #95 • Air Date: 9/27/52 • Host: Ella Raines • [Paley*, LOC, UCLA]
OTHER: Sleeping Baby [S, I]
   Parents try to quiet noisy neighbors, so their baby can sleep
PANTOMIME: Blind Date [S, I]
   Couple at the movies, as the man discovers that the woman is the Blind Date from Hell
FOREIGN FILM/DOUBLETALK: Le Honere de Julle (a.k.a. Port du Salut) [S, I, C, H] (YT, SC)
   A jewel thief discovers his lover has betrayed him to the police (French doubletalk)
GUEST SKETCH: Subway [S, I, GH]
   A man refuses to give up his seat for two women, who then make his life miserable
SONG/DANCE: Ragtime Melody [I]
MONOLOGUE: Jealous Husband [S]
   For the first time in 7 years, a man's wife is not there to greet him when he returns from work—she must be having an affair

Ep #96 • Air Date: 10/4/52 • Host: Wanda Hendrix • [Paley, LOC, UCLA]
At the Paley Center, Caesar's monologue is on the video for 10/29/51, a compilation of 8 monologues
HICKENLOOPERS: East Indian Restaurant [S, I, C]
   Doris drags Charlie to a new dining experience; he's wary of both the food and the waiter
PANTOMIME: Violin Recital (a.k.a. Music Recital) [S, I] (YT)
   A violinist's debut is ruined by his own ineptitude and his piano accompanist's antics

SPOOFS/PARODIES: Sudden Death by Killing [S, I, GH]
    A noirish scenario in which a husband is trying to kill his wife; the tension is broken somewhat when they keep accidentally stepping on a cat (sound effects supplied by Mel Brooks)
GUEST SKETCH: Wedding Rehearsal [S, I, C, H, GH]
    A pushy relative (Sid) completely disrupts it, in the process dismantling the prospective groom (Howie)
SONG/DANCE: You Belong to Me [I]
MONOLOGUE: Superstitious Man [S]
    A man who is afraid of everything, including revolving doors; a showcase for Sid's talents for both mime and sound effects ()

Ep #97 • Air Date: 10/11/52 • Host: Dennis O'Keefe • [Paley, LOC, UCLA]

HICKENLOOPERS: Parlor Games [S, I, C, H]
    At a party, Doris either spoils or refuses to play games; someone suggests Musical Chairs, which Charlie is determined to win at any cost (to other participants)
STRANGERS/CLICHES: Empire State Building [S, I]
    Trading trite observations from the top about New York and the views
GUEST SKETCH: The Celebrity [S, I, GH]
    A woman makes a fool of herself over a star in a restaurant, to her husband's embarrassment
FOREIGN FILM/DOUBLETALK: Der Busy Brain Doctor [S, I, C, H]
    A doctor has to follow the Hippocratic oath by operating on a rival for his wife's love; many sharp instruments are wielded improbably (German doubletalk)
SONG/DANCE: Swan Lake [I]
    Spoof in which Coca's swan molts and she employs her feathers like a fan dancer
MONOLOGUE: Man Who Can't Relax [S]
    A man obsesses about his business partner, whom he is sure is leading the company to ruin

Ep #98 • Air Date: 10/18/52 • Host: No guest host • [LOC, UCLA]

HICKENLOOPERS: Leaving Home (a.k.a. I'm Leaving You) [S, I]
    Doris threatens to leave Charlie because he's been seen with another woman; he threatens to leave because she doubts him
PROFESSOR: Sleep Expert [S, C]
SPOOFS/PARODIES: Dark Noon [S, I, C, H]
    Spoof of *High Noon* with Sid as the sheriff facing down outlaws alone, Imogene as the bride who wants to know why—"'Cause I'm stupid, Mary Ellen"
PANTOMIME: Starting a New Day [S, I]
MONOLOGUE: Life of a Fly [S]
    CaesarFly surveys his house, talks to other flies, and, on an excursion to a greasy spoon, ducks swatting

Ep #99 • Air Date: 10/25/52 • Host: Corinne Calvet • [Paley*, LOC, UCLA]

HICKENLOOPERS: Going to the Movies [S, I, C, H]
    The couple and friends try to decide on which movie to see; Doris, having seen them all, makes the process difficult

FOREIGN FILM/DOUBLETALK: Le Nu Automobile (a.k.a. New Automobile) [S, I, C, H]
 The arrival of a new car disrupts life in a small village (Italian doubletalk)
OTHER: The Birthday [S, I, C, H]
 8-year-old kids at a birthday party; chaos is the result
GUEST SKETCH: Count of Monte Carlo [S, I, C, GH]
 The efforts of a French duc to recoup his losses at the gambling table are foiled by two women
SONG/DANCE: The Magic Lamp [I]
 Coca in her tramp persona
MONOLOGUE: Man Without a Dime [S] (YT)
 Having forgotten his wallet, a man tries various methods to get a dime for the subway

Ep #100 • Air Date: 11/1/52 • Host: Jeffrey Lynn • [Paley*, LOC, UCLA]
HICKENLOOPERS: Symphony Hall [S, I, C, H]
 Doris drags Charlie to a symphony; both make life miserable for the patron sitting in the aisle seat
OTHER: New Faces [S, I, C, H]
 Two movie producers look for new talent in a diner, where they encounter unlikely prospects, a short-order cook and a waitress
SONG/DANCE: Glowworm [I]
 A number in which Coca does indeed glow—intermittently
MONOLOGUE: I've Caught a Cold [S]
 A man resorts to increasingly desperate measures to combat an uncommon cold ()

Ep #101 • Air Date: 11/8/52 • Host: Jane Wyatt • [Paley, LOC, UCLA]
HICKENLOOPERS: Chinese Food [S, I, C] (YT, SC)
 Doris has made an elaborate home-cooked meal, but Charlie brings home Chinese take-out; a neighbor solves the dilemma by consuming most of it
PANTOMIME: Sunday Driver [S, I]
 The usual driving misadventures, made worse by a total lack of adherence to the rules of the road
GUEST SKETCH: Shoe Repair [S, I, GH]
 Two women have difficulty with an uncooperative shoe repairman
SPOOFS/PARODIES: Twelve Little Words [S, I, C, H]
 Spoofing every vaudeville/Ziegfeld follies movie ever made: struggling composer makes good, marries star, loses her and his career, wins both back
MONOLOGUE: Husband's Third Complaint [S]
 A litany of complaints about an unsuitable wife, including having to purchase a bullet-proof vest

Ep #102 • Air Date: 11/15/52 • Host: Richard Ney • [Paley*]
HICKENLOOPERS: Baby in the Park [S, I]
OTHER: Phone Quarrel [S, I]
 After a fight, a couple want to make up, but telephone technology keeps preventing it

Appendix: Comedy Sketch Guide   209

GUEST SKETCH: French Without Food [S, I, GH]
SILENT FILMS: A Father's Love [S, I, C]
> A man gives up his daughter for adoption so that she can have a better life, then wants to win her back

SONG/DANCE: Crocodile Song [I]
MONOLOGUE: If I Only Had a Cigarette [S]
> Man resorts to desperate measures in search of a nicotine fix, including lighting up a too-short collection of scraps ("It tastes like burnt fingers!")

Ep #103 • Air Date: 11/22/52 • Host: Nancy Olson • [Paley, LOC, UCLA]

HICKENLOOPERS: Sunday Breakfast [S, I]
> The couple's attempts to construct a breakfast go awry, including making an egg dish that threatens to explode the oven

GUEST SKETCH: Angel and the Devil [S, I, C, GH]
> A man and a woman attempt courtship, with good and bad advice from an angel and devil on their shoulders

SPOOFS/PARODIES: Newspaper Movie (a.k.a. Five-Star Final) [S, I, C, H] (YT, SC)
> An ace reporter and his female rival try to get a big scoop, complicated by the arrival of gangsters who don't want them to get it

MONOLOGUE: Airplane Movies [S]
> Every cliché of World War II flying movies is taken on, as a lone pilot confronts the Luftwaffe

SONG/DANCE: Place Pigalle [I]

Ep #104 • Air Date: 11/29/52 • Host: Victor Jory • [Paley, LOC, UCLA]

OTHER: Goodbye at the Bar [S, I, C]
> After a wife tells her husband she wants a divorce, he's distraught (as is the waiter); drowning their sorrows repeatedly, they decide to reconcile

OTHER: Two Lions in the Zoo [S, I] (YT)
> A lion and lioness compare coats and fangs, comment on the other animals and humans at the zoo, and hope to be discovered by a movie producer

GUEST SKETCH: It's Certainly Been [S, I, GH]
> The Hickenloopers just can't convince a party guest to leave, even though it's 4 a.m.

FOREIGN FILM/DOUBLETALK: Bella Cara Mia [S, I, C]
> A man's search for a suitable wife (Italian doubletalk)

SONG/DANCE: Madame Galli [I]
> Spoof of opera divas

MONOLOGUE: If the Shoe Fits [S]
> A man purchases a spectacular pair of shoes, then must deal with the reactions of people (and a dog) to them

Ep #105 • Air Date: 12/6/52 • Host: Dave Garroway • [Paley, UCLA]
Sid and Imogene on vacation

Ep #106 • Air Date: 12/13/52 • Host: Nina Foch • [Paley, LOC]
Sid and Imogene on vacation

210   Appendix: Comedy Sketch Guide

Ep #107 • Air Date: 12/20/52 • Host: Maria Riva • [UCLA]
PANTOMIME: Restaurant Window [S, GH]
SPOOFS/PARODIES: Prison Walls [S, C, H, GH] (YT, SF, SC)
   A man imprisoned unjustly plans a breakout to join his girlfriend; things are not helped by his inept fellow co-conspirators
MONOLOGUE: Woman Getting Dressed [S] (YT)

Ep #108 • Air Date: 12/27/52 • Host: Faye Emerson • [Paley, LOC, UCLA]
OTHER: Big Business Conference [S, C, H]
   A meeting of the board to discuss the company's future is derailed when the boss suffers a series of physical mishaps; a Master Class in how to perform physical comedy ()
PANTOMIME: Movie Pest [S, GH]
   A woman's experience is ruined by a man's total lack of movie-going manners
SPOOFS/PARODIES: Foreign Agent [S, C, H, GH]
   The adventures of Agent B-59, sent by his superior ("Right, Chief!") to a dangerous assignment in Jargonia; intrigue and involvement with a female spy follow; the obvious origin of Mel Brooks' and Buck Henry's *Get Smart*
MONOLOGUE: A Bachelor's Day [S]
   A bachelor goes through his day of dirty laundry, no food in the house, etc., and ponders whether a care-free single life is all it's cracked up to be

Ep #109 • Air Date: 1/3/53 • Host: Glynis Johns • [Paley, LOC, UCLA]
OTHER: Old Friends at Bar [S, C, H]
   Two friends engage in one-ups-manship after reuniting at a bar
PANTOMIME: Boy at First Dance [S]
   A shy, awkward boy at his first dance; five years later, he's an assured ladies' man
OTHER: English Carnival [S, C, H, GH]
   A barker and his friends are outwitted by a woman who wins all the games she's bet on
FOREIGN FILM/DOUBLETALK: Es Ist Nicht Quiet on Vestern Front [S, C, H]
   Inept First World War German soldiers; including the germ of the later classic "German General" sketch, as Howie helps Sid get on his uniform
MONOLOGUE: Boy Growing Up [S]
   A father-to-be imagines what his son will be like, as it turns out, exasperating

Ep #110 • Air Date: 1/10/53 • Host: Michael Redgrave • [Paley, UCLA]
HICKENLOOPERS: The Maid Sketch (a.k.a. Doris Gets a Maid) [S, I] (YT)
   The couple acquires a maid; after initial reluctance, Charlie decides it's not a bad thing
PANTOMIME: In a Shoe Store (a.k.a. Shoe Clerk) [S, I] (YT)
   A clerk attempts to fit a fussy customer; mime at its best ()
GUEST SKETCH: Hocus Pocus [S, I, H, GH]
   A magician copes with the Hickenloopers' desire to join his act
SPOOFS/PARODIES: Birth of a Star [S, I, C]
   A Star Is Born, with Sid as an actor whose star dims as his newcomer wife Imogene becomes "America's Sweetheart"; superb comic acting by Imogene and

Appendix: Comedy Sketch Guide 211

this version features some of Caesar's best straight acting within a comedy sketch ()
MONOLOGUE: The Hangover [S]
After a wedding and a night of drinking, a man tries to remember what happened

Ep #111 • Air Date: 1/17/53 • Host: Frederick Franklin • [Paley*, LOC, UCLA]
HICKENLOOPERS: Silver Threads [S, I]
Doris is convinced she's growing old and tries to talk Charlie into feeling the same way; he convinces her otherwise by putting on a record and sweeping her up into a jitterbug
PANTOMIME: 1812 Overture [S, I] (YT, SC)
Sid and Imogene as percussionists in an orchestra mime their parts in the 1812 Overture
SPOOFS/PARODIES: Westward Whoa! [S, I, C, H]
The West's most inept wagonmaster tries to get the train to California, despite discontent over his leadership and Indian attacks; another in a series of *Your Show of Shows* send-ups of Westerns and their heroes ()
SONG/DANCE: I've Got a Lovely Bunch of Coconuts [I]
Music hall number
MONOLOGUE: English/French War Pictures [S] (YT)
Comparison of English and French war movies (French doubletalk)

Ep #112 • Air Date: 1/24/53 • Host: Robert Preston • [Paley*, LOC, UCLA]
PANTOMIME: Dance Hall Pick-up [S, I]
In search of a dance, a man is pestered by a woman he doesn't want as a partner
GUEST SKETCH: Priceless Possessions [S, I, GH]
An exuberant guest destroys the Hickenloopers' antiques; they eventually join in the breakage
SILENT FILMS: A Fool's Fate [S, I, C]
A man lured to his doom by a femme fatale
PROFESSOR: Space Travel (a.k.a. Professor Jet von Pulsion) [S, C] (YT, SF)
The Professor explains the mechanics of jet propulsion, complete with sound effects; exquisite comic timing from both Carl and Sid ()
SONG/DANCE: Bonnie, Bonnie Lassie [I]

Ep #113 • Air Date: 1/31/53 • Host: Marguerite Chapman • [UCLA]
OTHER: Goodnight in Vestibule [S, I]
PANTOMIME: Trained Seal [S, I]
GUEST SKETCH: Florida [GH]
SPOOFS/PARODIES: Gangster Movie [S, I]
MONOLOGUE: Just One of Those Days [S]

Ep #114 • Air Date: 2/7/53 • Host: No guest host • [LOC, UCLA]
OTHER: Suicide Sketch
OTHER: Burglar Sketch [S, I]
PANTOMIME: Cocktail Party [S, I] (YT, SC)
MONOLOGUE: The Cat [S]

Ep #115 • Air Date: 2/14/53 • Host: Jackie Cooper • [Paley, LOC, UCLA]
PANTOMIME: The Glamour Treatment [S, I]
    A woman in search of a new look; the stylist gives her an egg shampoo, complete with egg beater, and tweezes an eyebrow hair so long he can jump rope with it
GUEST SKETCH: The Drummer [S, I, GH] (YT)
    The Hickenloopers are seated all too close to a testy drummer at a theatre
SPOOFS/PARODIES: Broadway Rhapsody [S, I, C, H]
    A spoof of *42nd Street* with a bit of *Gold-Diggers of 1933* thrown in; a producer's difficulties in putting on a show are solved by the "kid in the chorus" whom he makes a star—and, of course, falls in love with ()
SONG/DANCE: Open Up Your Heart and Let Me In [I]
PROFESSOR: Child Psychologist [S, C]
    Advice on child-rearing from the Professor's book "Children are People—only Smaller"

Ep #116 • Air Date: 2/21/53 • Host: No guest host • [Paley*, LOC, UCLA]
HICKENLOOPERS: Late for the Theatre [S, I, C, H]
    Trying to eat fast at a restaurant with slow service
FOREIGN FILM/DOUBLETALK: Au Revoir Mon Cheri [S, I, C, H] (YT)
    Spoof of a World War I movie; a woman bids goodbye to her lover as he leaves for the front (French doubletalk)
PANTOMIME: Look, There's a Mouse! [S, I]
    Dealing with a recalcitrant rodent who just won't be caught
SPOOFS/PARODIES: A Place at the Bottom of the Lake [S, I, C, H]
    Parody of A Place in the Sun, in which the unhappy man just can't kill his obnoxious wife-to-be, despite his best efforts
SONG/DANCE: Artist's Life [I]
    Strauss spoof
MONOLOGUE: The Ring [S]
    A man purchasing a diamond for his girl when money is definitely an object

Ep #117 • Air Date: 2/28/53 • Host: Jan Sterling • [Paley, LOC]
Sid and Imogene on vacation

Ep #118 • Air Date: 3/7/53 • Host: Dave Garroway • [Paley, LOC]
Sid and Imogene on vacation

Ep #119 • Air Date: 3/14/53 • Host: Arlene Whelan • [Paley, UCLA]
HICKENLOOPERS: Dining Out [S, I, C]
    It's their 10th-anniversary dinner at a swanky restaurant and Charlie can't figure out how much to tip the imperious waiter ("What's the square root of 9?")
GUEST SKETCH: The Jealous Maid [S, I, GH]
    The actress playing the maid in a play, resenting her actor husband's attraction to the leading lady, takes her revenge, dramatically
SPOOFS/PARODIES: Sneaking Through the Sound Barrier [S, I, C, H]
    Sid as the heroic, though somewhat dense jet pilot ("Can't I have just a little

propeller?") who's attempting to break the sound barrier; Coca as his girl who can't understand why
SONG/DANCE: Lovely Weather for Ducks [I]
   Coca in her tramp persona
MONOLOGUE: Man Who Can't Relax [S]
   A businessman on vacation can't relax, as he worries about his business and his partner

Ep #120 • Air Date: 3/21/53 • Host: Kukla, Fran, and Ollie • [Paley, LOC, UCLA]
OTHER: Summer Romance [S, I]
   A man searching his black book for a date, finally comes up with a woman he had a summer romance with (she's on the last page—and finds out about it)
GUEST SKETCH: Movie Premiere [S, I, GH]
   The Strangers join Kukla, Fran, and Ollie to trade clichés about the movie, its cast, and Hollywood in general
SPOOFS/PARODIES: The Seventh Wail [S, I, C, H] (YT)
   Parody of *The Seventh Veil*, with Sid as the tyrannical piano master who terrorizes his ward Imogene into becoming a keyboard virtuoso; one of Caesar's best "saves" on live TV when the cane he's been thwacking the piano top with breaks ()
SONG/DANCE: San Antone [I]
MONOLOGUE: Man Getting Bald [S]
   Noticing his hairline receding and his side part growing larger, a man contemplates a follicly-challenged life

Ep #121 • Air Date: 3/28/53 • Host: Wendell Corey • [Paley, LOC, UCLA]
HICKENLOOPERS: Showing Home Movies [S, I, C, H]
   Charlie hauls out reels of home movies to "entertain" guests
GUEST SKETCH: The Movies [S, I, C, GH]
   A man and woman drive another patron batty with talking, eating, and blocking his view of the screen
OTHER: Pet Shop Window [S, I]
   Two puppies entertain each other by commenting on the people peering at them through the window while hoping to be adopted as a pair
FOREIGN FILM/DOUBLETALK: Readin,' Writin,' and Weltschmerz [S, I, C, H]
   A skewed anatomy lesson in a Heidelburg schoolroom with the teacher attempting to cope with his students (German doubletalk)
SONG/DANCE: Syncopated Rhythm [I]
MONOLOGUE: It'll Be Nice [S]
   A man about to walk down the aisle imagines married life—and starts worrying

Ep #122 • Air Date: 4/4/53 • Host: Marguerite Piazza • [Paley, LOC, UCLA]
GUEST SKETCH: The New Secretary [S, I, H, GH]
   Doris assists Charlie in interviews for a new secretary; unfortunately, one of them (Piazza) is a real knockout

PANTOMIME: Coney Island [S, I]
    A couple's adventures with attractions, particularly what seems to be the world's highest rollercoaster
SPOOFS/PARODIES: The Longest Show on Earth [S, I, C, H] (YT)
    Spoof of Cecil B. DeMille's *Greatest Show on Earth*, with Sid as the circus boss, Imogene and Carl as rival trapeze artists, and Howie as a clown
SONG/DANCE: Doll Song from Tales of Hoffman [I]
MONOLOGUE: Dance Hall Stag [S]
    A man is turned down repeatedly in his quest for a dance, to his increasing frustration; he finally gets one—with a male friend

Ep #123 • Air Date: 4/11/53 • Host: Diana Lynn • [Paley, UCLA]

HICKENLOOPERS: Spring Cleaning [S, I]
    Doris starts throwing things away in the Spring ritual; most of them are Charlie's
GUEST SKETCH: Sneezing Fit at Musical Soiree (a.k.a. The Music Salon) [S, I, C, GH]
    A man disrupts a piano recital when, after trying to smother a sneeze, he runs out of the room and succumbs to a truly epic sneezing fit; one of Caesar's most impressive sound effects-it lasts 30 seconds
SPOOFS/PARODIES: Hospital Movie [S, I, C, H, GH]
    An idealistic doctor tries to help an amnesiac recover her memory by the use of rather unorthodox methods
SONG/DANCE: Striptease [I]
    Coca does a striptease under a huge overcoat
MONOLOGUE: Man at the Bar [S]
    A man enters a bar, has seven shots, and his mood changes with each; a classic Caesar monologue, displaying his acting and physical comedy abilities ()

Ep #124 • Air Date: 4/18/53 • Host: Paul Douglas • [Paley*, LOC, UCLA]

HICKENLOOPERS: The Boarder [S, I, H] (YT)
    Charlie returns home to find a stranger sitting in his living room; Doris has taken in a boarder, who soon complicates their lives
GUEST SKETCH: The Truck Driver & the Lady (a.k.a. Magistrate's Court) [S, I, C, H, GH] (YT)
    A trucker and a woman involved in an accident take their case to court; a hapless eyewitness finds himself under attack by not only them, but the defense attorney as well
PROFESSOR: Fishing (a.k.a. Fishing Expert) [S, C] (YT)
    Epic tales of fishing experiences, including observation of the Flying Whale and meeting a mermaid
FOREIGN FILM/DOUBLETALK: Who Stole My Bicycle? [S, I, C]
    Spoof of *The Bicycle Thief*, with Coca as the wife who fancies it and Caesar as the husband who tries to control her (Italian doubletalk)

Ep #125 • Air Date: 4/25/53 • Host: No guest host • [Paley, LOC, UCLA]

HICKENLOOPERS: Leaping Lions [S, I, C, H]
    A movie audience marvels at the latest 3-D process; Charlie can't get his glasses on, and once he does, finds the action a bit too realistic

Appendix: Comedy Sketch Guide 215

PANTOMIME: Picnic [S, I]
    The usual al fresco mishaps
SPOOFS/PARODIES: Final Payment [S, I, C]
    Pitch perfect send-up of *Double Indemnity*; Sid's insurance salesman, seduced by sultry Imogene (in about 10 seconds flat), agrees to help murder her husband Carl ()
SONG/DANCE: Polka [I]
MONOLOGUE: Penny Chewing Gum Machine [S]
    The saga of a polite chewing gum machine in a subway station who comes to a bad end as a downtown slot machine

Ep #126 • Air Date: 5/2/53 • Host: Gene Nelson • [Paley*, LOC, UCLA]
HICKENLOOPERS: Dressmaking [S, I]
    Without telling Charlie, Doris decides to work from home; he's less than pleased to be turned into an impromptu dressmaker's dummy
PANTOMIME: Summer Resort [S, I]
    A couple participate in so many resort activities, they're too fatigued for a romantic dinner
OTHER: English Pub [S, I, C, H]
    A gambler and his cronies are bewildered by a woman who consistently bets on horses that shouldn't win—but they do
SONG/DANCE: To Be a Millionaire [I]
PROFESSOR: Royalty Expert [S, C]
    A disquisition on royal families and customs

Ep #127 • Air Date: 5/9/53 • Host: Ilona Massey • [UCLA]
HICKENLOOPERS: Nightclub Sketch [S, I]
GUEST SKETCH: The Gypsy Countess [S, I, GH]
SPOOFS/PARODIES: Barbary Coast [S, I, C, H]
MONOLOGUE: Man Getting Up in Morning [S]

Ep #128 • Air Date: 5/16/53 • Host: Jean Pierre Aumont • [Paley, LOC, UCLA]
HICKENLOOPERS: Cinder in My Eye [S, I]
    Doris tries to get something out of Charlie's eye, complicated by his being a big baby about it
STRANGERS/CLICHES: Superstitions–Tea Leaves [S, I] (YT)
    Couple meet at a gypsy tearoom and compare methods of warding off bad luck
GUEST SKETCH: The First Time I Saw Paris [S, I, GH]
    Charlie meets up with a Frenchman he knew in the war; Doris is promptly smitten
SILENT FILMS: The Sewing Machine Girl [S, I, C, H] (YT, SF)
    Sweethearts in a sweat-shop, whose relationship is doomed by the lascivious boss and her ominous cough
SONG/DANCE: Tell Us Where the Good Times Are [I]
MONOLOGUE: Coming Attractions (a.k.a. Gangster Movie) [S] (YT)
    Spoof of formulaic gangster movies, in which Sid meets a predictable bad end

Ep #129 • Air Date: 5/23/53 • Host: Andy Russell • [Paley, UCLA]
HICKENLOOPERS: Four Telephones [S, I, C]
   Rather sophisticated technology for 1953, as four people on three different screens try to decide about dinner plans
OTHER: The Four Englishman I (a.k.a. English Pantomime #1) [S, I, C, H] (YT, SF, SC)
   Four Englishmen whose upper lips are so stiff, their speech is unintelligible are served hors d'oeuvres at a party, then engage in a genteel food fight
SPOOFS/PARODIES: The Gangster and the Lady [S, I, C, H]
   A crime boss hatches a plot to discredit a reformer who threatens his business; he falls in love with her instead, much to the displeasure of his henchmen
SONG/DANCE: Maywalk [I]
   A young girl with her Maypole laments missing the dance
PROFESSOR: Archeology II (a.k.a. Archeology Expert) [S, C] (YT)
   Ludwig von Fossil explains archaeological techniques and describes his famous expeditions

Ep #130 • Air Date: 5/30/53 • Host: Brian Donlevy • [Paley, LOC, UCLA]
MONOLOGUE: Sunday Ride with Family [S]
   A man takes his extremely large family out for a drive, complicated by Jimmy, one of the brood, constantly taking the keys
SONG/DANCE: Ho-ho-diddle-di-di-di [I]
   Coca in her tramp persona
OTHER: The Four Englishman II (a.k.a. English Pantomime #2) [S, I, C, H] (YT)
   Four Englishmen in a manor hall sit quietly as the roof begins to leak; rain drips on, then soaks them, as they sit in imperturbable silence
GUEST SKETCH: Smalltown Jail [S, I, C, GH]
   Doris is picked up for speeding in a small town and argues her way into a cell; Charlie attempts to cope with the sheriff who put her there
SPOOFS/PARODIES: Starstruck [S, I, C, H]
   A Star Is Born with Sid as an actor whose star dims as his wife Imogene becomes "America's Sweetheart"

Season 5 (1953-54)

The show moves from the International Theatre in Columbus Circle to the Center Theatre in Rockefeller Center, which had more seating and greater space for production numbers. It now was aired three times a month (the usual schedule for NBC variety shows) rather than four; the running time remained the same (ninety minutes). There was an experiment with a new format: more guest stars rather than guest hosts and a shake-up in the running order. It lasted for only a month before returning to the more traditional format. Parodies become even longer; Caesar did fewer monologues. Two episodes (12/5/1953 and 6/5/1954) were telecast in color. The final three episodes of the show featured sketches requested by viewers.

Appendix: Comedy Sketch Guide 217

Ep #131 • Air Date: 9/12/53 • Host: No guest host • [Paley*, LOC, UCLA]
OTHER: Good Luck Opening [S, I, C, H]
   Everyone introduces themselves for the new season
PANTOMIME: Dentist's Apprentice [S]
   The misadventures of a dentist's janitor mimed to the music of "The Sorcerer's Apprentice"
SPOOFS/PARODIES: From Here to Obscurity [S, I, C, H] (YT, SF, SC)
   The classic takeoff of *From Here to Eternity*; the famous beach scene proceeds from the logical premise that, if you make love by the waves, you're going to get very, very wet ()
HICKENLOOPERS: Birthday Sketch [S, I]
PROFESSOR: Jet von Pulsion [S, C]
   The Professor explains the mechanics of jet propulsion, complete with sound effects
SONG/DANCE: I Love Only One Man [I]
   Coca's wide crinoline dress does battle with rose bushes and a trellis as she sings; they win

Ep #132 • Air Date: 9/19/53 • Host: No guest host • [Paley, LOC, UCLA]
HICKENLOOPERS: Birthday Present [S, I] (YT)
   Charlie has forgotten Doris's birthday—or did he? A charming détente after an argument—they weren't always the Bickersons ()
OTHER: Jazz Session [I]
   Imogene joins a jazz band, on trombone
OTHER: Englishmen at Track [S, I, C, H]
   The stiff-upper-lip quartet watching the races at Ascot and being pelted by the mud thrown up by the horses
SPOOFS/PARODIES: The Russian Arthur Godfrey [S, C, H] (YT)
   Talent scouts in Russia, with Carl as a contestant doing impressions and Sid absolutely nailing all of Godfrey's most irritating mannerisms (Russian doubletalk) ()
SPOOFS/PARODIES: Strange [S, I, C, H]
   Parody of *Shane*, with Sid as the less-than-heroic gunfighter and Imogene as the incredibly annoying boy who worships him ()

Ep #133 • Air Date: 9/26/53 • Host: No guest host • [Paley, UCLA]
HICKENLOOPERS: Restaurant [S, I, C, H]
   During dinner at a restaurant, Doris is convinced every man there, including a patron and the waiter, are flirting with her and demands Charlie do something about it
PANTOMIME: The Bavarian Clock [S, I, C, H] (YT, SF, SC)
   The classic pantomime in which a large clock in the town square malfunctions, as do the figures that come out to mark the hours ()
MONOLOGUE: I Can't Sleep [S]
   After an argument with his wife, a husband tries various methods to get some shut-eye

SPOOFS/PARODIES: Homicide 6-5300 [S, I, C]
   A semi-spoof of *Sorry, Wrong Number*, in which a man plans to kill his cheating wife, with much poking fun at the melodramatic music used in the genre

Ep #134 • Air Date: 10/10/53 • Host: Jean Pierre Aumont • [Paley, LOC, UCLA]
OTHER: Boxer [S, I, C, H]
   As he tries to relax before a title fight, a boxer has to contend with his annoying wife—"You always forget to bring home bread and milk after a fight" "You're always complaining--I have a headache. I have a concussion"
SONG/DANCE: Toddling [I]
SPOOFS/PARODIES: 12 Little Words [S, I, C, H]
   Spoofing every vaudeville/Ziegfeld follies movie ever made: struggling composer makes good, marries star, loses her and his career, wins both back
GUEST SKETCH: Bistro La Paris [S, I, GH]
   The Hickenloopers go to a bistro with a very handsome French singer; the effect on Doris is predictable
PANTOMIME: Woman Dressing in the Morning [S]
   A woman's morning routine, including getting into a dress with endless zippers in odd places

Ep #135 • Air Date: 10/17/53 • Host: Eddie Albert • [Paley, LOC]
HICKENLOOPERS: Get It Off Your Chest [S, I]
   Obviously not thinking this through, Doris suggests the couple share what they find most irritating about each other; discussions of her toothpaste tube-squinching and his soup-slurping follow
OTHER: Four Englishmen with Muggs [S, I, C, H]
   It takes more than a chimpanzee on the loose to ruffle the Four Englishmen
SPOOFS/PARODIES: I'm In Love [S, I, C, H]
   Elements of *The Blue Angel* and *Of Human Bondage* as a Heidelburg professor falls for a barmaid; loss of money and reputation soon follow ()
GUEST SKETCH: Friend in Need [S, I, GH]
   Charlie Hickenlooper is hit up for a loan by a friend, who requests it in the worst passive-aggressive way possible
SONG/DANCE: Give Me the Simple Life [I]
   Coca in her tramp persona

Ep #136 • Air Date: 10/24/53 • Host: No guest host • [LOC, UCLA]
OTHER: Bublitchki Follies
OTHER: The Four Cats [S, I]
OTHER: The Martians [S, I]
   Content unknown, but a still from a rehearsal suggests a pre–SNL Conehead sketch
PANTOMIME: Boy at First Dance [S]

Ep #137 • Air Date: 11/7/53 • Host: No guest host • [Paley, LOC, UCLA]
HICKENLOOPERS: The Matchmakers [S, I, C]
   After Charlie and Doris attempt to match a friend with several women, they disapprove of the one he finally does pick

Appendix: Comedy Sketch Guide 219

PANTOMIME: In the Subway [S, I] (YT)
    Two riders fight off fellow passengers—and each other—in an attempt to score a seat
SPOOFS/PARODIES: The Continental Express [S, I, C, H] (YT, SF, SC)
    Intrigue on the Orient Express, as a hapless spy tries to pass on secret plans to a confederate; matters become complicated when he shares a compartment with two enemy spies and a woman whose loyalties seem to be mixed
SONG/DANCE: Harrigan [I]
    Music hall number
PROFESSOR: Expert on Magic [S, C]
    Professor Hocus von Pocus returns to discuss famous magicians he's known and, once again, foul up the glass-and-bottle trick

Ep #138 • Air Date: 11/14/53 • Host: Nina Foch

PANTOMIME: String Quartet [S, I, C, H]
    Four musicians at a recital where a fire breaks out offstage; they carry on stoically, even while they're being soaked by the fire hoses
FOREIGN FILM/DOUBLETALK: Le Grande Amour [S, I, C] (YT)
    A baker talks down a woman who's going to jump into the Seine; attracted to her, he gives her a job in his shop; no good deed goes unrewarded as she flirts with his assistant (French doubletalk)
HICKENLOOPERS: The Sleep Sketch [S, I] (YT, SF, SC)
    Charlie has insomnia; Doris suggests taking a sedative the doctor prescribed, unfortunately he confuses Sleepos with Zippos and she has to contend with his high
MONOLOGUE: Man at Class Reunion [S]

Ep #139 • Air Date: 11/21/53 • Host: Margaret Hayes • [Paley, LOC, UCLA]

HICKENLOOPERS: Health Food Restaurant [S, I, H] (YT, SF, SC)
    Doris takes Charlie to a restaurant that's vegetarian with a vengeance; after trying a flower hors d'oeuvre, he rebels ("I'm going to Pepito's, you can go to the Botanical Gardens")
PANTOMIME: Four Turkeys [S, I, C, H]
    At Thanksgiving, one of the quartet is going to get the axe—maybe
SPOOFS/PARODIES: Invitation to Murder (a.k.a. Invitation to a Murder) [S, I, C, H] (YT, SC)
    Agatha-Christie style mystery in which guests invited to a mansion are murdered one by one
PANTOMIME: Blind Date [S, I]
    A man goes to the movies with the Blind Date from Hell

Ep #140 • Air Date: 12/5/53 • Host: Faye Emerson • [Paley*, LOC, UCLA]

Broadcast in color
HICKENLOOPERS: The New Location [S, I, C]
    The couple look at a house, which the high-pressure salesman wants them to buy immediately; they soon find out why, as it's not exactly prime real estate

OTHER: News Stand [S, I]
   The owner of a newsstand contends with an eccentric customer; featuring the perils of live TV, as Sid, ducking bales of newspapers thrown at him from a truck, takes one on the chin, opening a noticeable gash
PANTOMIME: Concert Recital [S, I]
   A violinist's debut is ruined by his own ineptitude and his piano accompanist's antics
MONOLOGUE: Marriage Proposal [S]
   A man rehearses various scenarios in which he'll ask his girl to marry him

Ep #141 • Air Date: 12/12/53 • Host: Claude Dauphin • [Paley, LOC, UCLA]
HICKENLOOPERS: The Lost Glove [S, I, C, H]
   Doris loses a glove at the movies; she and Charlie create chaos in the theatre and commit mayhem on the other patrons in an attempt to find it
GUEST SKETCH: Call a Doctor [S, I, GH]
   Charlie becomes ill on a trip to France and a doctor is summoned; Doris considers it a great opportunity to practice her high-school French, Charlie is not amused ("I'm dying and you're getting a French lesson!")
SPOOFS/PARODIES: Sidewalk Rhapsody [S, I, C]
   Two brothers from the tenements; one grows up to become a lawyer, the other a hood, and both are in love with the same girl
SONG/DANCE: Who Stole That Choo-choo? [I]
   Audience-participation number
MONOLOGUE: If the Shoe Fits [S]
   A man buys a particularly garish pair of shoes, then contends with his friends' reactions, the looks of passersby, and at least one inquisitive dog

Ep #142 • Air Date: 12/19/53 • Host: Bil and Cora Baird • [Paley, LOC, UCLA]
HICKENLOOPERS: Charming Charles (a.k.a. Handsome is as Handsome Does) [S, I, C]
   Charlie gets a swelled head when one of Doris's friends tells her that women find him attractive; he's convinced it's his new cologne "Tang of Burning Timber"
STRANGERS/CLICHES: Christmas Shopping [S, I]
   Trading clichés in a department store, while discussing the difficulties of gift-giving and observing shop-lifters
SILENT FILMS: The Drunkard's Fate [S, I, C, H] (YT)
   The perils of Demon Rum; Sid eventually loses his wife, daughter, dog, and canary (NBC got letters of complaint because it was shown during the holiday season)
OTHER: Big Business (a.k.a. What's on the Agenda) [S, C, H] (YT, SF, SC)
   A business lunch goes south when the delivery doesn't include the boss's sandwich; featuring overlapping dialogue and a hungry Sid's desperate attempt to get his mouth around a pickle waved in front of him by Howie
SONG/DANCE: Where Did My Snowman Go? [I]

Appendix: Comedy Sketch Guide 221

Ep #143 • Air Date: 1/2/54 • Host: Jayne Meadows • [Paley*, LOC, UCLA]
HICKENLOOPERS: Incinerator [S, I, C]
  Dealing with a neighbor who throws his trash into the hall instead of down the garbage chute; a garbage battle ensues
PANTOMIME: The Visit [S, I]
  A man's plans for a romantic afternoon with his girl are interrupted by her dog, which wants constant attention
HICKENLOOPERS: Bus Station (a.k.a. Which Way to Riverdale?) [S, I, H] (YT, SF, SC)
  In a bus station, the couple try to help a man searching for the one to Riverdale, get into an argument about which is the right route, and dismantle him in the process
PANTOMIME: Lionel the Great [S, I]
  A circus sketch, with Sid as the strongman who needs a lot of help from his assistant Imogene
OTHER: The Recital (a.k.a. Sunday Salon) [S, I, C, H] (YT, SF, SC)
  A man disrupts a vocal performance by various means; at least when he gets his finger caught in a cigarette lighter, he politely runs offstage to scream
SONG/DANCE: Wrap Your Troubles in Dreams [I]
  Coca in her tramp persona

Ep #144 • Air Date: 1/9/54 • Host: Marilyn Maxwell • [Paley, LOC, UCLA]
HICKENLOOPERS: The New Suit [S, I, C]
  Doris accompanies Charlie to a haberdashery; the result is several unsuitable outfits, including cuffed pants that don't break at the shoe heel but extend three feet beyond his shoes
PANTOMIME: Shoe Store [S, I]
  A clerk attempts to fit a fussy customer
FOREIGN FILM/DOUBLETALK: Der Prince and Der Papa [S, I, C]
  Conflict over a royal marriage, as the Prince (Sid) wants to marry a commoner (Imogene), to the disapproval of Der Papa (Carl)
OTHER: Order in the Court [S, I, C, H, GH]
  A judge (Sid) presides, more or less calmly, over a case involving non-payment of a debt to a dressmaker (Imogene)--until the attractive female defendant shows up; of the best pure slapstick sketches of *Your Show of Shows* ()
SONG/DANCE: This Can't Be Me [I]

Ep #145 • Air Date: 1/16/54 • Host: Charlton Heston • [Paley*, UCLA]
HICKENLOOPERS: The Letter [S, I, C]
  Doris finds a letter in a friend's coat pocket that seems to suggest he's having an affair; the couple are appalled—and fascinated
SPOOFS/PARODIES: Stranger in Danger [S, I, C, H, GH]
  Foreign intrigue in "occupied Europe" where it's up to Sid, a facial tissue salesman from Milwaukee, and Imogene, a singing spy, to save the Free World ()
SONG/DANCE: Ragtime Melody [I]

MONOLOGUE: Breaking the News [S]
A man prepares his parents for the announcement of his marriage

Ep #146 • Air Date: 1/30/54 • Host: Angela Lansbury • [Paley, LOC, UCLA]

HICKENLOOPERS: Cigar Fight (a.k.a. The Quarrel) [S, I, C] (YT)
The longest version of an epic argument over cigars and her cooking, culminating in his leaving to spend the night with a friend; the latter encourages him to return, if only so he can get a good night's sleep

SPOOFS/PARODIES: The Wembley Incident [S, I, C, H, GH]
English public school movie spoof; an educational reformer (Sid) helps a poor student (Imogene) who's accused of theft by a rich one (Lansbury), using unorthodox methods

OTHER: Bell Ringing [I]
Coca versus bells of various sizes

PROFESSOR: Mountain Climbing II (a.k.a. Mountain Climbing Expert) [S, C] (YT)
The best mountain-climbing Professor sketch, in which Ludwig von Snowcap offers advice on what to do if your rope breaks and describes his famous expedition to Mount Everest ()

Ep #147 • Air Date: 2/6/54 • Host: Margaret Truman • [LOC, UCLA]

HICKENLOOPERS: Going Out Saturday Night [S, I] (YT)
The saga of trying to find a parking place in Manhattan, featuring driving on the sidewalk and squeezing your car into very tight spaces

SPOOFS/PARODIES: Tall, Dark and Strange [S, I, C, H]
A stranger rides into a Western town and helps the local newspaper editor ("We'll print the truth even if we have to make it up") in his fight against corruption; of course he also falls in love with the editor's daughter

MONOLOGUE: Man Without a Dime [S]
Having forgotten his wallet, a man tries various methods to get a dime for the subway

Ep #148 • Air Date: 2/13/54 • Host: Eddie Albert • [Paley, UCLA]

HICKENLOOPERS: The Poker Game [S, I, C, H] (YT)
Charlie goes to a poker game—and forgets he was supposed to meet Doris

SPOOFS/PARODIES: Hired to Kill [S, I, C, H, GH]
Two gangsters come to a small-town diner, intent on eliminating a counter-man who was a witness to one of their crimes

SONG/DANCE: Scheherazade [I]
Coca as the story-teller

OTHER: Boss and Doctor [S, C]
A busy exec combines his annual physical and a board meeting

Ep #149 • Air Date: 2/27/54 • Host: Jackie Cooper • [LOC, UCLA]

OTHER: The Nervous Suitor [S, I, C] (YT)
SPOOFS/PARODIES: Broadway Rhapsody [S, I, C, H]

Appendix: Comedy Sketch Guide 223

Ep #150 • Air Date: 3/6/54 • Host: Zachary Scott • [Paley, LOC, UCLA]
HICKENLOOPERS: Breaking the News [S, I, C]
   After Doris finally admits to wrecking the car, the couple visit a new car salesroom with a pushy salesman
OTHER: The Long, Long Voyage [S, I, C, H, GH]
   A sailor who is shanghaied every time he gets drunk in a bar is headed for another voyage, until the barmaid falls for him and prevents it
SONG/DANCE: Torch Song [I]
PROFESSOR: Criminology Expert [S, C]
   Professor von Bloodhound on catching—and keeping—criminals

Ep #151 • Air Date: 3/13/54 •Host: Rhonda Fleming • [LOC, UCLA]
HICKENLOOPERS: Out of Town Buyer [S, I]
OTHER: The Innocent Bystander (a.k.a. At the Movies) [S, I, C, H] (YT, SF, SC)
   A man (Sid) goes to the movies and finds himself caught up in a quarrel between a man and a woman (Carl and Imogene); mayhem and manhandling follow
OTHER: The Brain

Ep #152 • Air Date: 3/27/54 •Host: Rita Gam • [Paley, LOC, UCLA]
HICKENLOOPERS: The Antique Auction [S, I]
   To furnish a new apartment, the couple go to an auction; Charlie is overcome by the excitement of bidding
SPOOFS/PARODIES: Newspaper Movie [S, I, C, H]
   An ace reporter and his female rival try to get a big scoop, complicated by the arrival of gangsters who don't want them to get it
SONG/DANCE: I've Got a Lovely Bunch of Coconuts [I]
   Music hall number
OTHER: How's Production? [S, C, H]
   A brainstorming session at the Acme Novelty Company

Ep # 153 • Air Date: 4/3/54 • Host: Phyllis Kirk • [UCLA]
HICKENLOOPERS: The Boarder [S, I, H]
   Charlie returns home to find a stranger sitting in his living room; Doris has taken in a boarder, who soon complicates their lives
FOREIGN FILM/DOUBLETALK: The Cobbler's Daughter [S, I, C, H] (YT, SC)
   A shoemaker tries to find a suitable catch for his daughter (Italian doubletalk)
SPOOFS/PARODIES: This Is Your Story [S, C, H] (YT, SF, SC)
   This Is Your Life, with Sid as the reluctant guest who attempts to flee the theatre, Carl as the smarmy MC, and Howie as Uncle Goopy, who can't—literally can't—be separated from his nephew; funniest 11 minutes ever shown on TV ()
PANTOMIME: Carnegie Hall [S, I]
   Couple seated next to each other at a symphony mirror the emotions of Tchaikovsky's "Romeo and Juliet"

Ep #154 • Air Date: 4/10/54 • Host: Jinx Falkenberg • [Paley, LOC, UCLA]
HICKENLOOPERS: The Good Investment [S, I, C] (YT)
   Doris persuades Charlie to take a flyer in the stock market, which promptly goes through minute-by-minute boom-bust cycles
SPOOFS/PARODIES: The 7th Wail [S, I, C, H]
   Spoof of *The Seventh Veil*; a tyrannical piano master terrorizes his ward into becoming a keyboard virtuoso
SONG/DANCE: Song Parody [I]
   Coca spoofs Yma Sumac, a Peruvian singer
OTHER: Twenty Minutes for Lunch [S, C, H] (YT, SC)
   A mild-mannered soul tries to get lunch in a crowded restaurant and takes every kind of abuse that can be dished out by the waitstaff; superb "reaction" slapstick ()

Ep #155 • Air Date: 4/24/54 • Host: Patricia Crowley • [Paley, LOC, UCLA]
HICKENLOOPERS: The Lost Diamond [S, I, C, H]
   Doris loses her ring; suspecting it happened while helping to prepare a neighbor's buffet lunch, Charlie proceeds to take it apart
SPOOFS/PARODIES: Emergency! [S, I, C, H, GH] (YT)
   An idealistic doctor tries to help an amnesiac recover her memory by the use of rather unorthodox methods; a good example of Caesar responding to a set malfunction, one of the perils of live TV, with a series of ad-libs ()
SONG/DANCE: Back in the Old Routine [I]
OTHER: Track Man on Subway [S]
   For some reason, a runner decides to make up a few laps using the subway

Ep # 156 • Air Date: 5/1/54 • Host: Louis Jourdan • [Paley*, LOC, UCLA]
HICKENLOOPERS: The Late TV Movie [S, I, C] (YT)
   Doris's insistence on watching an African explorer film on TV not only disturbs Charlie's sleep, but eventually the neighbors' as well
SPOOFS/PARODIES: Barbary Coast [S, I, C, H]
   Parody of the San Francisco Western with Sid as a saloon owner in competition with Carl; Imogene as the saloon singer with a heart of gold helps him win out
OTHER: Baseball Bleachers [S, I, C, H]
   A man's bleacher seat is a magnet for every ball successive batters foul off
SONG/DANCE: Maywalk [I]
   A young girl with her Maypole laments missing the dance

Ep #157 • Air Date: 5/8/54 • Host: Eddie Albert • [UCLA]
   Scripts indicate this episode contained the classic German General sketch, seen in video compilations of sketches. Long classified, incorrectly, as from a Caesar's Hour episode of September 1954
HICKENLOOPERS: Memories [S, I]
FOREIGN FILM/DOUBLETALK: The German General (a.k.a. German Slicking Up) [S, H] (SF, SC)
   A classic sketch with Sid as a German officer and Howie as his aide helping him into his uniform, with a twist ending
SPOOFS/PARODIES: Gangster and the Lady [S, I]

Appendix: Comedy Sketch Guide 225

Ep #158 • Air Date: 5/22/54 • Host: Patricia Neal • [Paley, LOC, UCLA]
HICKENLOOPERS: Birthday Present [S, I]
   Charlie has forgotten Doris's birthday—or did he?
SPOOFS/PARODIES: Homicide 6-5300 [S, I, C]
   A semi-spoof of *Sorry, Wrong Number*, in which a man plans to kill his cheating wife, with much poking fun at the melodramatic music used in the genre
SONG/DANCE: Anyone Here from Out of Town? [I]
   Audience-participation number
MONOLOGUE: 6-Month-Old Baby [S]
   Thoughts of a baby about his situation; in light of his treatment by his father and older cousins, "If I grow up, it'll be a miracle!"

Ep #159 • Air Date: 5/29/54 • Host: Marguerite Piazza • [Paley, LOC, UCLA]
HICKENLOOPERS: Poker Game [S, I, C, H]
   Charlie goes to a poker game—and forgets he was supposed to meet Doris
OTHER: Slowly I Turn [S, I]
   Adaptation of the old vaudeville routine; a man is assaulted by a crazed woman when he innocently says things that set her off
SONG/DANCE: Doll Song from Tales of Hoffman [I]
OTHER: What's on the Agenda [S, C, H]
   A business lunch goes south when the delivery doesn't include the boss's sandwich; featuring overlapping dialogue and a hungry Sid's desperate attempt to get his mouth around a pickle waved in front of him by Howie

Ep #160 • Air Date: 6/5/54 • Host: Faye Emerson • [Paley, LOC, UCLA]
Broadcast in color
HICKENLOOPERS: First Homecooked Meal [S, I]
   Charlie's attempts to deal with Doris' inedible food without hurting her feelings include tossing it out the window, with collateral damage to passersby
FOREIGN FILM/DOUBLETALK: Au Revoir Ma Cherie [S, I, C, H]
   Spoof of a World War I movie; a woman bids goodbye to her lover as he leaves for the front (French doubletalk)
PANTOMIME: 1812 Overture [S, I]
   Sid and Imogene as percussionists in an orchestra mime their parts in the 1812 Overture
SILENT FILMS: Sewing Machine Girl [S, I, C, H]
   Sweethearts in a sweat-shop, whose relationship is doomed by the lascivious boss and her ominous cough
SONG/DANCE: Wrap Your Troubles in Dreams [I]
   Coca in her tramp persona
OTHER: Four Englishmen: Leaky Roof [S, I, C, H]
   The quartet sit stoically in a manor hall as the rain drips, then pours, from a roof that leaks

Notes

Part I

1. In Fred Ferretti, "Playing Comedy Is No Laughing Matter," *New York Times*, 11/14/1982, Section 2, 22.
2. Paley Center retrospective on Sid Caesar, 7/16/2014, video panel discussion with Carl Reiner, Mel Brooks, Billy Crystal, and Eddy Friedfeld, Paley Center for Media in New York.
3. Neil Simon, *Laughter on the 23rd Floor* (Random House, 1995), 19; Act I.
4. Sid Caesar with Bill Davidson, *Where Have I Been?* (Crown Publications, 1982), 224–235. Further citations will be noted as "Caesar." His autobiography, in its account of his addictions, can be wrenching. It's also remarkably frank about at least some, if not all, aspects of his life. It's clear that he loved his wife Florence and his children, although there are intimations that he was not always faithful as a husband during *Your Show of Shows* (Letter from Mel Tolkin to Lucille Kallen, 4/19/1982, Box 2, Series 1: Correspondence—Mel Tolkin, 1969-1998 in Lucille Kallen Papers, 1938-1999, Billy Rose Theatre Division, New York Public Library for the Performing Arts) as well as after, and his crushing schedule frequently made him an absentee father as his children were growing up. As he ruefully acknowledged, his addictions would take a toll on his family as well as himself. His alcohol-fueled rages terrified his children when they were young and he was verbally abusive to his wife, although according to his son Rick, he was never physically abusive to either. After he achieved sobriety, he began to repair his relationships with his family, and his marriage to Florence would last 67 years, until her death in 2010.
5. Robin Meltzer, "The Name Remains the Same," *Mishpacha: The Journal of the Jewish Genealogical Society of Greater Washington, D.C.* (Spring, 2014), 10–11; Philip Sutton, "Why Your Family Name Was Not Changed at Ellis Island," New York Public Library, Division of Local History and Genealogy www.nypl.org/blog/2013/07/02/-name-changes . In 1881, Caesar's paternal relations would have arrived at the immigration center at Castle Island in the Battery, rather than Ellis Island, but family names were not generally changed there either.
6. Jhan and June Robbins, "I Grew Up Angry," *Redbook*, 108–109 (November 1956), 54. This is a valuable source for information about Caesar's early life, and was certainly given an appropriate title, taken from one of his comments in the interview.
7. Caesar, 14.
8. Caesar, 10
9. There was a fourth Caesar son, Milton, born after the first, Abe. He would have been another much older sibling but died of meningitis before Sid was born.
10. Caesar, 11.
11. Reiner, Paley Center retrospective. Although Carl doesn't mention the brothers' names, it's easy to figure out which, from his parenthetical comments, was probably the main instigator. Few, if any, of those associated with Caesar's siblings had anything but good things to say about Dave, and Sid always wrote of him with great love. One can guess that in this instance Abe took sibling rivalry to a rather cruel extreme.

227

12. "Comedian with Four-Figure Audiences and Six-Figure Income...," *Rochester Democrat and Chronicle*, 7/6/1950, F4, 67.

13. Caesar, 13.

14. Sid Caesar and Richard Gehman, "What Psychoanalysis Did for Me," *Look*, October 6, 1956, 49–52. The ironically titled article (it didn't do much in the long run) was reprinted and expanded in *Celebrities on the Couch*, ed. Lucy Freeman (Price/Stern/Sloan, 1967), 36.

15. Sid Caesar with Eddy Friedfeld, *Caesar's Hours* (Public Affairs, 2003), 9; "The Woes of a Sensitive Comedian," TV Guide Views: Sid Caesar by Richard Gehman, *TV Guide*, 2/23/1963, 21. It was an incident difficult for Caesar to let go: he had told the same story to Maurice Zolotow in 1953 for an article in the *Saturday Evening Post*, www.saturdayeveningpost.com/2016/04/21/history/post-perspective/-sid-caesar-king-comedy-television.

16. For this reason, Caesar's account of his childhood in *Caesar's Hours* should be read as a striking contrast with earlier ones, even his autobiography of 1982. In it, he changes many of the situations described, often leaving Max out of them entirely, or revises them significantly to put him in a better light. By 2003, he had either come to terms with the unpleasant aspects of his early life that he described in the 1950s or, consciously or unconsciously, chose to leave them out.

17. Caesar, 73.

18. David Marc, *Demographic Vistas: Television in American Culture* (University of Pennsylvania Press, 1996), 99–100,102.

19. Michael V. Tueth, *Laughter in the Living Room: Television Comedy and the American Home Audience* (Peter Lang, 2005), 48–50.

20. Nanette Fabray, Interviews, *The Sid Caesar Collection*, Vol. 3, DVD (NEWVIDEO/Creative Light), 2001. Just how uncomfortable he was being himself is seen vividly in his appearance on *Person to Person* in 1954; obviously ill-at-ease, he stumbles over introducing his wife ("this is my wife ...uh...this is Florence Caesar") and manages to knock a mounted deer head off a wall. You can't help thinking he agreed to appear only to plug the upcoming debut of *Caesar's Hour*. He had a reputation for being a tough interview;

he could occasionally give a lively one, particularly after he had conquered his addictions, but his shyness often got in the way. Dick Cavett, on whose show he appeared several times, called him "almost winsomely shy" as a talker. Dick Cavett, "Dick Cavett Remembers Sid Caesar's Brilliant Career and Chaotic Life," *New Republic*, 12/20/1982, rpt. 2/12/2014, https://newrepublic.com/article/116600/.

21. *Celebrities on the Couch*, 36.

22. In *Sid Caesar: Television's Comedy Genius*, A&E Biography, VHS (A&E Home Video, 1994).

23. *Celebrities on the Couch*, 35.

24. "I Grew Up Angry," 111.

25. Perhaps somewhere still floating around, most likely on 78s or LP collections of Big Band music, are two recordings made by the Shep Fields Orchestra in 1941 with a 17-year-old Sid Caesar on saxophone. And, perhaps, he appeared in a 5-minute short with the Orchestra, "Shep Fields New Music." There's a band member playing clarinet (which he did) with a sax in front of him who looks very much like Caesar; unfortunately, there are no full-face shots to make identification certain.

26. Caesar's Catskills experience would change his life in another way. Appel was responsible for his getting his last summer booking at Avon Lodge. It was there he met Florence Levy, the attractive niece of the owner; they would marry a year later. Sid would also change someone else's life at Avon Lodge that summer. Appel introduced him to a 14-year-old *tummler*, one Melvin Kaminsky, from a nearby lodge. After the war, Kaminsky, now Mel Brooks, would renew their acquaintance backstage at the Copa where Caesar was appearing in 1947—it was the beginning of a mutually beneficial relationship, particularly for Brooks, who would begin to supply material for Sid on *The Admiral Broadway Revue* and gain ultimate entry into the writing staff of *Your Show of Shows*.

27. Caesar, 47.

28. In *Sid Caesar: Television's Comedy Genius*, A&E Biography.

29. Martha Schmoyer LoMonaco, *Every Week, a Broadway Revue: The Tamiment Playhouse, 1921–1960* (Greenwood Press, 1992), 2. This is an invaluable source for Liebman's career at Tamiment and his role

in discovering and promoting Playhouse alumni, not to mention employing them in his later TV ventures.

30. Interviews, *The Sid Caesar Collection*, Vol. 1, DVD (NEWVIDEO/Creative Light, 2000).

31. Although, for some reason, a poster advertising *Tars and Spars* shows him playing the saxophone, something that doesn't occur in the film.

32. Caesar, 74.

33. One reason may have been the nature of his representation. He had signed a contract with Milton Bren, the producer of *Tars and Spars*, in which Bren was supposed to serve as a kind of agent and also employ Caesar in films for Bren's own unit, Capitol Pictures. Nothing much beyond *Janet Ames* ever materialized, nor was Bren active as a producer. After Caesar returned to New York and began to make it big, he was sued by Capitol for $250,000 for breach of contract; Caesar's defense, besides claiming that Bren had breached it by trying to loan him out and not getting him work at Capitol, was that the contract was signed when both were in the Coast Guard and Bren was his commanding officer. It was finally settled, one suspects, after a federal judge permitted Sid's "Coast Guard" defense to stand (*Variety*, 2/22/1950; 3/15/1950; *Billboard*, 1/19/1952). He would be much shrewder in signing future contracts.

34. *Variety*, 1/8/1947, 264.

35. Patrick McGilligan, in his biography of Mel Brooks, *Funny Man* (HarperCollins, 2019), says that Caesar had been under personal contract to Max Liebman ever since *Tars and Spars* (p. 52). A contract does indeed appear to have existed, but perhaps not that far back. After the revue was put together, Max returned to New York. At the end of the revue's tour, Sid stayed in California for the filming of it and *Janet Ames* and doesn't mention any contact with Liebman until he asked for his help in putting together an act for his Copa engagement in early 1947. Given the circumstances, entry into a personal contract with Liebman at that point would be eminently plausible. (It also would seem hardly a coincidence that Bren would sue Sid for breach of contract in 1947—see note above.)

36. *New York Times*, 1/16/1948; *Variety*, 1/21/1948.

37. There was an off-Broadway revival in 2012; its music and lyrics were praised, but a number of '40s-specific sketches were dropped and, despite attempts to stress common Manhattan themes of 1948 and today, much of the appreciation was for a charming period piece.

38. Jeff Kisseloff, *The Box: An Oral History of Television 1920-1961* (ReAnimus Press, 2013 ed.), 307.

39. Jack Gould, "Television in Review," *New York Times*, 2/6/1949.

40. In Kisseloff, *The Box*, 307-308.

41. In *The Box*, 309.

42. "Lavish New Television Review," *Life*, 3/7/1949; Larry Wolters, "A Caesar Rises in Television: Comic Named Sid," *Chicago Tribune*, 3/27/1949, 10

43. Caesar, 89-90.

44. "Admiral Sells Television Through Television," *Broadcasting* 1/23/1950, 64-65.

45. Sid probably was not worried: There was talk of a picture-a-year deal with 20th Century Fox, and, more interestingly, a pitch for a situation comedy, "Great Caesar," to be written by Mel Tolkin and Abe Ginnes. *Variety*, 6/8/1949, 3; 2/1/1950, 36. If the latter had come to fruition, an account of Caesar and early television might have been very different from this one.

46. Pat Weaver with Thomas M. Coffey, *The Best Seat in the House: The Golden Years of Radio and Television* (Knopf, 1994), 179.

Part II

1. "Variety Marathon," *New York Times*, 3/5/1950, X 11.

2. Eddy Friedfeld, Paley Center retrospective on Sid Caesar, 7/16/2014, video panel discussion with Carl Reiner, Mel Brooks, Billy Crystal, and Eddy Friedfeld. Paley Center for Media in New York.

3. Script information, including references to ad-libs, deviations from script, etc., unless otherwise noted, is based on the 20-box collection in the Sid Caesar Papers, 1950-1963; Series 1: *Your Show of Shows*, 1950-1954. Manuscript Division, Library of Congress, Washington, D.C. Subsequent references will be to "Sid Caesar Papers."

4. "The Things That Were Caesar's," *Esquire*, May 1972, 145.

5. David Hinckley, "The Glory of Caesar," *Daily News* (New York), 12/18/2000, 34.

6. Andrew Sarris, "Your Show of Shows Revisited," *Television Quarterly*, 10, No. 4 (Summer 1973), 49. Sarris, no great fan of Caesar's, nonetheless makes a series of good observations about him—his lack of a comedic persona and his ultra-professionalism—but this isn't one of them.

7. Sid Caesar with Eddy Friedfeld, *Caesar's Hours* (Public Affairs, 2003), 249. In his description, Sid recalls the mix-up in sketch running order correctly (corroborated if you watch the entire episode), but misremembers the nature of the bus station sketch that follows. (Forgiveable, as it *was* almost 50 years after the fact.)

8. Sid Caesar Papers, Box 15, #120.

9. "Your Show of Shows," *Emmy Magazine*, March–April 1982, 52.

10. Lawrence R. Samuel, *Brought to You By: Postwar Advertising and the American Dream* (University of Texas Press, 2001), 27–30.

11. Samuel, 37–38. Many of *Your Show of Shows*' sponsors continued throughout the program's run. One that did not was Snow Crop, maker of frozen foods, including the first frozen orange juice. It dropped its early sponsorship not because of discontent with the program or its ratings, but for a very 1950s reason: Because the show aired on Saturday nights, the company was concerned that the audience would be unable to run out and purchase their products the next day, Sunday, when most stores would be closed. *Billboard*, 2/17/1951, 5.

12. Caesar would once make a joke about a brand product, sort of, in a Professor sketch of 5/23/53, although it was probably not to the sponsor's liking. As an "expert" in engineering, the Professor was asked to straighten out the leaning Tower of Pisa; his solution was to attach a team of camels to the Tower by chains around their humps and had them tug away at it for three weeks. Reiner asks whether the Tower was straightened and Sid replies, "No, but the camels were." And then ad-libs, "You want to buy some smooth camels, kid?" For a second, any Camel ad-rep watching might have thought at long last, Sid might give a plug for one of the show's major sponsors, R.J. Reynolds. But, no, as he then goes on, "... Smooth and fully packed." As any '50s audience would have known, "So Round, So Firm, So Fully Packed" was a slogan for a Camels competitor—Lucky Strike.

13. Robert Pondillo, *America's First Network Censor: The Work of NBC's Stockton Helffrich* (Southern Illinois University Press, 2010), 69.

14. Script #18, Box 5, folder 15, Series IV-Television, in Lucille Kallen papers, 1938–1999, Billy Rose Theatre Division, New York Public Library for the Performing Arts, New York, NY. Kallen's papers contain scripts for *The Admiral Broadway Revue* comedy sketches, as well as those for the 1950 season of *Your Show of Shows*.

15. Pondrillo, 186.

16. Pondrillo, 70.

17. The only exception to never showing a couple in bed together was in *Mary Kay and Johnny*, a little known and largely forgotten TV series (almost all of the kinescopes of it were destroyed). It aired initially in 1946 in 15-minute segments on DuMont, primarily in the New York area. It starred a real-life couple as well.

18. Script #138 in Max Liebman Collection, Box 8, A-988, Moving Images Section, Library of Congress, Washington, D.C.

19. About the only exception, and even here it's somewhat of a stretch, was in a sketch where Sid, as a be-medalled German officer, thinks his authority is being challenged. Pointing to one of the medals, he inquires, "What does this look like—a Dewey button?"

20. Sid Caesar with Bill Davidson, *Where Have I Been?* (Crown Publishers, 1982), 40.

21. Harry Stein, "My Father, *Fiddler*, and the Left," *City Journal*, Summer 2014, www.cityjournal.org/2014/24-3-urb-joseph-stein, 6.

22. Katherine Brodsky, "Dick Van Dyke and Carl Reiner on Pushing 100, Charming the FBI, and Falling in Love Again," www.theguardian.com/tv-and-radio/2016/May/31.

23. Pat Weaver with Thomas M. Coffey, *The Best Seat in the House: The Golden Years of Radio and Television* (Knopf, 1994), 238–239.

24. A story Sid told to Jane Klain, Manager of the Research Division, The Paley Center for Media in New York, related in a conversation of 11/2016.

25. Fred Ferretti, "Playing Comedy Is No Laughing Matter," *New York Times*, 11/14/1982, Section 2, 22.
26. "The Things That Were Caesar's," 147.
27. The line comes from "Casabianca," an 1826 poem elementary school students often encountered in readers up to the 1950s. Its subject was rather grim: a young boy, the son of a ship's captain, perishes because he refuses to give up his post as the ship burns. Apparently, elementary school age students back then were made of sterner stuff. Its meter (The boy stood on the burning deck/whence all but he had fled) bore an unfortunate resemblance to that of "Mary Had a Little Lamb." Sid would invariably come up with something like "The boy stood on the burning deck/his feets were white as snow."
28. Descriptions of the Writers' Room are many; this one is drawn from, unless otherwise noted, the interviews in "The Things That Were Caesar's," *Esquire*, May 1972, 138-149; Fred Feretti, "Playing Comedy Is No Laughing Matter," *New York Times*, 11/14/1982, Section 2, 1,22; Lucille Kallen, "Comedy Writer Remembers Her Favorite Years," *New York Times*, 11/29/1992, Section 2, 5-6.
29. "The Things That Were Caesar's," 145.
30. "Playing Comedy is No Laughing Matter," 22; Caesar, *Where Have I Been?*, 99.
31. Bernard Weinraub, "Great Caesar's Toast; New Attention Burnishes the Reputation of a TV Pioneer, *New York Times*, 11/15/2000, www.nytimes.com/2000/11/15/arts/great-caesar-s-toast-new-attention-burnishes-the-reputation-of-a-tv-pioneer.
32. *Where Have I Been?*, 99.
33. Undated typescript draft for an article/essay, Series VIII: Other Writings 1969-1986, Box 40, Lucille Kallen Papers, NYPLPA.
34. Margalit Fox, "Lucille Kallen, 76, Writer for 'Show of Shows' Dies," *New York Times*, 1/21/1999, www.nytimes.com/1999/01/21/arts/lucille-kallen-76-writer-for-show-of-shows-dies; Dana Gold, "Unrecognized Genius," *Moment Magazine*, 12/5/2014, rpt. 8/29/2017, http://momentmag.com/unrecognized-genius-franklin-schwartz-kallen/.

35. Kallen, "Comedy Writer Remembers Her Favorite Years," 5-6; Fox," Lucille Kallen, Writer for 'Show of Shows" Dies," https://interviews.televisionacademy.com/interviews/lucille-kallen#people-clips.
36. Bill Davidson, "Hail, Sid Caesar!" *Collier's*, 11/11/1950, 51.
37. In Jeff Kisseloff, *The Box: An Oral History of Television 1920-1961* (ReAnimus Press, 1995), 311. Kallen regarded it as an illustration of performers' resentment of their dependence on writers. If so, Caesar would not have been the first comedian to feel that way, but none of the other writers mention in their interviews circumstances in which they perceived it. He might have been just angry and frustrated, which would have hardly been unusual.
38. Neil Simon, *Rewrites: A Memoir* (Simon & Schuster, 1996), 115-116; *Laughter on the 23rd Floor* (Random House, 1995), 19; Act I. The dangers involved in treating fiction as fact are obvious; in this case, however, the play is only a slight exaggeration of the real Writers' Room and the people in it. I'll go with Mel Tolkin's assessment after he saw the play: "Not a single word said onstage was ever uttered by any of us. But all of it is true." (Margalit Fox, "Mel Tolkin, Lead Writer for "Your Show of Shows," Dies at 94," *New York Times*, 11/27/2007, Section B, 7.
39. Television Academy Foundation: The Interviews: Lucille Kallen http://interviews.televisionacademy.com/interviews/lucille- kallen#people-clips
40. In Kisseloff, *The Box*, 310.
41. Weaver, *The Best Seat in the House*, 201.
42. "The Things That Were Caesar's," 149; *Where Have I Been?*, 146.
43. In *Hail Sid Caesar! The Golden Age of Comedy*, DVD (Creative Light, 2002).
44. "The Things That Were Caesar's," 146; *The Box*, 311.
45. Caesar always wrote about Liebman in terms of the greatest respect in both *Where Have I Been?* and *Caesar's Hours*; he realized how much he owed him, not just in shaping his career from the Coast Guard to *Your Show of Shows* but in teaching him how a successful TV show was put together. However, it's clear that, after the first season, their views on what made for effective comedy began to diverge. (Sid Caesar

with Eddy Friedfeld, *Caesar's Hours: My Life in Comedy* (Public Affairs, 2003, 125.) You can indeed see a shift from the first season to the second, with far fewer of the *Admiral Broadway Revue*-type broad comedy sketches.

46. Neil Simon wrote for Gleason briefly and never forgot his dismissive attitude toward his writers: "nobody who respected our contribution could have treated us that way." Simon would even "credit" Gleason for his later career as a playwright: "I did not want to get to be a middle-aged man waiting for the phone to ring so I could go to work writing gags for some abusive, unappreciative shit like Jackie Gleason." William A. Henry III, *The Great One: The Life and Legend of Jackie Gleason* (Doubleday, 1992), 169; 249–250. It should be noted that Simon wasn't the only one of Jackie's writers who felt that way.

47. *The Box*, 320–322.

48. *Caesar's Hours*, 102; Fox, "Mel Tolkin, Lead Writer for 'Your Show of Shows,' Dies at 94"; James Robert Parish, *It's Good To Be The King: The Seriously Funny Life of Mel Brooks* (John Wiley & Sons), 65. Mel Brooks said many times, "No Caesar, No Brooks." He was right. Liebman never saw the talent behind Mel's often outrageous behavior and *chutzpah*. Caesar did. Although he initially regarded Brooks as a "kind of groupie" who was funny and shared his sense of humor (Caesar, 92), he quickly came to realize his ability to come up with the perfect topper or line in a sketch when progress on it was at a standstill. Without Sid's support and backing, it's doubtful that Liebman would have finally relented and put Mel on the payroll during *Your Show of Shows*' first full season.

49. *The Box*, 305.

50. Glenn Collins, "Caesar's Commentaries: Unraveling Source of Genius," *New York Times*, 11/14/2000, Section B, 6.

51. It can be followed in Glenn Collins, "Mother Lode of TV Comedy Is Found in Forgotten Closet," *New York Times*, 11/14/2000, 1; Section B, 6 and "Key's Holder Unlocks Mystery of TV Treasure," *New York Times*, 11/19/2000, 51 in which Max Liebman's last assistant, Barry Jacobsen, revealed not only the key, but the reason the closet was locked for so long.

52. Lisa Schwarzbaum, "What We Did Last Saturday Night," *Daily News* (New York), 4/8/1990, 249.

53. Max Liebman, "A Broadway Revue Every Week," *Theatre Arts* (May, 1953), 75–77. This account of the show's weekly schedule leaves you in admiration of Liebman's management and production skills.

54. Sid Caesar Papers, Box 2, #9; Box 13, #110.

55. Sid Caesar Papers, Box 17, #142.

56. Sid Caesar Papers, Box 16, #133.

57. Sid Caesar Papers, Box 2, #9.

58. Sid Caesar Papers, Box 18, #147; Lucille Kallen Papers, Box 5, folder 2, Series IV-Television.

59. Sid Caesar Papers, Box 12, #98.

60. Script #153 in Max Liebman Collection, Box 41, A-1070, Moving Images Section, Library of Congress, Washington D.C.; *Caesar's Hours*, 255–257; Morris interview in *The Sid Caesar Collection*, Vol. 1, DVD (NEWVIDEO/Creative Light, 2000); Reiner interview in *Hail Sid Caesar! The Golden Age of Comedy*.

61. Dick Cavett, "He Came, He Saw, He Conquered ... Hilariously," *New York Times*, 2/20/2014, www.nytimes.com/2014/02/01/opinion/cavett-he-came-he-saw-he-conquered-hilariously.

62. In *The Sid Caesar Collection*, Vol. 3, DVD (NEWVIDEO/Creative Light, 2001).

63. Carl Reiner, *My Anecdotal Life: A Memoir* (St. Martin's Press, 2003), 1,15,32.

64. Margalit Fox, "Howard Morris, an Actor in Television Comedies, Dies at 85," *New York Times*, 5/25/2005.

65. One of the fullest accounts of Coca's early life can be found in Karen Adir, *The Great Clowns of American Television* (McFarland Press, 1988), 89–96.

66. Mark Evanier and Jim Brooks, "The Comedy Interview: Sid Caesar," *Comedy* Vol. 1, No.1 (Summer, 1980), 18.

67. If you want to get technical about it, *Mary Kay and Johnny*, which aired in 1946 on DuMont, was the first domestic sitcom, although its initial audience was a limited one. See Note 12.

68. Karen Adir, *The Great Clowns of American Television* (McFarland Press, 1988), 45; *Caesar's Hours*, 91.

69. In a later episode of *The Honeymooners*, Alice briefly gets a job. Ralph's reaction mirrors Charlie's—it's a threat to his status as breadwinner.

70. Sid Caesar Papers, Box 6, #53.
71. *Caesar's Hours*, 134–35.
72. "The Comedy Interview: Sid Caesar," 18.
73. *Where Have I Been?*, 136.
74. And also based on a real-life incident, another indication of the writers, in this case Tolkin and Caesar, using something that had happened to them as inspiration for a sketch. Mel and Sid were with their wives having dinner in a restaurant when firemen with axes, dragging a hose, went through the dining room on their way to the kitchen to put out a small fire. And no one paid any attention, continuing to eat (of course, it was New York). The next day, they turned it into "The String Quartet." Max Wilk, *The Golden Age of Television: Notes from the Survivors* (Dell, 1976), 168.
75. Liebman, "A Broadway Revue Every Week," 76.
76. Bill Hayes & Susan Seaforth Hayes, *Like Sands Through the Hourglass* (New American Library, 2005), 108–09.
77. Davidson, "Hail, Sid Caesar!" 51.
78. Unfortunately, you can't see her routines from *Your Show of Shows* on video, only on complete episodes, which are rare outside the Paley; fortunately, some of her numbers (including the famous topcoat striptease) from *The Admiral Broadway Revue* can be seen on YouTube and DVDs.
79. Ted Sennett, *Your Show of Shows* (Macmillan, 1977), 60.
80. Barry Putterman, *On Television and Comedy: Essays on Style, Theme, Performer, and Writer* (McFarland Press, 1995), 71–72; 77–78.
81. Albert Goldman, "Laughtermakers," in *Jewish Wry: Essays on Jewish Humor*, ed. Sarah Blacher Cohn (Indiana University Press, 1987), 84.
82. *Caesar's Hours*, 219.
83. Erskine Johnson, syndicated column *Johnson in Hollywood*, *Long Beach Independent*, 10/21/53, 24.
84. www.law.justia.com/cases/federal/district.courts/FSupp/137/348/1480440. Few legal opinions are funny; Exhibit B of this one is (unintentionally), as it dryly dissects every plot point and character of "From Here to Obscurity." As usual with matters legal, the issue was a bit more complicated than the necessarily brief summary given. The same judge had ruled only a few months before that Jack Benny and CBS were guilty of copyright infringement in a parody of MGM's film *Gaslight*; the issue was that the parody had taken too substantial an amount of material from it. Benny had appealed and the judge was obviously hoping that Columbia would appeal his decision in the Sid Caesar case, so that a higher court could make a definitive ruling for both. However, that didn't happen: Columbia didn't appeal and Benny lost his. It would not be until 1986 that a more definitive parody test would be determined. (Charles J. Sanders and Steven R. Gordon, "Strangers in Parodies," *Entertainment, Media & Intellectual Property Law Forum*, 1, No. 1 [1990], 23–25.)
85. *Caesar's Hours*, 219–220.
86. J. Hoberman and Jeffrey Shandler, eds., *Entertaining America: Jews, Movies, and Broadcasting* (Princeton University Press; The Jewish Museum, NY, 2003), 144–45. Although not all the Jewish writers were American-born: Mel Tolkin was born in Ukraine and emigrated to Canada; Lucille Kallen was also Canadian.
87. David Margolick, "The Deep Jewish Roots of Television's Caesar," *Tablet*, 2/14/2014, www.tabletmag.com/jewish-arts-and-culture/163060/sid-caesar-show-of-shows/; Michael Auslin, "Sid Caesar and His World," *Commentary*, 4/1/2014, www.commentarymagazine.com/articles/sid-caesar-and-his-world.
88. "Comedian with Four-Figure Audiences and Six-Figure Income …" *Rochester Democrat and Chronicle*, 7/6/1950, F4, 67. George Burns and Jack Benny would indeed reminisce about growing up Jewish in, respectively, New York City and Waukegan, Illinois but not until decades later (in, for example, Burns' *The Third Time Around* (1980) and *All My Best Friends* (1989) and Benny's *Sunday Nights at Seven*, his unfinished memoir supplemented by the reminiscences of his daughter Joan, published in 1990). Barry Rubin, *Assimilation and its Discontents* (Times Books/Random House), 68–69.
89. *Entertaining America*, 145.
90. My thanks to Gary Westin for drawing this interview to my attention. "Celebrating 30 Years of 'Fresh Air': The Carl Reiner Interview: NPR," 8/25/2017 (originally broadcast in 1988), www.npr.org/templates/transcript.php?storyID=546065955.

91. Goldman, "Laughtermakers," 84.
92. Television Academy Foundation: The Interviews: Mel Tolkin, http://interviews.televisionacademy.com.
93. Caesar could imitate for friends a Jewish union leader riding the subway to a strike (Margolick, "The Deep Jewish Roots of Television's Caesar,") or do doubletalk in Hebrew, but in the outside world, he didn't tend to poke fun at that sort of thing or to wear his Jewishness on his sleeve. In both *Where Have I Been?* and *Caesar's Hours*, he briefly mentions his bar mitzvah, attending *shul*, and observing Yom Kippur, but if you're looking for some kind of disquisition on What Judaism Means to Me, you won't find one. In one of his last interviews, although admitting that he didn't "live a very Jewish lifestyle," he repeated the simple statement that he had made frequently throughout his life, that he was proud to be Jewish. (Barbra Paskin, "Interview: Sid Caesar, *JC: The Jewish Chronicle*, 10/7/2010, www.thejc.com/culture/interviews/interview-sid-caesar-1.18603.
94. Undated typescript, b. 40, Lucille Kallen Papers, NYPLPA.
95. Margolick, "The Deep Jewish Roots of Television's Caesar."
96. *Entertaining America*, 145.

Part III

1. Fred Ferretti, "Playing Comedy Is No Laughing Matter," *New York Times*, 11/14/1982, Section 2, 22.
2. In Jeff Kisseloff, *The Box: An Oral History of Television 1920–1961* (ReAnimus Press, 1995), 308. And then Stein added a familiar Caesar observation: "Except one thing, he couldn't stand up and tell jokes ... he had a lot of difficulty talking as himself."
3. Steve Allen, *The Funny Men* (Simon & Schuster, 1955), 115.
4. Richard Corliss, "Great Caesar's Ghost," *TIME*, Feb. 13, 2014, http:/entertainment.time.com/2014/02/13-sid-caesar/remembrance.
5. See, for example, Neil Simon's account of Caesar's DIY sink removal. (Neil Simon, *Rewrites: A Memoir* (Simon & Schuster, 1996), 116.
6. Sid Caesar and Eddy Friedfeld, *Caesar's Hours* (Public Affairs, 2003), 137.

7. There are slightly different versions of this story, although the core action—Sid attempting to extricate the cab driver—remains the same. This is, I think, a plausible amalgam of Brooks' story in *The Sid Caesar Collection*, Vol. 2 DVD (NEWVIDEO/Creative Light, 2001) and the one Dick Cavett relates ("Dick Cavett Remembers Sid Caesar's Brilliant Career and Chaotic Life," *New Republic*, December 20, 1982, 3). Caesar told a similar story, with a slightly different situation, but with many of the same elements, i.e., hauling someone from a car through the window. (Television Academy Foundation: The Interviews: Sid Caesar http://interviews.televisionacademy.com/people). In any event, it's safe to say that, even if you were in the presumed safety of a car, it was generally not a good idea to provoke him.
8. The incident obviously made an impact on his writers. Mel Brooks would adapt it for *Blazing Saddles* (1974), where Alex Karras knocks out a horse with a right cross.
9. In Kisseloff, *The Box*, 311.
10. Earl Wild and Michael Rolland Davis, *A Walk on the Wild Side* (Ivory Classics Foundation, 2011), 287–88. My thanks to Richard Camhi, who knows far more about music than I ever will, for his observation on Caesar's miming skill on the cadenza.
11. Carl Reiner, Interviews, *The Sid Caesar Collection*, Vol. 2 (DVD) (NEWVIDEO/Creative Light, 2001); Maurice Zolotow, "TV Gives Him Nightmares" (May 16, 1953), www.saturdayeveningpost.com/2016/04/21/history/post-perspective/sid-caesar-king-comedy-television.html.
12. *Caesar's Hours*, 237.
13. Lucille Kallen, "Comedy Writer Remembers Her Favorite Years," *New York Times*, 11/29/1992, Section 2, 5–6; Undated typescript for an article/essay, Series VIII: Other Writings 1969–1986, b. 40, Lucille Kallen Papers, New York Public Library For the Performing Arts, New York, New York.
14. Bill Hayes and Susan Seaforth Hayes, *Like Sands Through the Hourglass* (New American Library, 2005), 102.
15. For just one instance, watch the aptly titled "The Sneeze Sketch" aka "The Hypochondriac" (10/21/50). Caesar's facial contortions in his attempt to stifle a sneeze are

funny enough; his failure results not so much in a sneeze as a whole-body explosion.

16. Cited in Gerald Nachman, *Seriously Funny: The Rebel Comedians of the 1950s and 1960s* (Pantheon Books, 2003), 103.

17. For an example of Caesar's incredible skill with sound-effects, see the description in Part 1 of a monologue featuring them that he did on *The Admiral Broadway Revue*.

18. Sid Caesar Papers, 1950–1963; Series 1: *Your Show of Shows*, 1950–54. Manuscript Division, Library of Congress, Washington, D.C. Box 2, #39.

19. *New York Times*, 2/13/2014. NY Times.com/2014/02/13/arts/television/sid-caesar-comic-who-blazed-tv-trail-dies.

20. "The Things That Were Caesar's," *Esquire*, May 1972, 142.

21. Allen, *Funny Men*, 114.

22. In *Sid Caesar: Television's Comedy Genius*, A&E Biography VHS (A&E Home Video, 1994).

23. Sid Caesar with Bill Davidson, *Where Have I Been?* (Crown Publishers, 1982), 130, 153.

24. My thanks to Barry Jacobsen for showing me his recording of the *Revue*.

25. Mark Evanier and Jim Brooks, "The Comedy Interview: Sid Caesar," *Comedy* Vol. 1, No. 1 (Summer, 1980), 19.

26. In Kisseloff, *The Box*, 315.

27. "The Comedy Interview," 17.

28. In Kisseloff, *The Box*, 311.

29. Sid Caesar Papers, Box 10, #86

30. Sid Caesar Papers, Box 13, #110.

31. "The Comedy Interview," 19–20.

32. Again, my thanks to Gary Westin for providing the Chaplin references. Just to forestall the perhaps inevitable "Didn't Danny Kaye do Russian?" question, Kaye would use a few Russian words in songs or, in his best-known bit, recite the names of Russian composers. The speed of the latter is impressive, but neither is technically doubletalk.

33. In *Hail Sid Caesar!: The Golden Age of Comedy*.

34. Television Academy Foundation: The Interviews: Lucille Kallen, http://interviews.televisionacademy.com/interviews/lucille-kallen#people-clips.

35. *Where Have I Been?*, 102.

36. Maurice Zolotow, "TV Gives Him Nightmares" (May 16, 1953).

37. Sid Caesar Papers, Box 10, #87; Box 15, #123.

38. Ted Sennett, *Your Show of Shows* (Collier Books, 1977), 41.

39. "Latenite Killed the Vaudeo Star," *Variety*, 5/30/2007, A11.

40. "The Things That Were Caesar's," *Esquire*, May 1972, 147.

Part IV

1. "Sid Caesar and Imogene Coca to Quit as Team," *Los Angeles Times*, 2/26/1954, 4.

2. Theo Wilson, "Tears Flow as Imogene and Sid Come to Parting of TV Waves," *Daily News* (New York), 2/26/1954, 76.

3. Coca's differing versions of events may be found in "The Things That Were Caesar's," *Esquire* (May, 1972), 149; Karen Adir, *The Great Clowns of American Television* (McFarland Press, 1988) 104; Jeff Kisseloff, *The Box: An Oral History of Television, 1920–1961* (ReAnimus Press, 2013 ed.), 312.

4. Pat Weaver with Thomas M. Coffey, *The Best Seat in the House: The Golden Years of Radio and Television* (Knopf, 1994), 249–50.

5. In *Hail Sid Caesar!: The Golden Age of Comedy*, DVD (Creative Light, 2002); "What's Going to Happen to *Show of Shows*," *TV Guide* (July 31, 1953), 7.

6. "Your Show of Shows," *Emmy Magazine* (March-April, 1982), 53; Sid Caesar with Bill Davidson, *Where Have I Been?* (Crown Publications, 1982), 136–37.

7. In *The Box*, 312. Interestingly, Morris never seems to have repeated this in any earlier or subsequent interviews, including one a year before his death.

8. "Sid Caesar and Imogene Coca to Quit as Team," 4

9. In *The Box*, 312.

10. Lisa Schwarzbaum, "What We Did Last Saturday Night," *Daily News* (New York), 4/8/1990, 249.

11. "What's Going to Happen to *Show of Shows*," 7; Erskine Johnson, "Crystal Ball Hints New Format for Caesar Show," *Los Angeles Daily News*, 6/16/1953, 15.

12. "Your Show of Shows," 52.

13. "Celebrating 30 Years of 'Fresh Air': The Carl Reiner Interview: NPR," 8/25/2017 (originally broadcast in 1988),

www.npr.org/templates/transcript.php?storyID=546065955.

14. "The Things that were Caesar's," 192.

15. Max Wilk, *The Golden Age of Television: Notes from the Survivors* (Dell, 1976), 168.

16. Weaver, *The Best Seat in the House*, 173.

17. *Where Have I Been?*, 139.

18. Walter Ames, "Sid Caesar Says He Won't Replace Imogene Coca with a New Partner," *Los Angeles Times*, 9/19/1954, 117.

19. Jack Gould, "Television in Review: Ave Caesar," *New York Times*, 3/1/1954, 23.

20. Harvey Sheldon, *The History of the Golden Age of Television* (Sheldon, 2013), 24–28.

21. See "What's Going to Happen to Show of Shows," 5–7; Arthur Gelb, "Why's and Wherefore's for a Revised Format," *New York Times*, 9/6/1953, Section 2, 9.

22. Coca in particular may have felt those restrictions keenly. According to one report, she was "not anxious to renew her contract with *Your Show of Shows* because she wants to do a Broadway show." *Radio-TV Mirror*, May 1953, 21.

23. Arthur Frank Wertheim, "The Rise and Fall of Milton Berle," 69–70 in *American History/American Television*, ed. John E. O'Connor (Frederick Ungar Publishing Co., 1983); *The Columbia History of American Television*, ed. Gary Edgerton (Columbia University Press, 2007), 103.

24. Wertheim, "The Rise and Fall of Milton Berle," 74, 78 n37.

25. Larry Gelbart, *Laughing Matters* (Random House, 1998), 183.

26. Gilbert Millstein, "TV's Comics Went Thataway," *New York Times*, 2/2/1958, 107/Arts Section, 14. The title of the article refers to yet another cycle in TV programming, the rise of the Western, which swamped comedy shows and would dominate the ratings for the next several seasons. At that point, in 1958, Caesar was the longest-running comedian in television.

27. Things were not helped by Caesar himself, who later said that, after 9 years of live TV, "I was out of it. I was just too tired." https://interviews.televisionacademy.com/shows/sid-caesar-invites-you. Imogene Coca was alarmed by something else: his mental state. He was so manic she feared he was having a breakdown. Adir, *The Great Clowns of American Television*, 106.

28. George Rosen, "Pricing TV Off the Market," *Variety*, 3/4/1953, 38.

29. "Liebman to Produce NBC 'Spectaculars,'" *Variety*, 4/28/1954, 10; "NBC Not Happy with Caesar's Salary of $25,000 a Show," *Sponsor*, 7/13/1953, 183.

30. My thanks to Barry Jacobsen for providing access to the letter.

31. "Last Time Together for a Great Pair," *Life*, 6/21/1954, 63.

32. Gilbert Seldes, *The Public Arts* (Simon and Schuster, 1956), 139.

Afterword

1. https://interviews.televisionacademy.com/interviews/lucille-kallen#people-clips; interviews.televisionacademy.com/interviews/max-wilk?clip=65676#.

2. https://interviews.televisionacademy.com/shows/sid-caesar-imogene-coca-carl-reiner-howard-morris-special.

3. Lorraine Ali, "Flying Without Her Net," *Los Angeles Times*, 5/13/2018, E3. Sid would appear on the show three times.

4. www.cc.com/video/the-daily-show-with-jon-stewart-moment-of-zen.

5. In *Hail Sid Caesar! The Golden Age of Comedy*, DVD (Creative Light, 2002).

Bibliography

Primary sources include scripts from *Your Show of Shows*, contained in the Sid Caesar Papers and the Max Liebman collection in the Library of Congress, Washington, D.C.; and scripts and unpublished material and correspondence from the Lucille Kallen and Max Liebman Papers in the New York Public Library for the Performing Arts. Box or folder numbers are supplied in the notes. I have also made extensive use of contemporary, and later, articles in newspapers, magazines, and journals; complete citations for these as well as video interviews are also found in the notes.

Adir, Karen. *The Great Clowns of American Television*. Jefferson, NC: McFarland, 1988.

Allen, Steve. *The Funny Men*. Simon & Schuster, 1955.

Brooks, Tim and Marsh, Earle. *The Complete Directory to Prime Time Network and Cable TV Shows 1946-Present* (ninth edition). New York: Ballantine Books, 2007.

Caesar, Sid, with Bill Davidson. *Where Have I Been? An Autobiography*. New York: Crown Publishers, 1982.

Caesar, Sid, with Eddy Friedfeld. *Caesar's Hours: My Life in Comedy*. New York: Public Affairs, 2003.

Cohn, Sarah Blacher, ed. *Jewish Wry: Essays on Jewish Humor*. Bloomington: Indiana University Press, 1987.

Edgerton, Gary, ed. *The Columbia History of American Television*. New York: Columbia University Press, 2007.

Freeman, Lucy, ed. *Celebrities on the Couch: Personal Adventures in Psychoanalysis*. Los Angeles: Price/Stern/Sloan, 1967.

Gelbart, Larry. *Laughing Matters*. New York: Random House, 1998.

Hayes, Bill, and Susan Seaforth Hayes. *Like Sands Through the Hourglass*. New York: New American Library, 2005.

Henry, William A., III. *The Great One: The Life and Legend of Jackie Gleason*. New York: Doubleday, 1992.

Hoberman, J., and J. Shandler, eds. *Entertaining America: Jews, Movies, and Broadcasting*. Princeton, NJ: Princeton University Press; The Jewish Museum of New York, 2003.

Kisseloff, Jeff. *The Box: An Oral History of Television 1920-1961*. Golden, CO: ReAnimus Press, 2013 ed.

LoMonaco, Martha Schmoyer. *Every Week a Broadway Revue: The Tamiment Playhouse, 1921-1960*. New York: Greenwood Press, 1992.

Marc, David. *Demographic Vistas: Television in American Culture*. Philadelphia: University of Pennsylvania Press, 1996.

McGilligan, Patrick. *Funny Man: Mel Brooks*. New York: HarperCollins, 2019.

Nesteroff, Kliph. *The Comedians: Drunks, Thieves, Scoundrels and the History of American Comedy*. New York: Grove Press, 2015.

O'Connor, John E. *American History/American Television: Interpreting the Video Past*. Frederick Ungar Publishing, 1985.

Parish, James Robert. *It's Good to Be the King: The Seriously Funny Life of Mel Brooks*. Hoboken, NJ: Wiley & Sons, 2007.

Pondillo, Robert. *America's First Network Censor: The Work of NBC's Stockton Helfrich*. Carbondale: Southern Illinois University Press, 2010.

Putterman, Barry. *On Television and Comedy: Essays on Style, Theme, Performer, and Writer.* Jefferson, NC: McFarland, 1995.

Reiner, Carl. *My Anecdotal Life: A Memoir.* St. Martin's Press, 2003.

Samuel, Lawrence R. *Brought to You By: Postwar Television Advertising and the American Dream.* Austin: University of Texas Press, 2001.

Seldes, Gilbert. *The Public Arts.* New York: Simon & Schuster, 1956.

Sennett, Ted. *Your Show of Shows.* Springfield, OH: Collier Books, 1977.

Simon, Neil. *Laughter on the 23rd Floor.* New York: Random House, 1995.

Simon, Neil. *Rewrites: A Memoir.* New York: Simon & Schuster, 1996.

Tueth, Michael V. *Laughter in the Living Room: Television Comedy and the American Home Audience.* Series: Pop Culture and Everyday Life, Vol. 8. New York: Peter Lang, 2005.

Weaver Pat, with Thomas M. Coffey. *The Best Seat in the House: The Golden Years of Radio and Television.* New York: Knopf, 1994.

Wild, Earl, and Michael Rolland Davis. *A Walk on the Wild Side.* Ivory Classics Foundation, 2011.

Wilk, Max. *The Golden Age of Television: Notes from the Survivors.* New York: Dell/Delta, 1976.

# Index

Page numbers in **_bold italics_** indicate pages with illustrations

ABC 67; *Sid Caesar Invites You* 162
The Admiral Broadway Revue: Avera in 29, 31; "Better Go Now" 32; Brooks writing for Caesar 28, 228n26; Caesar in 11, 19, 27–36; Coca in 27–29, 31–32, 90; comedy sketches in 30–31; dance sequences 31; doubletalk in 140; film noir parody 34–35; "Five-Dollar Date" 32–33; Kallen and Tolkin writing for 28, 30; Liebman and 27–32; monologues 33–34, 63; Morris in 30–31; "Penny Gum Machine" 32–33; production costs 36; "The Schmoe" 34;scripts for 60; sponsorship 35–36; variety acts 28–29
Admiral Corporation 27, 35–36
The Adventures of Ozzie and Harriet (TV show) 77
The Al Jolson Story (film) 24
Albert, Eddie 47
All Star Revue (TV show) 158–159, 163
Allen, Steve 115, 132
Appel, Don 21, 228n26
Arnaz, Desi 43, 46, 72
Arthur Godfrey's Talent Scouts (TV show) 107
Avera, Tom 29, 31

Ball, Lucille 43, 46; comparison of Lucy Ricardo on *I Love Lucy* with Coca's Doris Hickenlooper 72–73, 77–78
Ballero, Marc 23
Bellamy, Ralph 44
Benny, Jack 18, 43, 95, 108, 233n84, 233n88
Berle, Milton: *The Buick-Berle Show* 161; comic persona 18, 37, 110, 134; off-color comedy and 45; relationship with writers 59; *Texaco Star Theatre* 30, 43, 59, 111, 163
Billy Williams Quartet 6, 158
blacklisting 46–47
Blair, Janet 23
Blazing Saddles (film) 234n8
Bock, Jerry 22

Bowman, Lee: as guest host, unscripted praise of Caesar 90
Brando, Marlon 106, 107, 132
Bren, Milton 229n33
Brooks, Mel: *The Admiral Broadway Revue* writing (for Caesar) 28, 228n26, *Blazing Saddles* 234n8; on Caesar as musician 23; on Caesar's abilities 113; Caesar's anger and 56, 117; on Caesar's inner demons 12; *Get Smart* 99, 168; *Imogene Coca Show* writing 167; Professor sketch writing 81–82; relationship with Caesar 59, 232n48; television writing 4, 36–37; 51; as *tummler* in Catskills 228n26; Writers' Room 36–37, 51–52, **_54_**, 56, 82, 228n26
The Buick-Berle Show (TV show) 161
Burnett, Carol 71, 149, 159, 169
Burns, George 108, 233n88
The Burns and Allen Show (TV show) 43
Burton, Robert 32

Caesar, Abe (brother): 14; bullying of Sid 15, 227n11
Caesar, Dave (brother) 14–15, 227n11
Caesar, Florence (wife) 47–48, 77, 227n4, 228n26
Caesar, Ida (mother) 5, 13–14, 16, 133
Caesar, Max (father): marital relationship 14–16; physical discipline of Sid 5, 14, 16–17; relationship with Sid 13–14, 16–17, 19–20, 228n16
Caesar, Rick (son) 12, 227n4
Caesar, Sid: addictions 12, 127, 157, 227n4; anger issues 6, 12, 14, 17, 115, 117; childhood 5, 12–18, 228n16; Donaldson Award 26–27, 32; Emmy and Sylvania awards 165, 168; family name 13, 227n5; financial aid to writers 59; generosity toward fellow actors 58, 156–157; inner demons and personality contradictions 11–12, 17–18; music and

239

240 Index

19–23, 141, 228*n*25; music as entrée into comedy 20, 21; physicality and strength 6, 115, **116**, 117–119, 234*n*5; politics of in '50s 46; relationship with father 5, 14–17, 19–20, 228*n*16; relationship with Max Liebman 22, 25, 56–57, **57**, 58, 229*n*35, 231*n*45; shyness 5, 11–12, 14, 19–20, 69, 76, 159, 228*n*20; start in Catskills Mountain resorts 11, 21, 228*n*26; World War II service in Coast Guard 21–23
Caesar, Sid, comedy: "Birth of a Star" 138–139; characterizations 141–143; clown character of Professor 80–81; as comic actor 132–149, 169; doubletalk 22, 33–34, 49, 63, 70, 109, 139–141; "A Drunkard There Was" (*Caesar's Hour*) 133; "I'm in Love" 137–138; Jewishness and 108–110, 234*n*93; lack of comedic persona 18; as Method comedian and actor 6, 132–133; mimicry in childhood 15; portrayal of emotions 135–136; range of talents 5; sound effects and 34–35, 130, 145, 235*n*17; staying in character 134–135; straight acting within comedy 133, 136–139; strength and 115, **116**, 117–119; theatrical acting and 134; voice and accent 129–130 "Das Vorgessenor Symphony" 136–137; *see also* Hickenlooper sketches; monologues; pantomime; parodies; physical comedy; Professor sketches
Caesar, Sid, films, revues: *The Guilt of Janet Ames* 24–25, 229*n*33, 229*n*35; *It's a Mad, Mad, Mad, Mad World* 25; *Make Mine Manhattan* 26, **26**–27, 32–33, 134; nightclub acts 25, 69, 134; *Six On, Twelve Off* (Coast Guard variety show) 21–22; *Tars and Spars* (Coast Guard revue) 12, **17**; *Tars and Spars* (film) 22–25, 57, 134
Caesar, Sid, television: comic acting abilities and 134, 136; familiarity with technical aspects 134; NBC contract and 155, 160, 163; on *Texaco Star Theatre* 27; *see also Admiral Broadway Revue*; *Caesar's Hour*; *Sid Caesar, Imogene Coca, Carl Reiner, and Howard Morris Special*; *Sid Caesar Invites You*
Caesar, Sid, *Your Show of Shows*: comedy sketch ensemble **58**, 67–71; demands of live TV in 39–41; end of show and 153, 154–156; "Hobo Ballet" 93–94; improvisation and ad libs in 41–42, 60, 61–66; "Lily of Laguna" 92–93; mishaps and "saves" 41–42; "Over a Bottle of Wine" 92–93, **116**; pairing with Coca 4, 31–32, 61–62, 70–80, 85–86, 91–94, 166; pairing with Reiner 80–85; refusal to incorporate advertising in 43–44; relationship with Coca 76–77, 156–157; relationship with writers 58–59, 231*n*37; song and dance routines 91–94; temperament and 56; Writers' Room 3, 51–53, **54**, 55–59; *see also* Hickenlooper sketches;

monologues; pantomime; parodies; physical comedy; Professor sketches
Caesar's Hour (TV show): "Aggravation Boulevard" 129–130, 168; cast relationships on 157; development of 157–158; doubletalk in 140; "A Drunkard There Was" 133; Emmy awards 168; female comedy writers on 54, 167; "Gallipacci" 42; "Grieg Piano Concerto" 120; improvisation 42; Nanette Fabray and 89, 123, 157, 167–168; "On the Docks" 106, 168; pantomime 123, 168; piano miming on 120; Reiner and 168; silent movie sketches 133, 135–136; writers for 167
Caesar's Hours (Caesar and Friedfeld) 7
Carney, Art 51, 71, 73
The Carol Burnett Show (TV show) 51, 71, 159, 169
Carson, Jack 89
Catskill Mountains resorts ("Borscht Belt") 21, 228*n*26
Cavalcade of Stars (TV show) 71
Cavett, Dick 64, 228*n*20, 234*n*7
CBS 27, 47, 67, 71, 169
censorship 44–46
Champion, Gower 28
Champion, Marge 28
Chaplin, Charlie 119, 139
Clift, Montgomery 96, 100, 132
Coca, Imogene: background 69; comedy sketches 3–4; Emmy award 165; Liebman and 69, 71; musical comedy 29, 90; pantomime 121–122, **122**, 123–124; Peabody award 165; professional dance 90; pursuit of Broadway career 29, 69, 160, 236*n*22; shyness 69, 76, 159; Tamiment Playhouse and 22, 27, 69, 76, 159
Coca, Imogene, plays: *New Faces of 1934* 69; *New Faces of 1936* 69; *The Straw Hat Revue* 29, 69
Coca, Imogene, television: *The Admiral Broadway Revue* 28, 29, 31, 32, 67, 69, 90; *Imogene Coca Show* 167; *Sid Caesar, Imogene Coca, Carl Reiner, and Howard Morris Special* 168; *Sid Caesar Invites You* 162, 236*n*27
Coca, Imogene, *Your Show of Shows*: ballet parodies, *Afternoon of a Faun* 91; comedy sketch ensemble 4, 29, **58**, 63, 67–70; end of show and 153, **154**–156; "Hobo Ballet" 93–94; "Lily of Laguna" 92–93; "Over a Bottle of Wine" 92–93, **116**; pairing with Caesar 31–32, 41–42, 48, 58, 61–62, 70–80, 85–86, 91–96, 166; physical comedy 48, 61, 70, 93, **116**, 117–121; relationship with Caesar 156–157; 176–77; song and dance routines 61, 90–92; *see also* Hickenlooper sketches; pantomime; parodies
Cohn, Harry 104

Index

Coleman, Deborah 154, 160
Colgate Comedy Hour (TV show) 158–159, 163
Columbia Pictures Corp. v. National Broadcasting Co. aka The Sid Caesar Case 106
Cooper, Jackie 89
Corey, Irwin 80
Corliss, Richard 6, 115, 132
Crosby, John 126–27
Crowley, Patricia 41–42
Crowther, Bosley 23–24

Dahl, Arlene 128
Dann, Mike 156
Diamond, Selma 54, 167
The Dick Van Dyke Show (TV show) 162, 168
Dietz, Howard 22
Donaldson Award 26–27, 32
doubletalk 22, 33–34, 49, 63, 70, 109, 139–141
Douglas, Melvyn 19, 24, 46
Drake, Alfred 23
Duke, Vernon 21–22
DuMont Television Network 11, 27, 71

Emerson, Faye 89, 165
Emmy awards 165, 168

Fabray, Nanette: appearances on *Your Show of Shows* 48, 89; on Caesar and introductions 19; on Liebman and Caesar 57; pantomime and 89, 123; working with Caesar 157; *see also Caesar's Hour*
Father Knows Best (TV show) 77, 80
Ferrer, Jose 47, 88
Fine, Sylvia 22
Ford Television Theatre 35–36
Four Englishmen sketches 86–88, 233*n*74
Francis, Arlene 89
Funny Man (McGilligan) 233*n*35
Furness, Betty 89

Gahagan (Douglas), Helen 46
Garrett, Betty 22
Garrison, Greg 22, 134
Gelbart, Larry 162, 167, 169
Get Smart (TV show) 99, 168
Gleason, Jackie: comedic talents and characters 18, 71–73, 141; comparison of Ralph Kramden on *The Honeymooners* with Caesar's Charlie Hickenlooper 71–72, 74; mistreatment of writers 58–59, 232*n*46; popularity of in Northeast 161; Stein writing for 113
Gobel, George 59
Godfrey, Arthur 43, 107
Goodman, Benny 23
Green, Alfred 24
The Guilt of Janet Ames (film) 24–25, 229*n*33, 229*n*35

Harrison, Rex 89
Hayes, Bill 6, 89
Hickenlooper sketches **68**; arguments in 74–76, 127; "The Birthday Present" 75; Caesar and Coca pairing in 71–80; "Divorce" 74–75; domestic comedy in 4, 67, 71–80; "Get It Off Your Chest" 76; influence on sitcoms 71–73; "It's Only a Movie" 79–80; as observational comedy 71–72; physical comedy and 130; "The Point Killer" 74; Reiner in 70; tight scripting for 61; twin bed sleeping rule in 46; urban humor in 161; "The Wife Works" 78–79; working women in 78–79; writing in 53, 55, 73, 78
Hope, Bob 134
Horne, Lena 47
Hunter, Kim 47

Imogene Coca Show (TV show) 167
It's a Mad, Mad, Mad, Mad World (film) 25

The Jack Benny Show (TV show) 43
The Jack Carter Show (TV show) 37
Jacobsen, Barry 171, 232*n*51
Janis, Hal 155
Jenkins, Dan 163–64
Jewishness: Caesar and 108–110, 234*n*93; comedy and 110–111; in sketches 109–111; writers and cast 108–110, 233*n*86, 233*n*88; Yiddishness and 108–109, 111
Johnson, Judy 6, **154**
Jory, Victor 44

Kallen, Lucille: *The Admiral Broadway Revue* writing 28, 30; on Caesar's miming 123–124; *Imogene Coca Show* writing for 167; Tamiment Playhouse and 22, 27; Writers' Room 4, 30, 36–37, 44, 51–54, **54**, 55, 78–79, 231*n*37
Kaye, Danny 22, 51, 110, 139
King, Dennis 89
Klain, Jane 60, 230*n*24

Lahr, Bert 144
Laughter on the 23rd Floor (play) 12, 47, 51, 56, 231*n*38
Levy, Florence *see* Caesar, Florence (wife)
Lewis, Jerry 18, 110, 113
Library of Congress 7
Liebman, Max: *The Admiral Broadway Revue* 27–32, 35; Caesar and 56–57, **57**, 58, 229*n*35; on Caesar's miming 124; Coca and 69, 71, 90, 92; comedy sketch ensemble and 69, 71; end of *Your Show of Shows* and 153–155; guest hosts and 88–90; *Make Mine Manhattan* 26; mentorship of Caesar 8, 22, 25, 56–57, 228*n*35, 231*n*45; packaging of *Revue* for prospective sponsorship 27; as

producer/director 4, 6–7, 61, 232n53; "spectaculars" and 153, 155, 167; *Star Spangled Revue* 134; *The Straw Hat Revue* 29; Sylvania award 165; Tamiment Playhouse and 22, 27; *Tars and Spars* 22–23; *Ten from Your Show of Shows* 167; as USO show director 22; Writers' Room 51–52, 55–58; *Your Show of Shows* 36, 39, 60, 71, 153, **154**, 155, 157, 159, 163–164

Make Mine Manhattan (Broadway revue) 11, **26**, 26–27, 32–33, 134
Marc, David 18
Marx brothers 111
Mata and Hari 6, 27–28
McCarthy, Joseph, and McCarthyism 46–47
McCarty, Mary 29, 36, 92
Meadows, Audrey: comparison of Alice Kramden on *The Honeymooners* with Coca's Doris Hickenlooper 71–72
Meredith, Burgess 47
monologues **140**; ad-libbing in 63; *The Admiral Broadway Revue* 33–34; characterizations and 6, 18, 141–144; comic energy and 5, 32, 131, 149; "Dance Hall Stag" 142–143; domestic situations in 144–145; doubletalk in 140–141; "Man at the Bar" 147–148; memorization and 123, 146; mime in 120, 145; "A New Leaf" 148; "Penny Gum Machine" 32–33; repetition and "drilling down" in 146–147; sound effects and 145; total immersion into characters 142–143; Writers' Room and 55
Morris, Howard "Howie": acting training and 70; *The Admiral Broadway Revue* 28–31, 67, 68; on Caesar's abilities 149; comedy sketch ensemble 4, **58**, 67–70; doubletalk 140; end of show and 155; physical comedy and 70, 118–119; *Sid Caesar, Imogene Coca, Carl Reiner, and Howard Morris Special* 168; *Your Show of Shows* 48–49, 62, 64–66, 86–87, 97–98, 103, 118–119, 165
Munshin, Jules 22
My Favorite Year (film) 51

NBC: *The Admiral Broadway Revue* 11; Caesar contract with 155,160; censorship and 45, 57; Coca contract with 160; Code directives and 44–46; comedy-variety shows on 158–159, 162; loyalty oaths and 47; production costs and 163; *Saturday Night Revue* 37; sponsorship and 43; Weaver and 27, 36, 153, 155; *Your Show of Shows* 36–37, 80; *Your Show of Shows* end 153, 155–156, 160–162, 164, 167

Omnibus (TV show) 162

Paley Center for Media 7
pantomime: "Bartered Souls" (ensemble) 130; "Bavarian Clock" (ensemble) 55, 58, 62; "Boy at First Dance" (Caesar) 120, 123; Caesar 119–122, **122**, 123–124; Caesar and Coca 3, 121–122, **122**, 123–124; "1812 Overture" (Caesar and Coca) 3; "The Foundling" (ensemble) 119; "In a Shoe Store" (Caesar and Coca) 62, 121; Kallen on Caesar's miming 123–124; Liebman on Caesar's abilities in pantomime 124; "The Paraders"/marching band (Caesar and Coca) 121–122; Reiner and 122; Reiner on Caesar's talent 123; "The Sewing Machine Girl" (ensemble) 118, 123
parodies: appeal of to Caesar and writers 94–95; "Broadway Rhapsody" 103–104; characteristics of 95–96; film noir/crime parodies 100–103; "The Final Payment"/*Double Indemnity* 96, 102; "Foreign Agent" 99; foreign film parodies 106–107; "From Here to Obscurity"/*From Here to Eternity* and copyright infringement suit 104, **105**, 106; "A Place at the Bottom of the Lake"/*A Place in the Sun* 96, 100–102; "Russian Arthur Godfrey"/*Arthur Godfrey's Talent Scouts* 107; "Strange"/*Shane* 97–99; "A Stranger in Danger" 99–100; "This Is Your Story"/*This Is Your Life* 63–66; "Westward Whoa!" 96–97
Peabody award 165
physical comedy: "Big Business Conference" 125–126; "Boy at First Dance" 62, 131; Caesar and 31, 43, 61, 88, 93, 115, **116**, 117–121, 125–131; Coca and 48, 61, 70, 93, **116**, 117–121; "The Heiress" 118; "I Object" 124; "A Man Coming Down with a Cold" 126; Morris and 70, 118–119; "The New Neighbor" 128; "The Photographer" 70; Reiner and 4, 70, 102, 118–120; slapstick and 48, 124–126; "Twenty Minutes for Lunch" 125, 160; *Your Show of Shows* 49, 61–65, 70, 115, 117–124
Piazza, Marguerite 6, 89, 159
Pons, Lily **154**, 160
Professor sketches: **81**; ad-libbing in 63, 83–84; Brooks and 81–82; Caesar and 4, 18, 55, 80–85; Caesar's clown persona in 80–81; comedy in 49, 85; "Mind Over Matter" 82–83; mountain climbing sketch 83–84; professor as standard comic figure 80; Reiner in 80–85; roving reporter in 4, 28, 80–81; on "Space Travel and Jet Propulsion" 84–85

Reiner, Carl **154**; on Caesar as musician 23; on Caesar's childhood 15; *Caesar's Hour* 162, 168; on Caesar's miming 123; comedy sketch ensemble on *Your Show of Shows* 4–5, 39, **58**, 67–70; *The Dick Van Dyke Show* 162,